IMAGES
of America

IRA TOWNSHIP

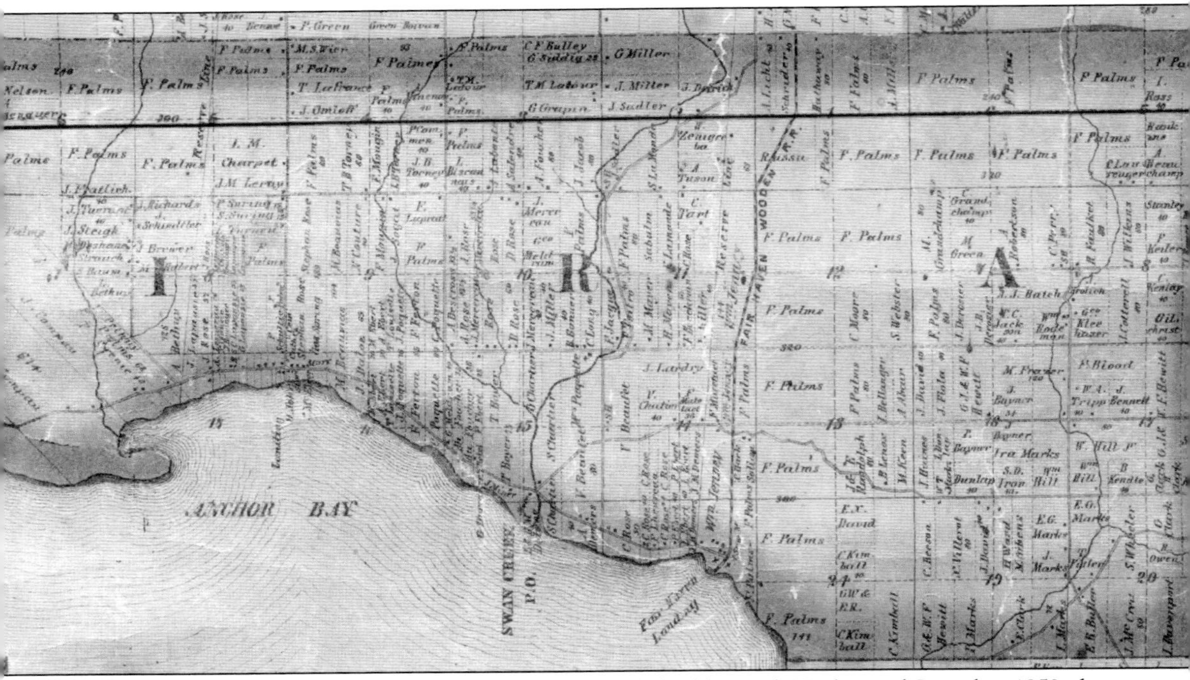

This 20-square-foot plat map of Ira Township, published by Geil, Harley and Siverd in 1859, shows the sections of land that were purchased by the early pioneers and includes their names. The Indian Reserve in Ira Township was disposed of between May 15, 1839, and October 30, 1848. The total area of the township is 21.6 square miles; the land area equals 17 square miles, and the water area is 4.6 square miles. (Courtesy of Bob Mack.)

On the Cover: This is an early 1900s photograph of the general store and saloon located in Anchorville at the corner of M-29 and Church Road. In the store's history, it saw fur trappers buying supplies and Native Americans canoeing from Walpole Island to shop, sell, and trade. Today, its employees use computers to track sales. Among the many store owners were George Christie, A.J. Christie, Adolph Eckhout, George Hart, Jack Gougeon, the Kandlers, and the D Brothers. From 1951 to 1990, the store was known as the Village Market. (Courtesy of Bob Mack.)

IMAGES
of America

IRA TOWNSHIP

Paul Torney, Lynn Lyon, Richard Gonyeau,
Bob Mack, and Gail Zabowski

ARCADIA
PUBLISHING

ISBN 978-1-4671-1315-1

Published by Arcadia Publishing
Charleston, South Carolina

Printed in the United States of America

Library of Congress Control Number: 2015936364

For all general information, please contact Arcadia Publishing:
Telephone 843-853-2070
Fax 843-853-0044
E-mail sales@arcadiapublishing.com
For customer service and orders:
Toll-Free 1-888-313-2665

Visit us on the Internet at www.arcadiapublishing.com

This book is dedicated to Ira Township pioneer Stephen Rose and to the generations that followed and shared his long line of ancestry, and to the memory of Carl Beauvais and Mae Vernier.

For the people who live in Ira Township, this quote from Elwin Vigneron goes out to them: "Be careful who you talk with, they may be your cousins."

Contents

Acknowledgments

There are many accounts that have provided information on the history of Ira Township. These include *The Heritage of Ira: A Sesquicentennial History*; *Immaculate Conception Parish 150-Year Anniversary and History Book*; *History of St. Clair County*; *Life on the Flats*; and *History Stories of New Baltimore*. They are all excellent sources. Also instrumental was Richard Gonyeau's original research into the newspapers and other source material of the past, which first appeared as history columns in the local newspapers *The Anchor Bay Beacon* and *The Bay Voice*, and Greg Furtah's work in saving and archiving the original articles. Paul Torney, Gail Zabowski, and Bob Mack's photographic archives were the core resources for this book, without which it would not have been possible.

An interesting discovery was a long-lost cache of approximately 700 French letters found in the Savoyard family barn and shared with Paul Torney. The letters were accounts of Savoyard's and Torney's ancestors in the early days of Ira Township. Thanks to Lois Similuk who translated a few Old French letters into modern English. Special thanks go to Alan Naldrett for his knowledge and expertise of writing history and to everybody else who donated pictures and information.

Unless otherwise noted, all images appear courtesy of the collections of Bob Mack, Paul Torney, and Gail Zabowski.

INTRODUCTION

After the glaciers began to recede from Michigan in the most recent ice age about 14,000 years ago, Native Americans were the first to settle the area now called Ira Township. With the region's many amenities, including a lake, rivers, creeks, and rich forestlands with a variety of animals, members of the Algonquin tribes dwelled here for thousands of years. The chief tribe of the area was referred to as the Swan Creek Ojibwas, for Ira Township's Swan Creek. Ojibwa was the French name; the English called them the Chippewa, which could refer to the whole tribe or just one person. Other tribes in the area included the Ottawa and Pottawatomie. The Pottawatomie tribe dwelt mainly on nearby Walpole Island in Ontario, Canada.

After the area was discovered by French explorers Father Louis Hennepin and Robert de La Salle in 1679, French explorers and pioneers began to arrive. They intermingled and learned from the Native Americans as they trapped and hunted furs and harvested salt from the Salt River. After the French and Indian War of the 1750s, a conflict that was an extension of the Seven Years' War between France and England in Europe, the English began to take control of the area. After the American Revolution, the area reverted to the new country, the United States. It was governed as part of the Northwest Territory, and life for the settlers continued as before. This all changed in 1807, when the Treaty of Detroit was signed between the Native American tribes and the US government. In the treaty, the chiefs ostensibly signed away their rights to the land and agreed to confine themselves to designated reservations. From 1807 to 1835, most of Ira Township was one of three Native American reservations in southwest Michigan, referred to on maps of the time as the "Indian Reserve" (the other two were in nearby Chesterfield Township, one by the Aux Vasse River and one by present-day Brandenburg Park). However, this arrangement was short-lived, as Ira resident Stephen Rose tells in his eyewitness account. He was paid by the government in 1845 to transport the Native Americans to Port Huron. From there, they were moved to the Omaha Territory, now Kansas. Many of these Swan Creek Chippewa moved instead to nearby Walpole Island, as did most of the Ottawa tribe—this is where their descendants live today. The last head of this tribe was Chief Francois Maconce, who taught the early settlers Native American knowledge, including herbal medicine using local fruits and fauna. Maconce, widely known as a doctor, saved the life of Stephen Rose's father, among others. Today, there is an elementary school in Ira Township named for him.

In its infancy, Ira Township was a lot larger, including parts of neighboring Clay and Cottrellville Townships and part of the City of New Baltimore. First established as part of St. Clair County by territorial governor Lewis Cass in 1821, the area's first constable was early settler Ira Marks. Since he was the predominant settler in the area and was present at the meetings establishing boundaries, the new township was given Marks's first name. He was also Ira Township's first postmaster in 1851 and was the township supervisor in 1855.

A great deal of Ira Township's early growth as a community was centered on the area's Catholic church, which came to be known as Immaculate Conception. As the church grew, a school was added nearby for the children of the settlers of the growing parish. More growth saw a general store, hotel, blacksmith, and other businesses arise in Anchorville.

Au Lac and Riviere au Cygne, as the areas were first known, became Anchorville and Fair Haven, respectively. As these villages developed along M-29, (also referred to as Dixie Highway and the Dyke Road), the Swan Creek settlement began to grow. Palms Road, located in Fair Haven, was named for Francis Palms, the largest landholder in the area. At one time, the Fair Haven Wooden Railroad came down Palms Road, drawn by oxen. It brought lumber and other resources from the north to the barrel stave mill located at the end of Palms Road, right on Anchor Bay. A boat launch now occupies the location of the former mill. Early maps designated this particular area as Fair Haven Landing.

The first Fair Haven post office was called Swan Creek (the English translation of Riviere au Cygne) and was started October 17, 1857. Due to other Swan Creeks in Michigan, the name was changed to Fair Haven on February 11, 1862, to denote the fact that boats could come to the enclave for protection during storms. Although the bay is somewhat protected from bad weather, many major storms have battered the bay. There were severe storms in 1929 and another in 1955.

In the early 20th century, an interurban railroad ran along the shoreline of Ira Township, with local stops in Anchorville and Fair Haven and others at Rose, Mills, Perch Point, and Bay View. In Anchorville, the train broke off on an express route, with one set of tracks continuing along the lake, and the other going inland—thereby creating a shortcut to Marine City. These tracks ran parallel to Meyer Road, which, because of the route of the railroad, came to be known as Short Cut Road (commemorating its years as a quicker route by train to Detroit). The remnant of these old railroad tracks was locally known as the "Indian Trail." The railroad contributed greatly to the settlement of the area. In the early years of the township, people from the Detroit area would come and build resort cottages on the waterfront. As the area grew, many more permanent structures were built as more people moved to Ira Township to live.

Because of its proximity to Anchor Bay, one of the largest businesses in Ira has been shipbuilding, with Mayea Boats operating in Ira Township for over 100 years.

Due to its excellent location on Lake St. Clair, Ira Township will continue to be a center of sports in the winter months, while water fun, including boating, fishing, and water-skiing, continue to dominate the rest of the year. As Fair Haven, Anchorville, and Ira Township have progressed, raising a family is still the main business. Family fun can be seen in the many parades and carnivals hosted in Ira Township over the years. For these and many other reasons, history will continue to be made in Ira Township for a long time!

—Alan Naldrett

One

Native Americans, French Explorers, and the First Settlers

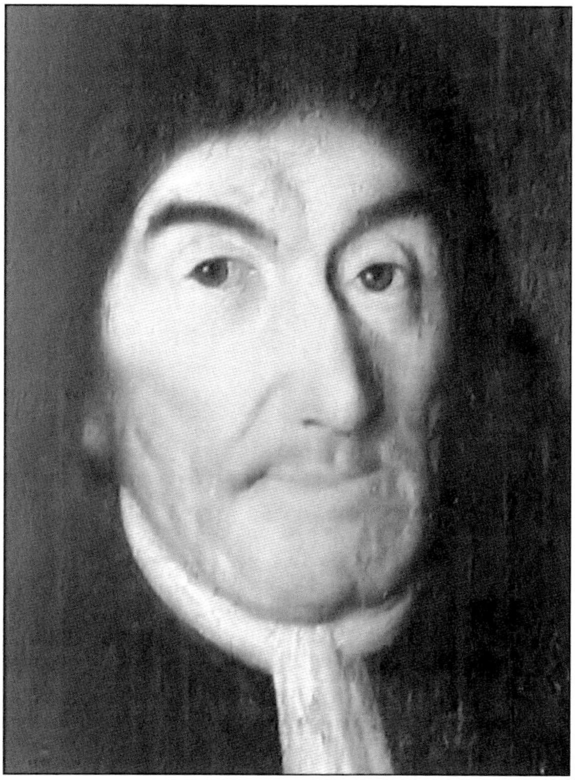

In 1679, Father Louis Hennepin, a Belgian missionary of the Franciscan Order, planted a cross on the shores of Anchor Bay and claimed the land for France. Hennepin sailed on the *Griffin* (*Le Griffon*), the first sailing ship to enter the Great Lakes. It was captained by the explorer Robert de La Salle. Father Hennepin is also credited with the discovery of Niagara Falls.

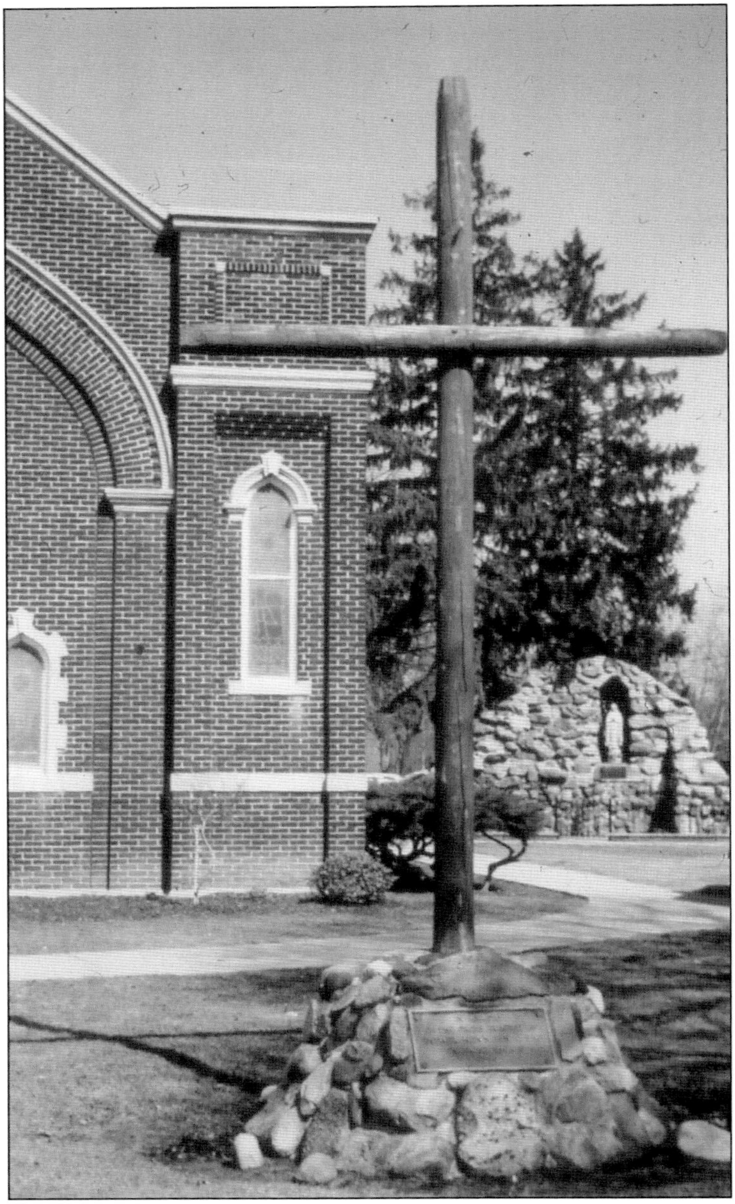

A cross honoring Father Hennepin stands in front of Immaculate Conception Church in Anchorville. The plaque on it reads: "In Memory of the Cross Erected by Father Hennepin O.F. M. on these Shores, 1679." Spreading faith was only part of the objective of early missionaries. They were explorers of new land for potential development and public-relations agents attempting to present their findings in the best light possible. Father Hennepin's first account of the area surrounding Lake Otsekita (now known as Lake St. Clair) described it as a land of "panoramic plenty." Of the wildlife, he wrote that it "abounds in stags, wild goats, and bears," also "turkey cocks and swans," along with "several other beasts and birds that we could not identify but were extremely relishing." The flora, too, was promoted by Hennepin, who noted, "The forests are chiefly made up of walnut trees, chestnut, plum and pear trees loaded with their own fruit." Addressing reluctant immigrants, Hennepin offered another incentive: "an abundance of timber for building houses for those who will be fortunate enough to inhabit this noble country."

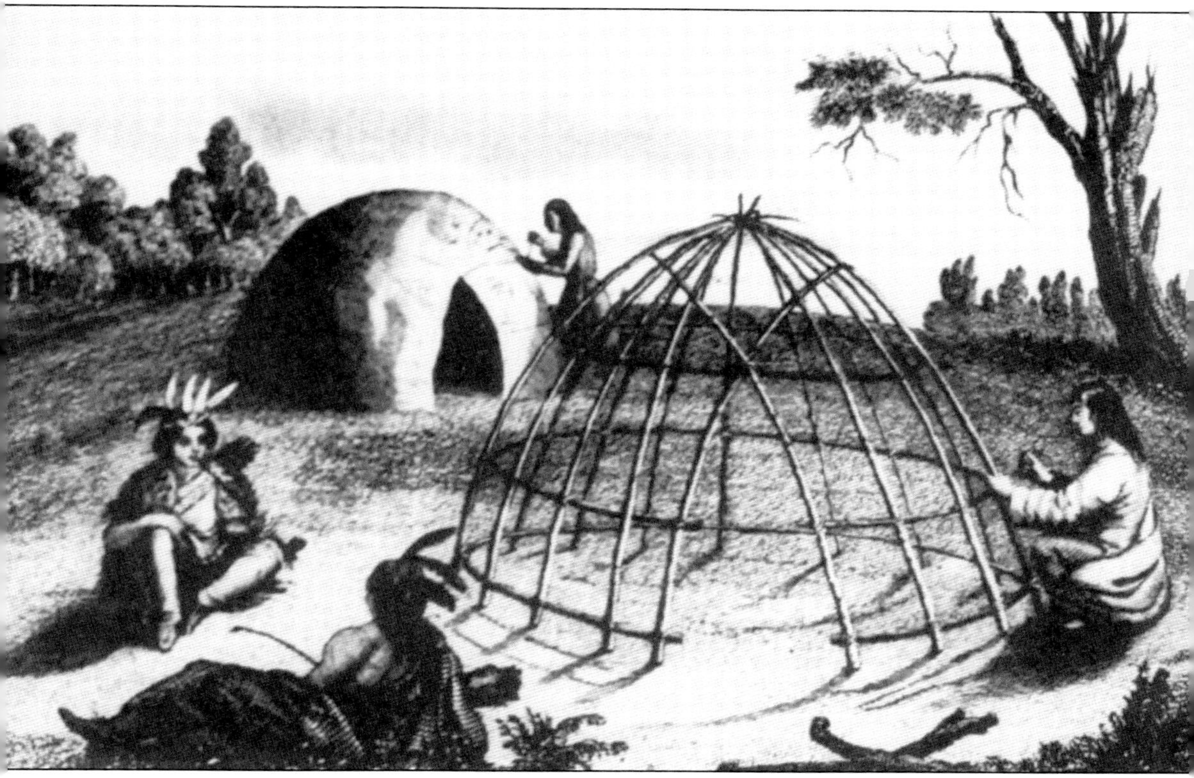

All Native Americans of Michigan were part of the Woodlands area and known collectively as "Algonquians." One tribe was known as Chippewa by the English and Ojibwa by the French. In 1807, they signed the Treaty of Detroit, which gave them $10,000 and confined them to three area reservations, two of which were in the area now known as Chesterfield Township. The other one took up almost the whole landmass of Ira Township, from Bethuy Road to Palms Road on one side and from Marine City Highway to Anchor Bay on the other. This area was referred to as the Indian Reserve. Besides Chippewa (Ojibwa), Native Americans in the area included members of the Ottawa, Pottawatomie, and, earlier, the Huron tribes. Following Hennepin, the first French to traverse this area were the Coureur de Bois (woodsmen), who took on native ways and often married native wives, and the Voyagers, who paddled large canoes loaded with beaver pelts back to Trappers' Alley in Detroit.

Smallpox epidemics were common all over the world in the 17th, 18th, and 19th centuries. Only one in ten Native Americans survived a case of smallpox, because they had no immunity to the disease. In 1872, twenty-nine people died of smallpox out of a population of 1,583 in Ira Township. The following list, taken from the St. Clair County, Michigan, death records, includes the names of the residents who died from the disease between May and December 1872, in chronological order: Anthony Bethuy, Joseph Beauvais, Anna Pelton, Joseph Marcereau, Mary Peterprin, Charles Rose, Mathilda Rose, Napoleon Bethuy, Timothy Boyer, Catherine Petitpren, Stephen Rose, Mary Pelton, Adaline Rose, John Pelton, Stephen Rose, George Solgat, Mathilda Boyer, Alexander Boyer, Timothy Boyer, Francis Boyer, Mary Petitpren, Mrs. Louisa Laprathe, Louis Charrot, John Harner, Francis Destraze, Ida Gohsmann, Anna Pelton, John Pelton, and Mira Pelton. Shown here is the headstone of Napoleon Bethuy, buried in St. Mary's Cemetery in Anchorville.

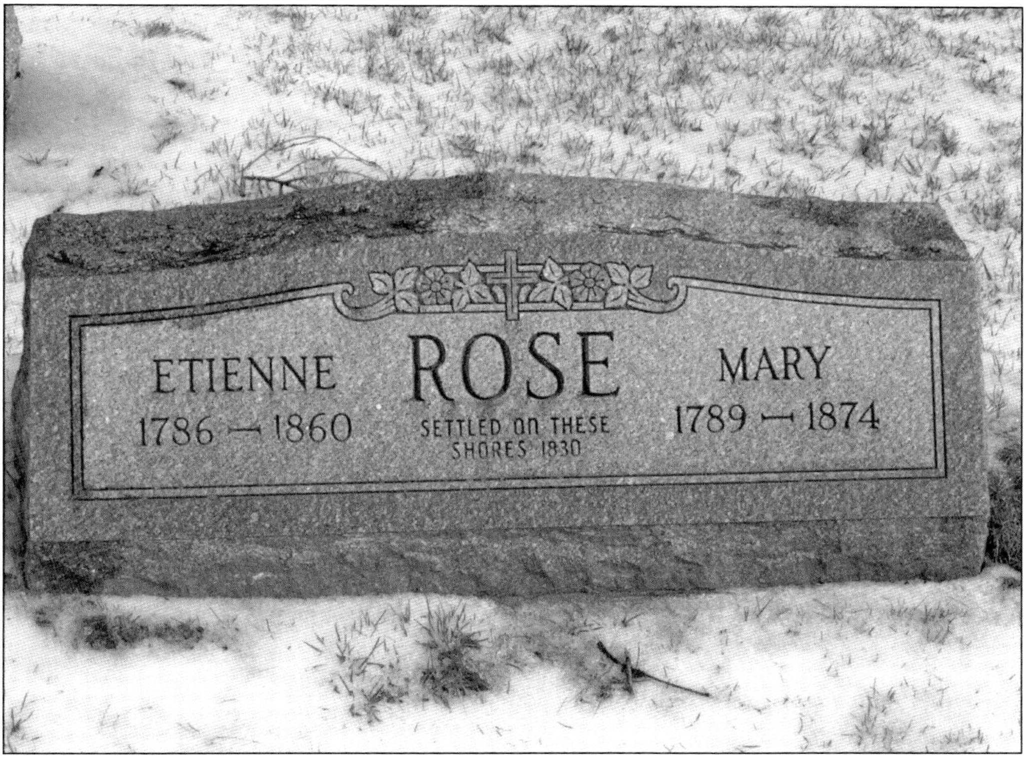

A headstone commemorating the original resting place of early settlers Etienne and Mary (Burt) Rose was placed in Saint Mary's Cemetery in Anchorville by Fred Rose, a parishioner of Immaculate Conception and a grandson of the couple. A Frenchman, Etienne was born in Montreal, Canada. His wife, Mary, of English descent, was from Boston. They lived with Etienne's brother Peter in the Swan Creek Indian Reserve (now Ira Township) in the 1830s. A great deal of their livelihood came from cutting and selling cordwood. Much of the wood was carried to Detroit on a scow that Peter had built.

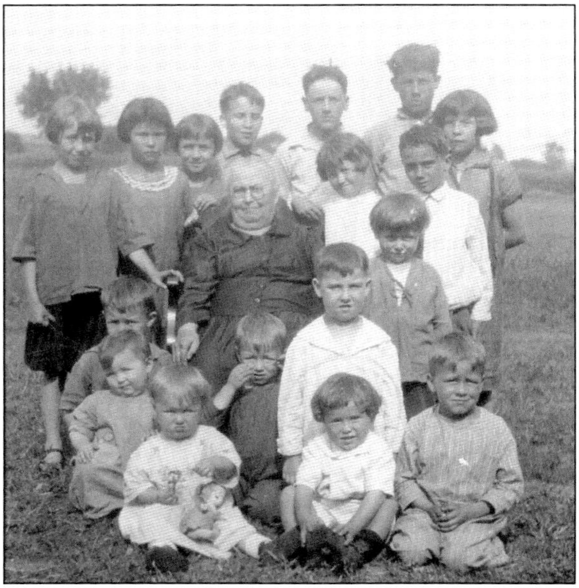

Old family names in Ira, such as Rose, Marcero, Faucher, Meldrum, Savoyard, Beauvais, Chartier, Furtah, Torney, and Vigneron (spellings vary) represent immigrants from Canada, France, Scotland, Germany, and Switzerland. Settling in this area, they often encouraged family and friends to come and join them. As the families grew, their children began to intermarry. Within a few generations, almost everyone was a "cousin" to everyone else. This photograph of "Grandma" Louise (Marcerau) Rose with some of her descendants includes children of the Rose, DeMars, Vigneron, and Deimel families.

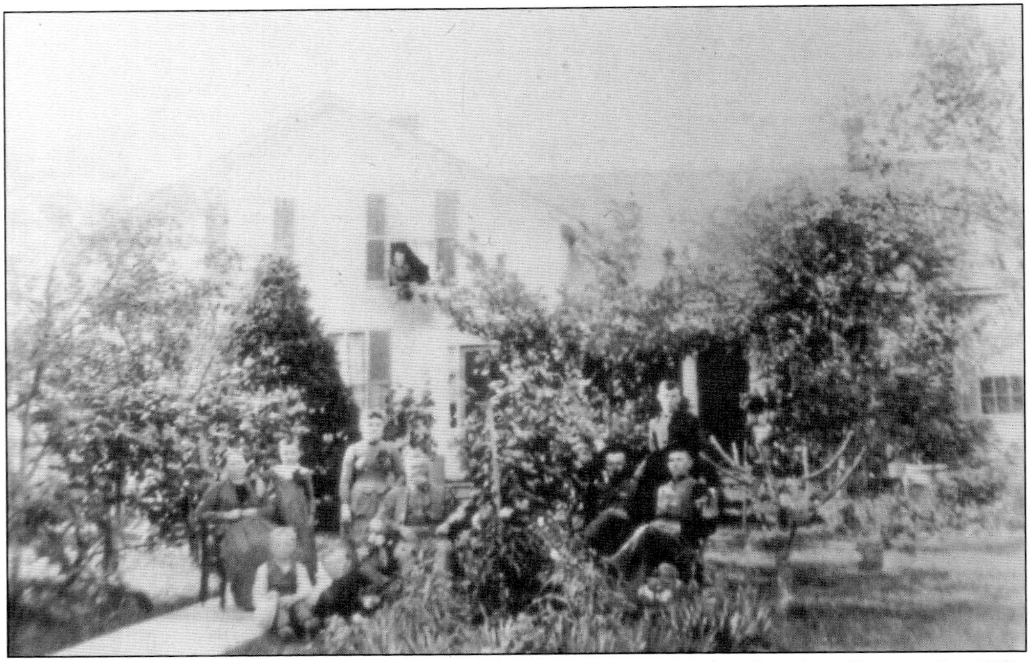

Early settler Henry Neddermeyer emigrated from Germany and first lived in Detroit. In 1853, he bought land in Ira Township and, around 1856, moved into a log cabin on Short Cut Road. Neddermeyer was supervisor of Ira Township from 1864 to 1871 and served four terms as justice of the peace. He and his wife, Mary, had 12 children. The Neddermeyer family is seen here at their house, which was built in 1875.

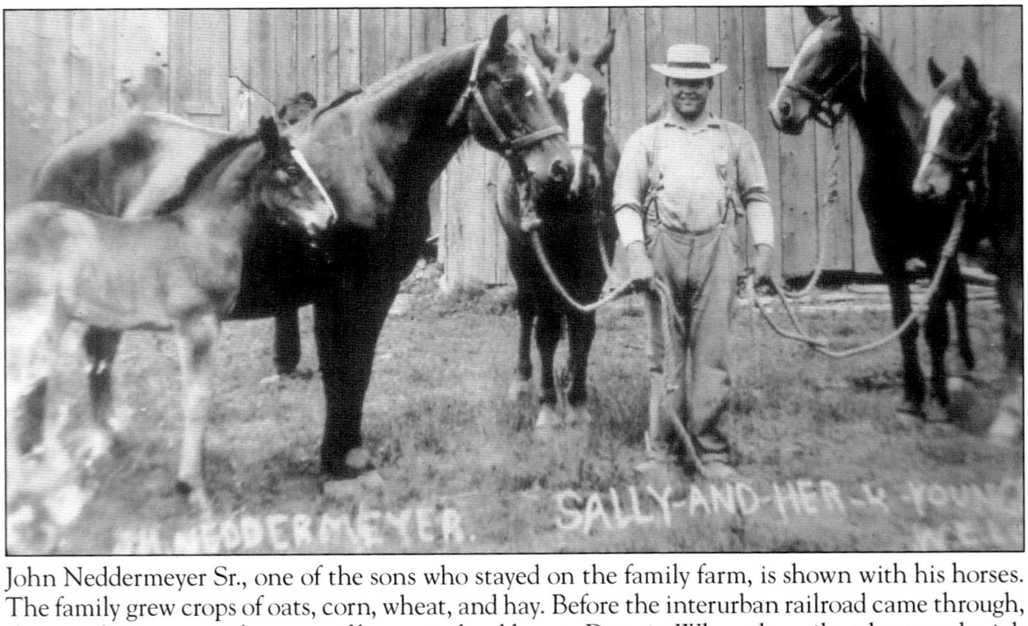

John Neddermeyer Sr., one of the sons who stayed on the family farm, is shown with his horses. The family grew crops of oats, corn, wheat, and hay. Before the interurban railroad came through, they used a wagon and a team of horses to haul hay to Detroit. When the railroad came, the job was made easier. They had the hay baled and taken to Fair Haven or Anchorville and loaded on freight cars.

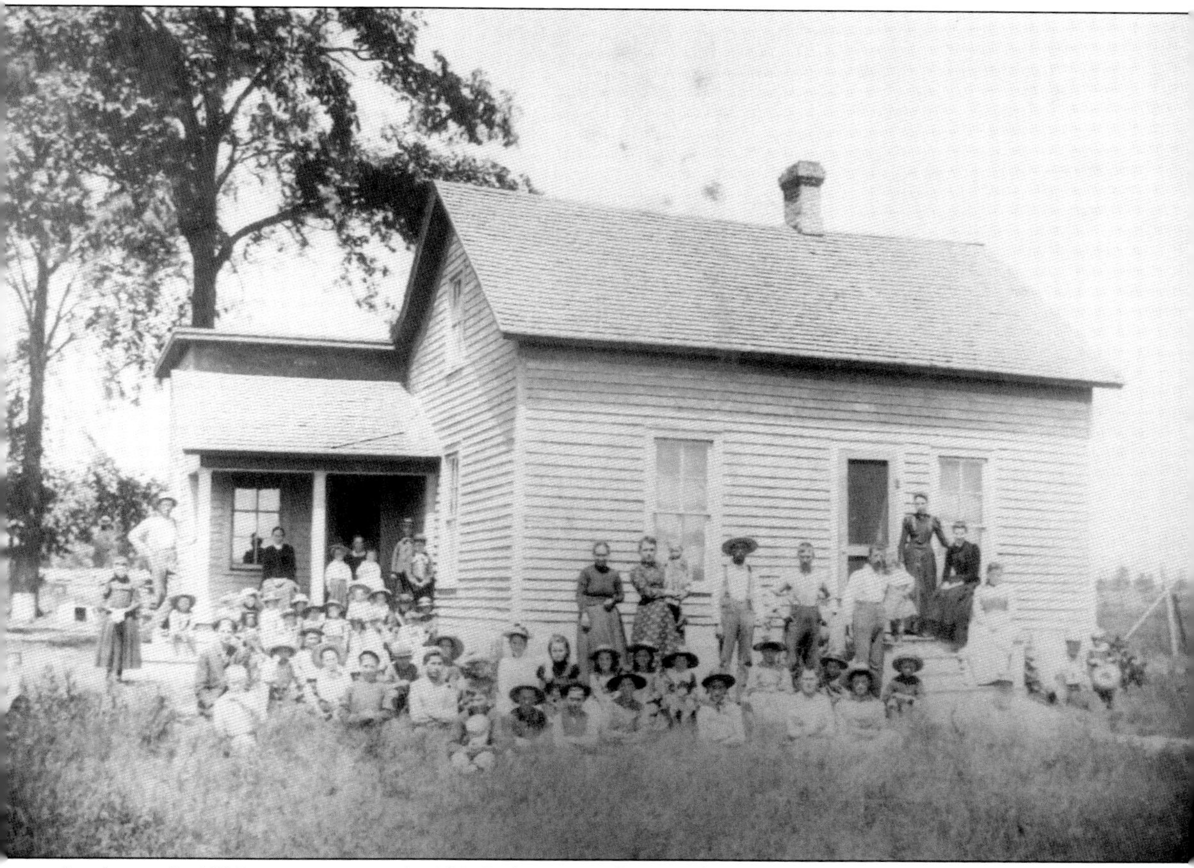

In the early 1830s, approximately 180 Ojibwa people were living in the Anchor Bay area. An unknown number perished in a cholera epidemic in 1832. Of the survivors, there were about 50 people who were to be removed and resettled in the Kansas Territory. Francois Maconce (Eshtonoquot) was their leader and chief. In the Treaty of Chicago of 1836, the Swan Creek band surrendered its reservation in Ira Township. Stephen Rose, son of early settler Etienne Rose, was paid $15 per day in 1845 to transport the Ojibwa from their reserve on the Swan Creek to Port Huron in his schooner *General Warren*. He got them drunk for the first leg of their removal west to keep them from leaving the ship. A later account by Stephen Rose describes the close relationship early settlers had with the natives. They shared a mutual respect and at times intermarried. The removal of the Swan Creek tribe not only divided friends, it divided families. Stephen Rose wrote with remorse regarding his part in this. In this photograph of an early Ira family, faces indicate the presence of some Native American blood, but not enough that they were forced to leave. (Courtesy of Bond Schnoor.)

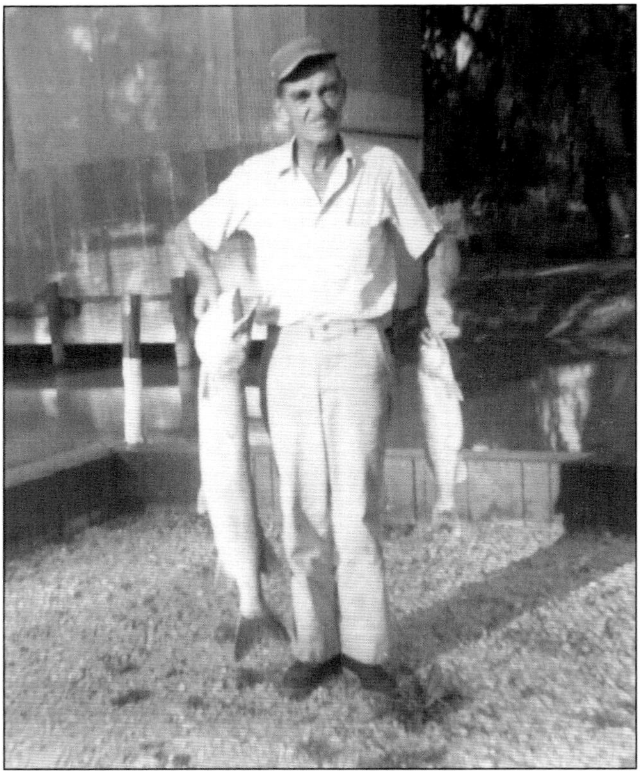

Ira Township has 17 square miles of land with an abundance of woods and wildlife, such as deer, pheasants, quail, ducks, squirrels, and turkeys. It also has 4.6 miles of water. Many of North America's freshwater fish species can be found in Lake St. Clair, providing good fishing throughout the seasons. Among them are perch, muskellunge (muskie), walleye, bluegill, bass, northern pike, and catfish. The photograph at left shows Hal Evoy holding a big muskie on the left and a bass caught in Anchor Bay. Originally from Oil Springs, Ontario, Evoy so enjoyed the amenities of the area that he moved to Fair Haven and became a naturalized citizen in the 1960s. Below, local resident Johnny Krauss holds a nice-sized muskie caught in the North Channel near Anchor Bay.

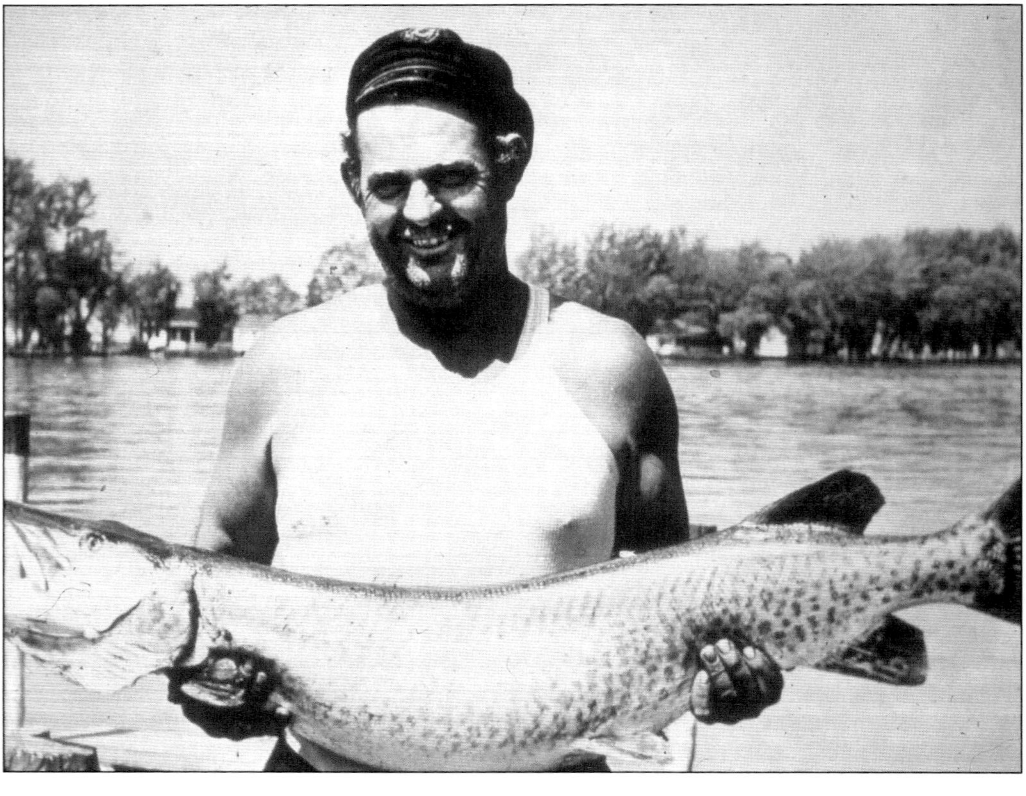

Two

The Catholic Church of the Immaculate Conception

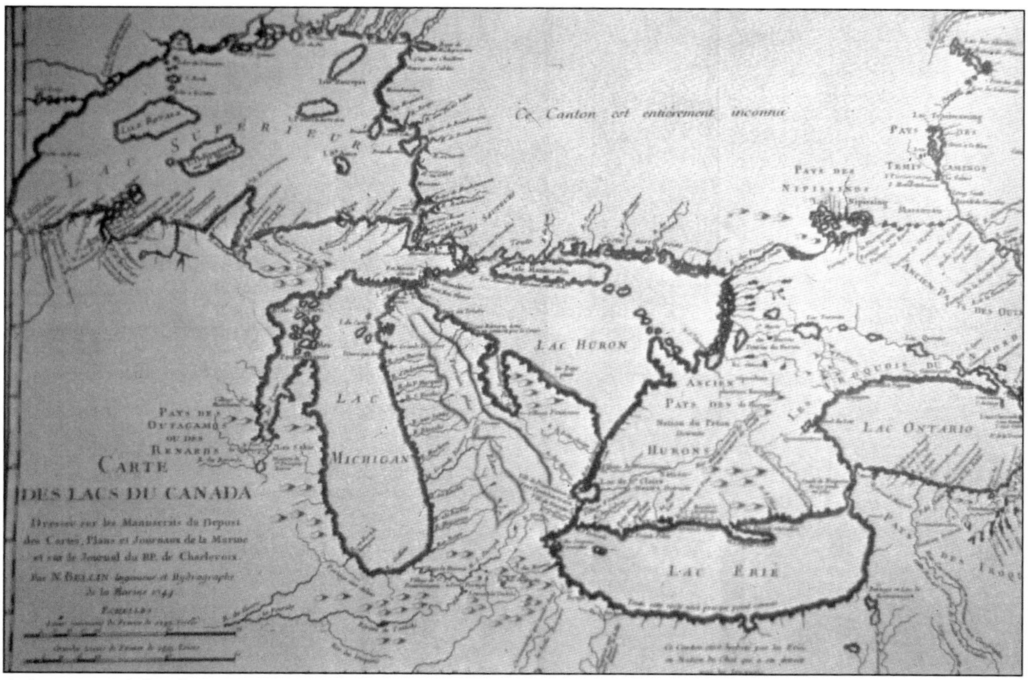

A history of the formation of the church of Anchorville necessitates a return to the 18th century, when the first Catholic settlers landed from Canada. At intervals, they were visited by missionary fathers from Canada, who ministered to their spiritual needs, and by French priests from Detroit, who were later replaced by the clergy from the surrounding parishes of Mount Clemens, Marine City, and Grosse Pointe. This Canadian fur trapper's map of 1744 illustrates the way the region was looked upon.

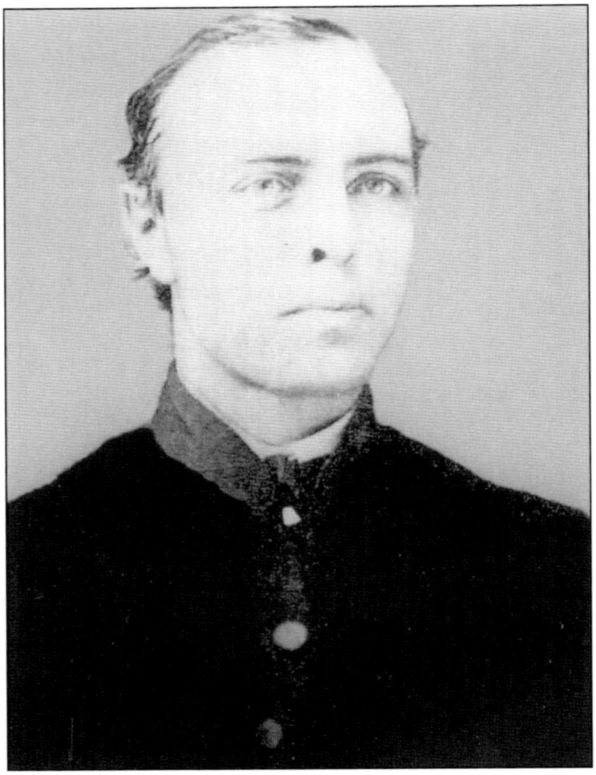

In 1845, Stephen Rose, one of the first settlers from Montreal, deeded a portion of his land for a church and also property for a cemetery. In 1853, Right Reverend Peter P. Lefevere, then bishop of the Detroit Diocese, deemed it expedient to send to the people of this infant land a permanent priest, in the person of Father Charles Chambille (pictured). During his early ministry, services were held in various private residences until Chambille succeeded in finding a central location in which to establish a parish.

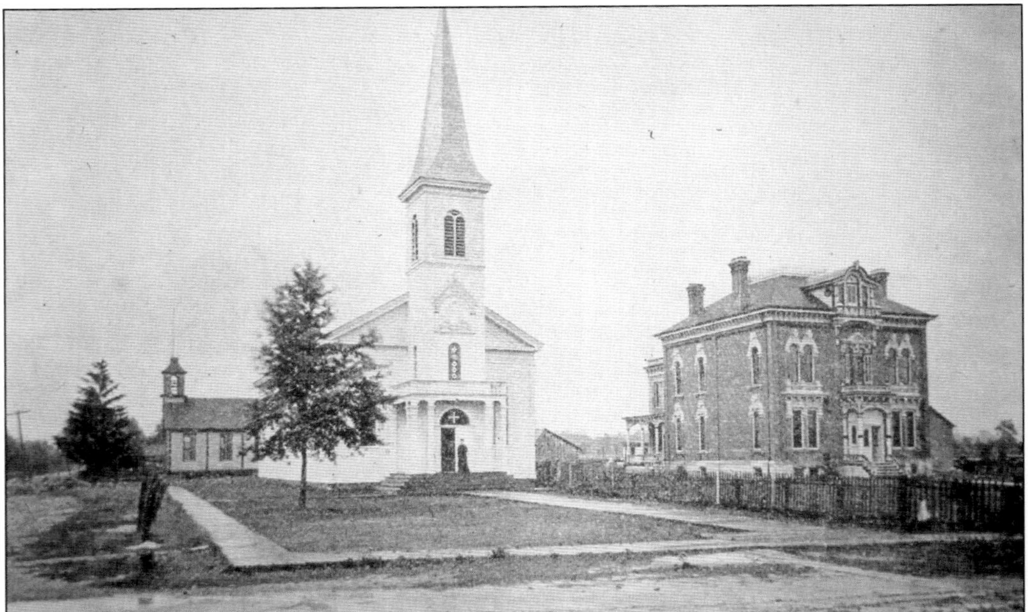

The new church was built on the corner of M-29 and Church Road and dedicated on October 15, 1854, to the Immaculate Conception of the Blessed Virgin Mary. There are only a few historical records telling of the work of Father Chambille; they indicate that he was an eloquent speaker. The only records kept were of the baptisms, marriages, and deaths in the parish. These are available in the Burton Historical Collection at the Detroit Public Library.

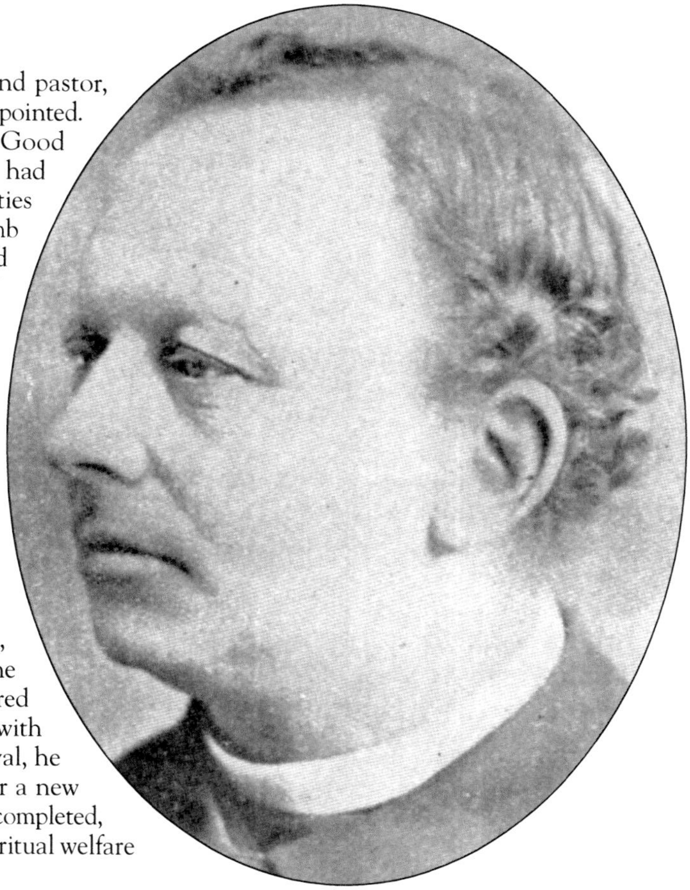

On March 20, 1859, the second pastor, Father Theophilus Buyse, was appointed. He became known as "The Good Father Buyse." At one time, he had within his boundaries five counties and forty-six stations in the thumb of Michigan. He was considered "a missionary sent from heaven." The trips undertaken by him sometimes lasted three months, but never a complaint was heard from his lips. There were feelings of joy and jubilation in the hearts of the people of Anchorville when their beloved pastor returned after his long journeys. "Father Buyse," like St. Paul, was "all to all." Before his departure and by most strenuous efforts, he succeeded in establishing the Catholic school known as Sacred Heart Institute (below). In 1892, with Father Henry H. Meuffel's arrival, he quickly discovered the need for a new school building, which was soon completed, so that educational as well as spiritual welfare was met.

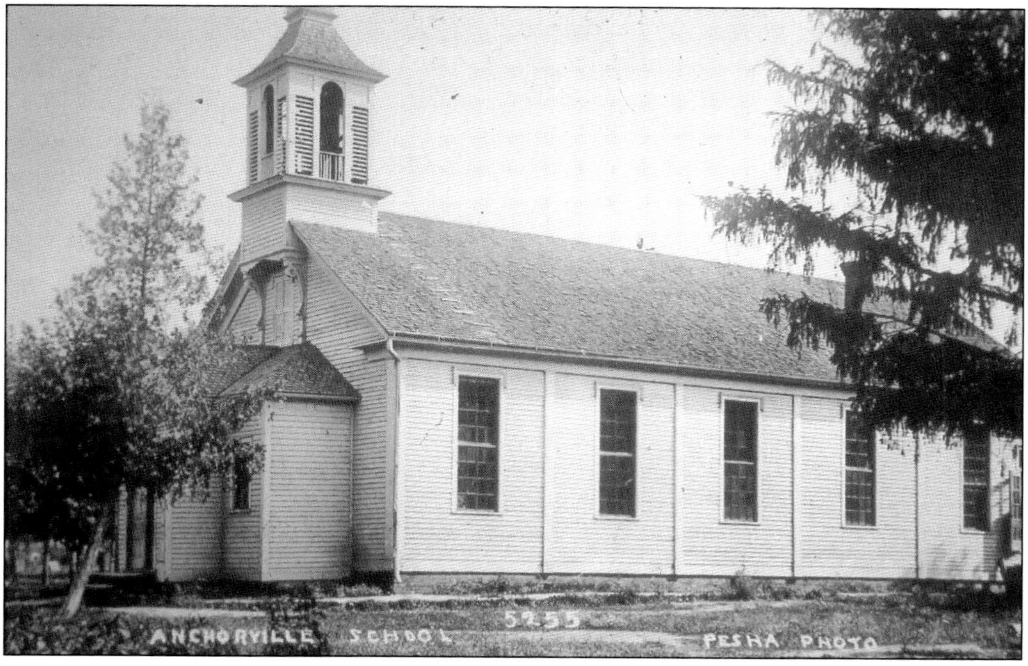

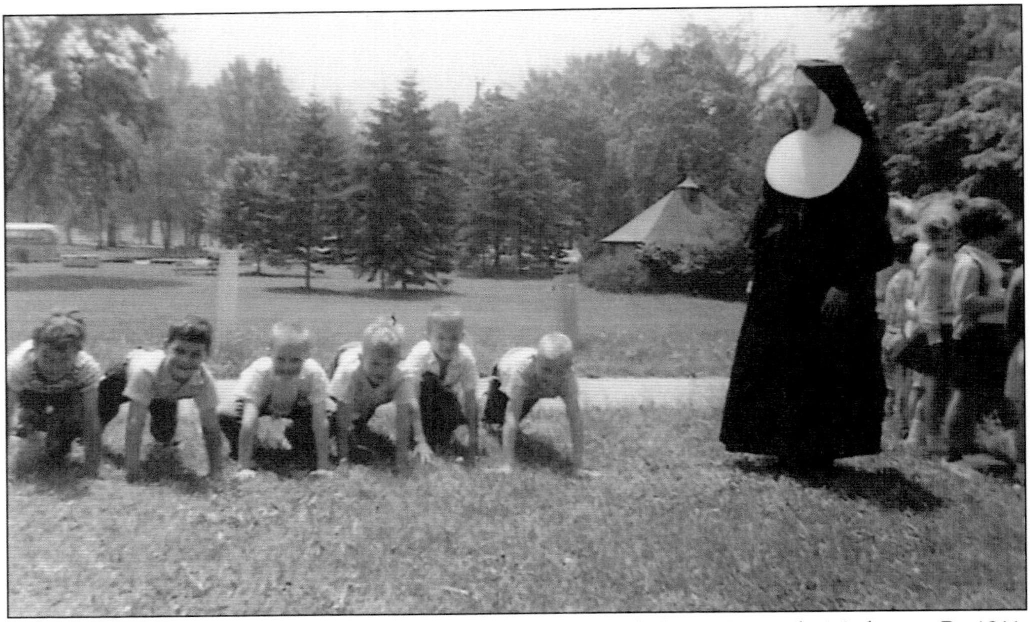

The year 1906 brought the arrival of the Sisters of St. Joseph from Nazareth, Michigan. By 1911, the sisters were operating a music school. They served until 1969—a total of 63 years. The church acquired two cemeteries. St. Mary's (now called the "old cemetery"), on the east side of Church Road, was given to the church by Stephen Rose sometime in the late 1840s. The graves of many early French Canadian pioneers are located there, but that was not the first cemetery. The first was located on the shore of Lake St. Clair, about 1,000 feet east of the church and across Dixie Highway (M-29). As the shoreline eroded and the water approached the graves, they were moved to the new location of St. Mary's Cemetery. Father Downey obtained the second and new cemetery on the west side of Church Road in 1914. It is known as Sacred Heart Cemetery.

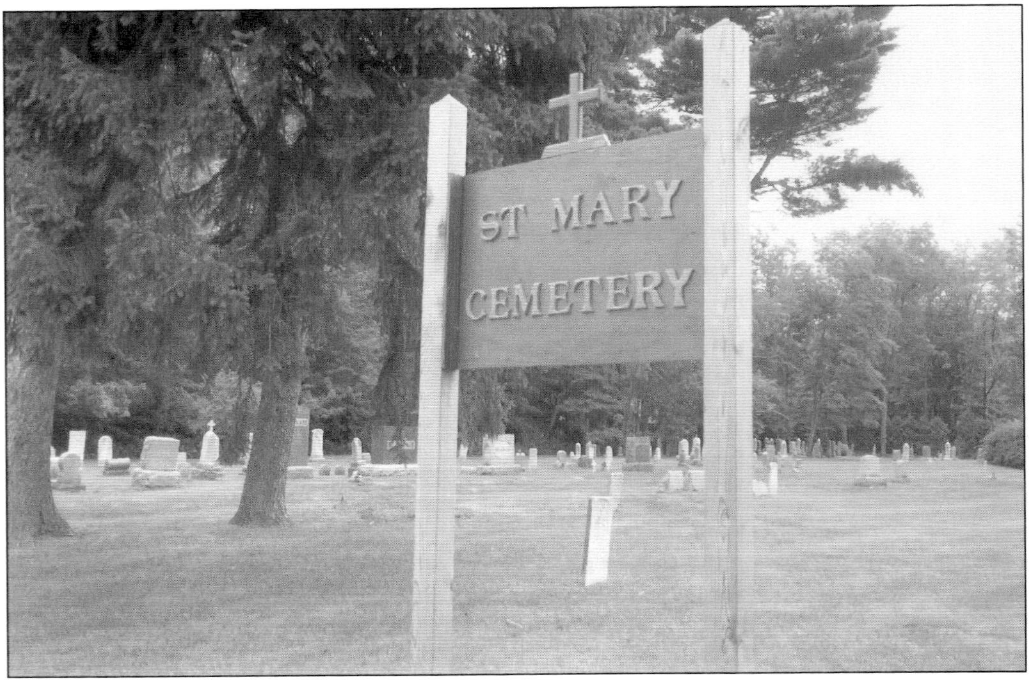

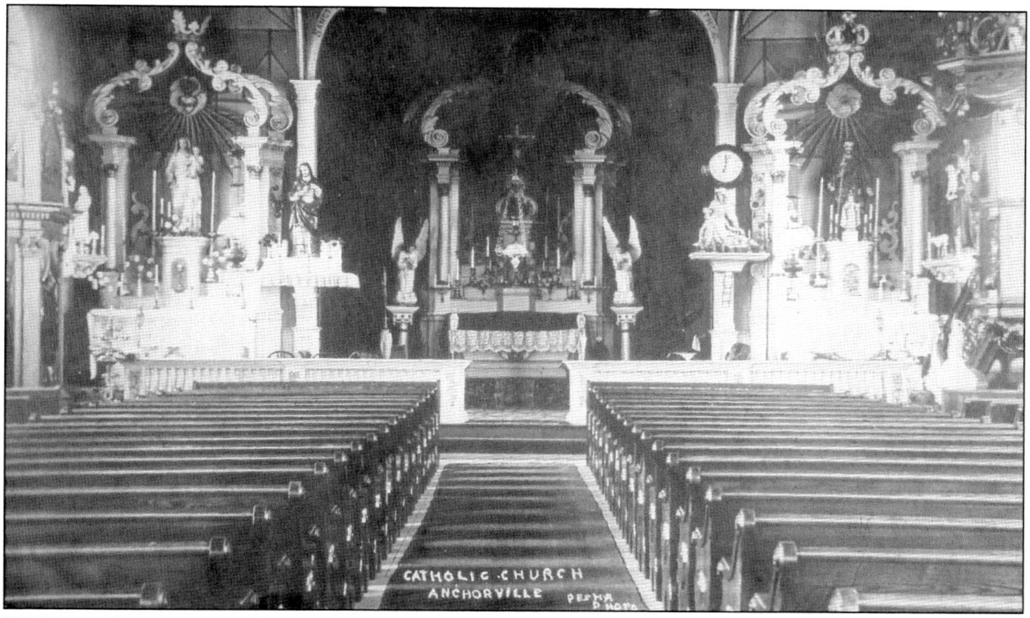

In September 1913, Father James Downey became the first American-born man to become pastor of Immaculate Conception Church. He succeeded Father Henry DeGryse, who served from 1892 to 1913. Father Downey had an affable disposition and endeared himself to the people of the parish. Shown here is the interior of the original church before the 1917 fire.

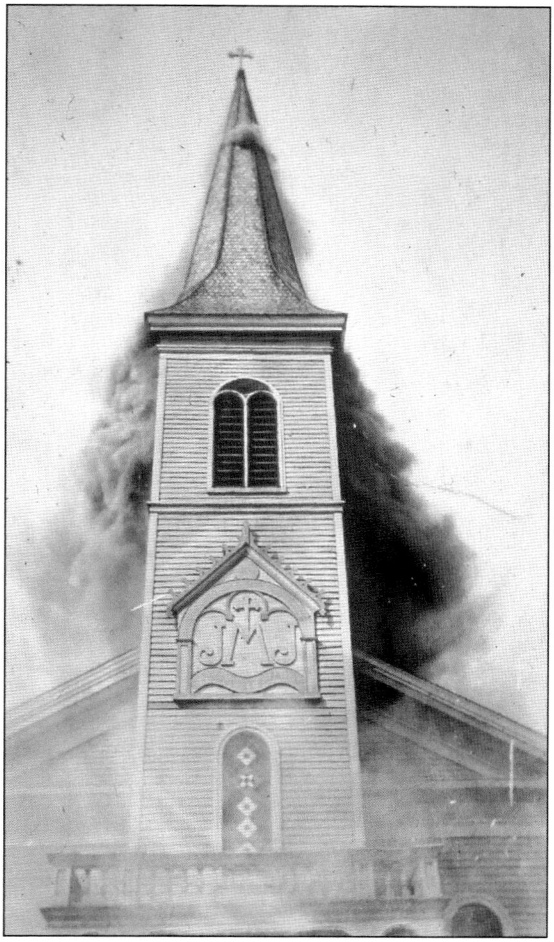

Few priests experience the heartbreak of seeing their entire parish destroyed. On Sunday, August 26, 1917, at 2:20 p.m., fire claimed all of the parish buildings: the convent, rectory, school, and the church. The flames endangered the general store of A.J. Christie, directly across the street, but the wind turned in time to prevent any great damage. Not a single thing was saved in the church or the convent, and there was no fire protection.

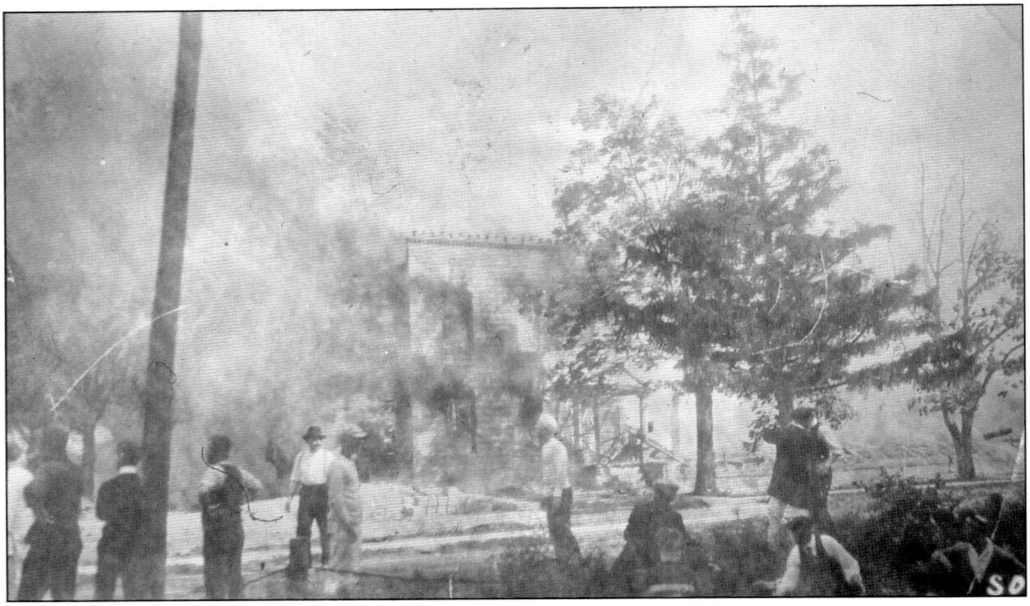

Crescentia Hahn, an eyewitness, gives this account of the fire: "We ran in the church and saw the altar ablaze, then they pulled Father Downey from the church and sat him down outside." Someone rang the bell, and within minutes, there were at least 1,000 people there. Parishioners desperately formed a bucket brigade using water from Lake St. Clair. However, the flames were out of control and destroyed the buildings within a few hours.

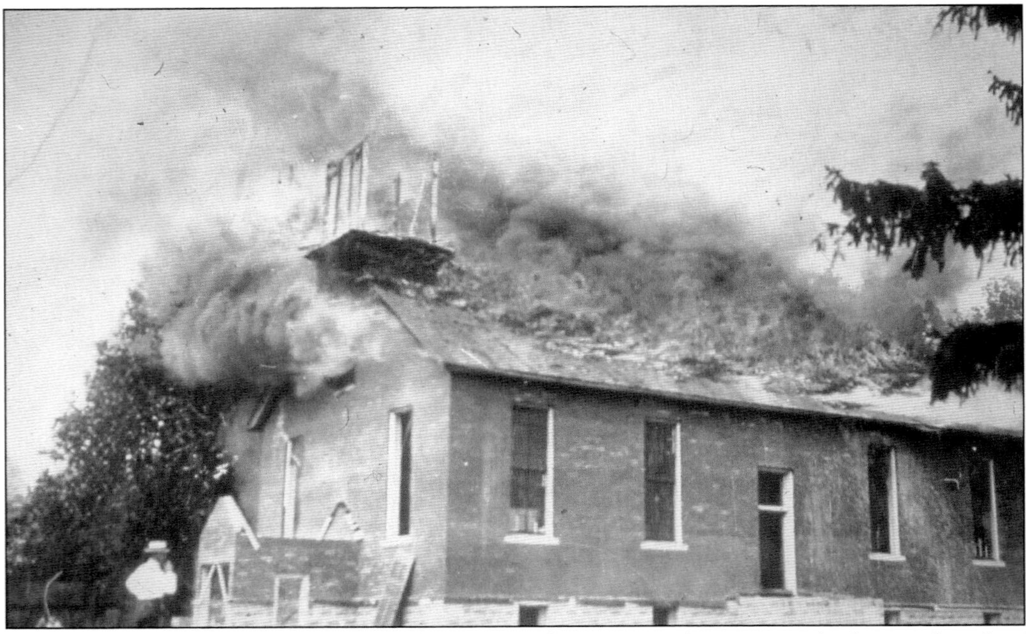

The damage was estimated at between $75,000 and $100,000. Father Downey had many friends of all faiths and an ingenious way of begging that always brought results. Within a year, the church and school were rebuilt. The new church bell was raised in 1921. There are 16 rings of 70 names encircling the bell. The top ring reads, "This bell is to the memory of the men and women whose names are here printed."

Father Downey served the parish for a total of 22 years (1913–1935), the longest of all the pastors at Immaculate Conception. It was in this era that the church was known as St. Mary's. This became confusing. It is not clear how it came about, but, in 1953, when the eighth pastor, Father John Koezler, arrived, he took the initiative and wrote to the archdiocese of Detroit and had the name changed back to Immaculate Conception.

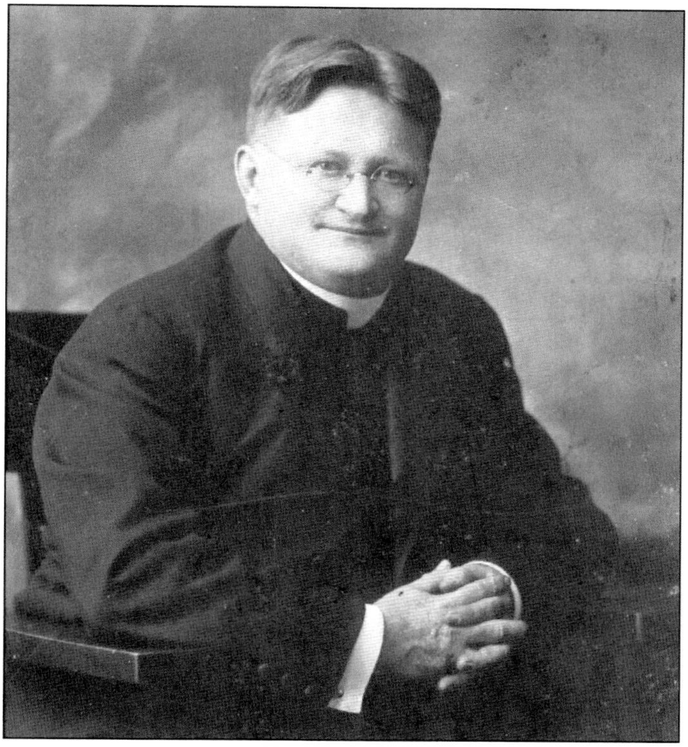

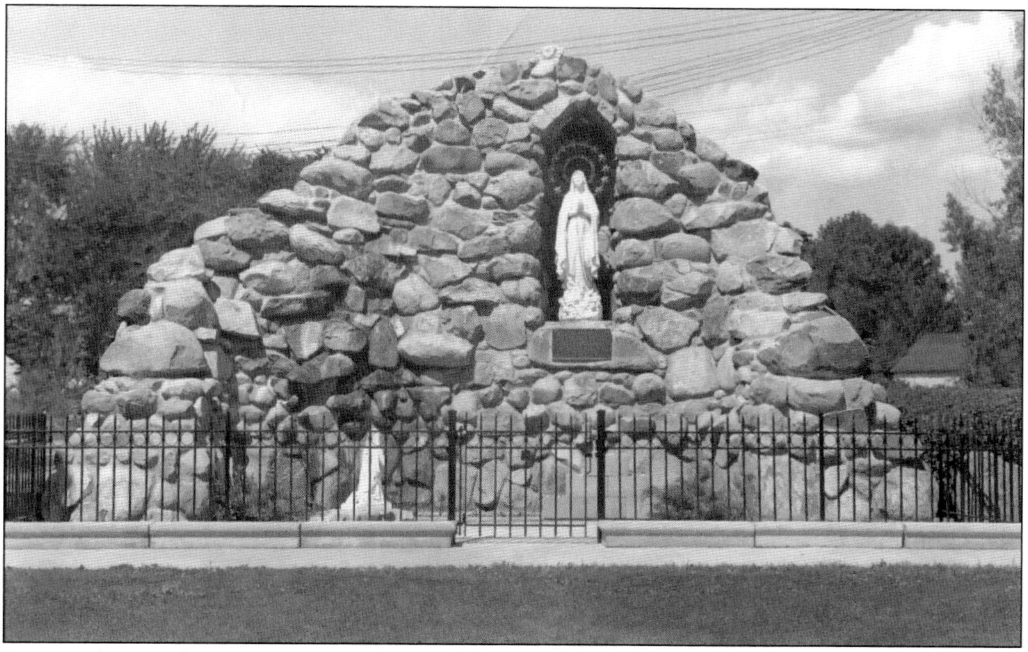

During the 100th anniversary of the church, Father Koezler directed the building of a grotto in honor of Our Lady of Lourdes. It was dedicated "in memory of the Pioneers of 1853 by the parishioners of Immaculate Conception of 1953." The fieldstone and boulders used to build the grotto were taken from various local parishioners' farmland. Joe Furtah, Paul Beauvais, and Roy Binge went on a road trip to the Alaskan Highway and gathered rocks to add.

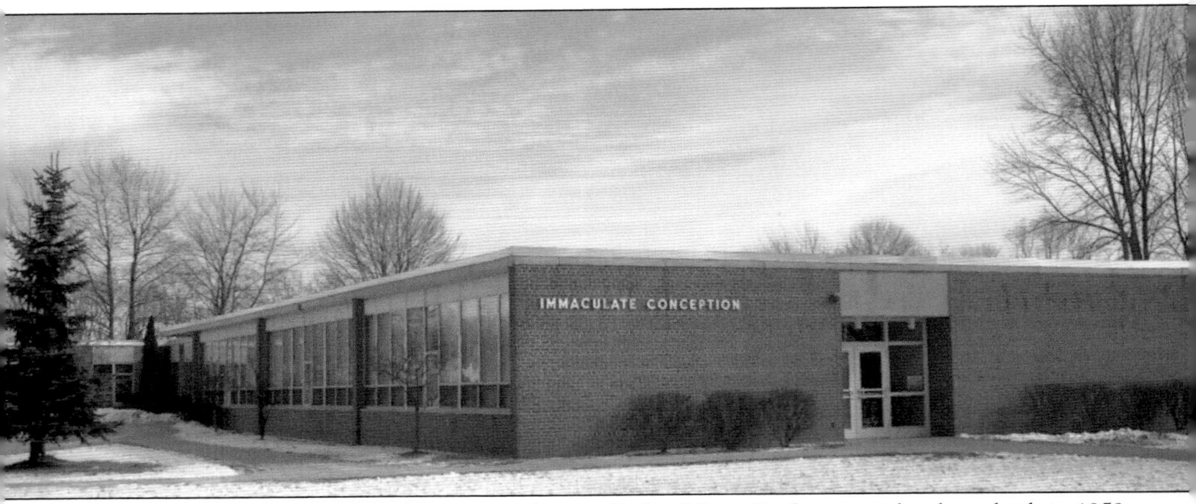

Under the leadership of newly appointed pastor Father Harry Paul, a new school was built in 1959, and a newsletter, *The Shrine Spotlight*, was first published. In 1967, Father Andrew LeFebvere was appointed associate pastor of Immaculate Conception Parish and served the parish for 11 years. In 1969, Father Paul and Father Andrew laid the groundwork for the first Parish Council. After months of preparation, an election was held and the first meeting took place on July 1, 1970. Father Paul also made the necessary arrangements to enlarge Sacred Heart Cemetery. After 22 years of dedicated service (1955–1977), Father Paul retired as pastor of Immaculate Conception Parish. He died on March 20, 1996, and his funeral was held in Anchorville at the Immaculate Conception Church.

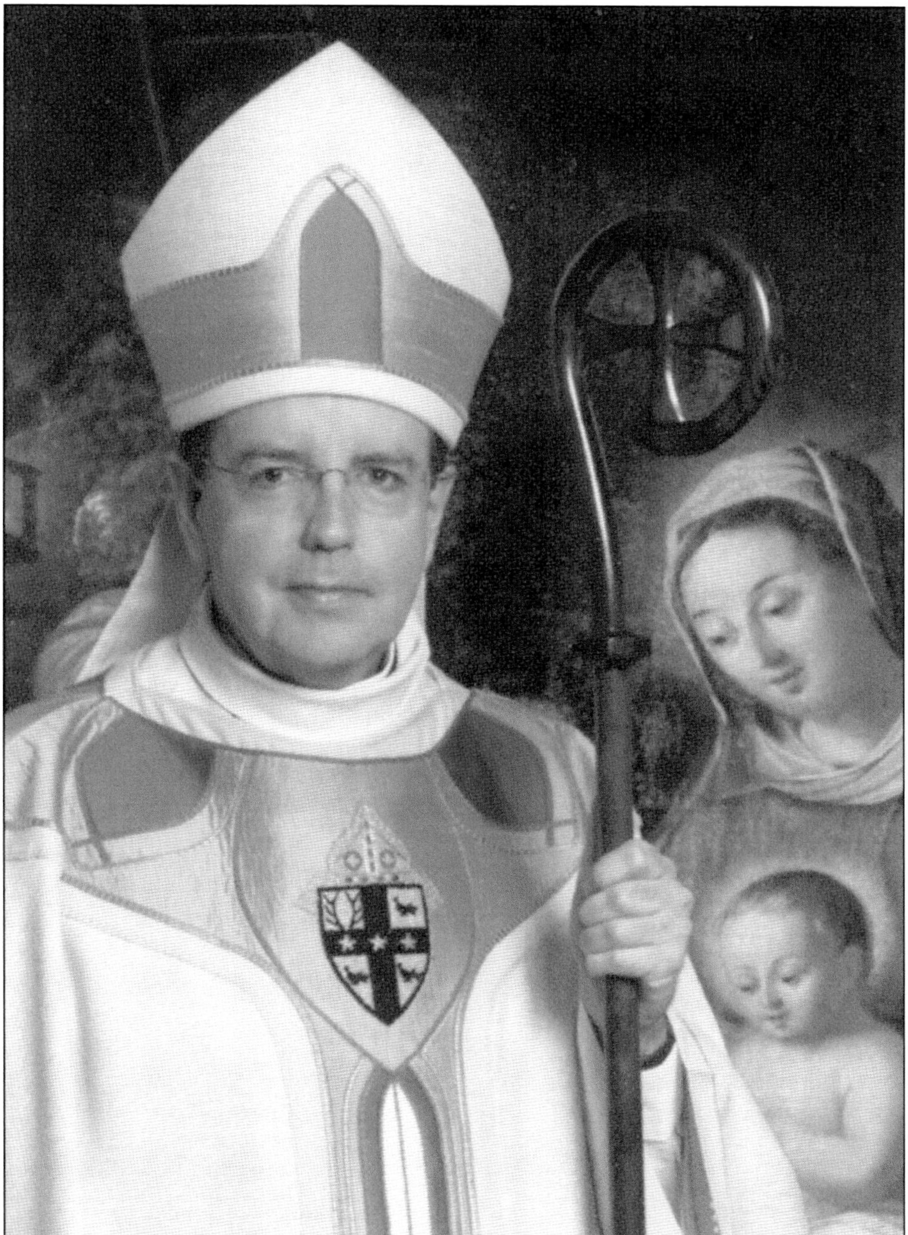

The Most Reverend Allen H. Vigneron (pictured), Archbishop of Detroit, the son of Elwin and Bernadine Vigneron of Fair Haven, attended Immaculate Conception School for eight years. As a young boy, he wanted to become a farmer, but by the age of seven, he had set his sights on becoming a priest. With encouragement from his parents and Father Harry Paul, Vigneron was ordained a priest in Detroit on July 26, 1975. He went on to be ordained auxiliary bishop of Detroit on July 9, 1996, and was appointed coadjutor bishop of Oakland, California, on January 10, 2003. He later succeeded as third bishop of Oakland on October 1, 2003, and was appointed tenth ordinary and fifth archbishop of Detroit on January 5, 2009. Vigneron was installed as archbishop of Detroit on January 28, 2009. His parents, Elwin and Bernadine Vigneron, were overjoyed at the honor bestowed upon their son.

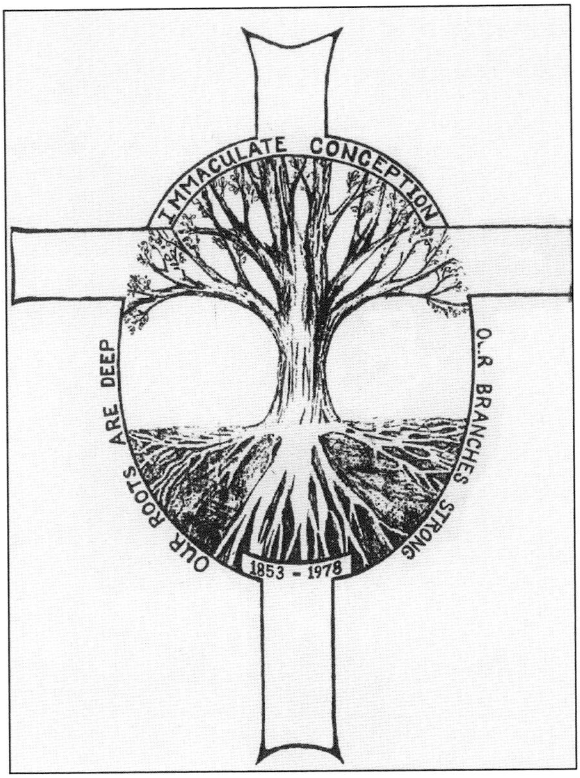

Father Daniel Bogus, who served from 1977 to 1991 as pastor, helped celebrate the 125th anniversary of Immaculate Conception Parish with a history book, *Our Roots Are Deep—Our Branches Strong*. He oversaw the building of a chapel, donated anonymously, at the Sacred Heart Cemetery. It serves the funerals held in the church.

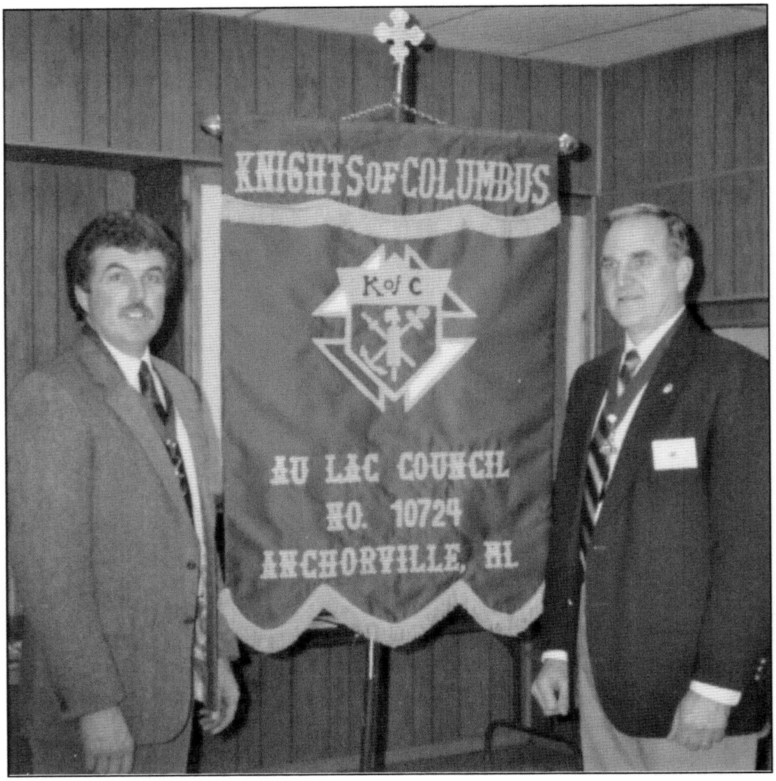

The Knights of Columbus was chartered on December 8, 1991. The charter date, on the feast of the Immaculate Conception, was selected to honor Mary, the patron of the church. Joe Kay (left), Tom Nofs (right), and Father Philip Briffa worked together to form the new council, which took the name Au Lac in honor of the village's name prior to 1876.

From 1993 to 1999, Father Zigismund Kowalczyk ("Father Sig") was the 12th pastor to serve at Immaculate Conception Church. At the time of Father Sig's arrival, the number of registered families was estimated to be about 700. He established the Living Waters prayer group and oversaw one of the best-known renovations to the church.

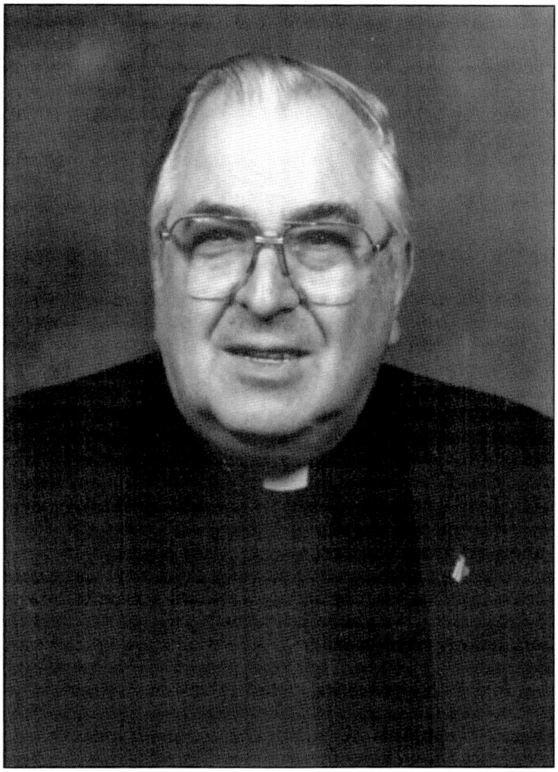

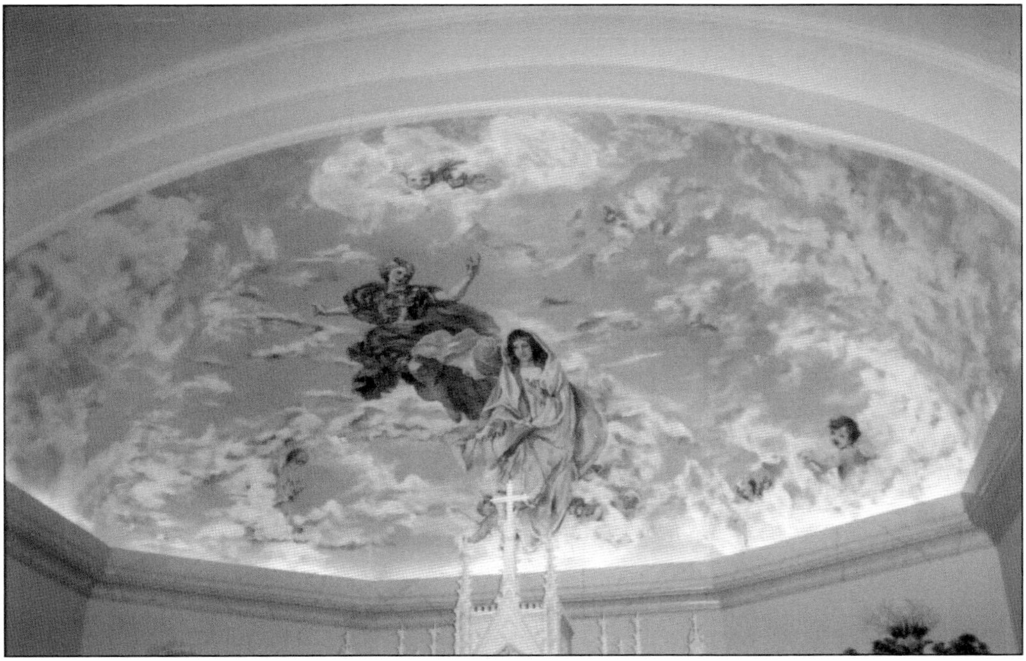

The church's restoration turned into inspiration. Eileen Fischer was chosen by Father Zigismund Kowalczyk, in 1996, to paint the ceiling dome in the church sanctuary. The task, which took 72 days to complete, was a labor of love. It depicts the moment the Virgin Mary learned she was chosen to give birth. The finished mural is stunning and admired by all who view it.

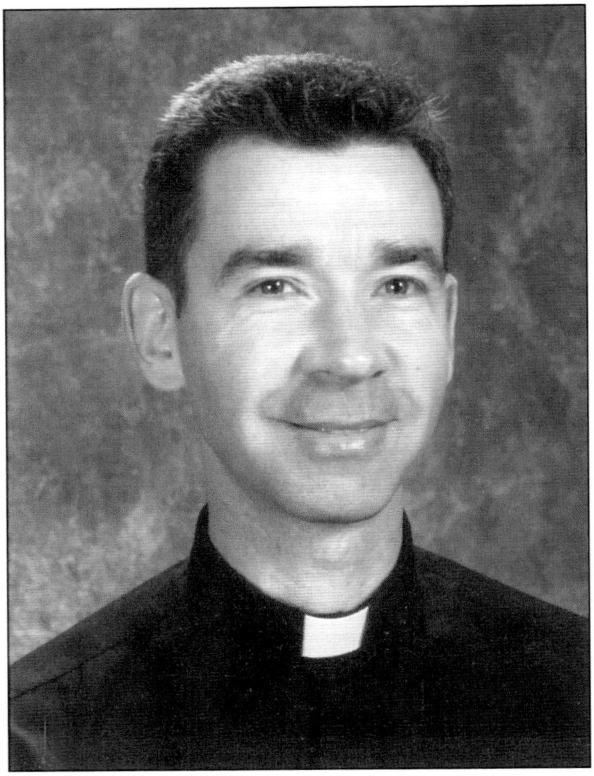

In 1999, Father David Burgard (left) arrived as the new pastor. He quickly anticipated the continued growth in the Anchor Bay area, and saw the need to expand the parish campus. It had been almost 35 years since any physical construction had taken place. After establishing a long-term planning committee, ground was broken for a new parish hall and gymnasium. The new buildings (below) were dedicated in 2005. In 2003, the church celebrated its 150th anniversary. As part of the festivities, a celebratory mass was said by Cardinal Maida, bishop of the Archdiocese of Detroit at the time. Also, a contest was initiated for all parishioners to use their talent to come up with a fresh logo. Father David announced the winning logo, and a new design was published, which declared, "Grounded in Hope, Nurtured in Faith."

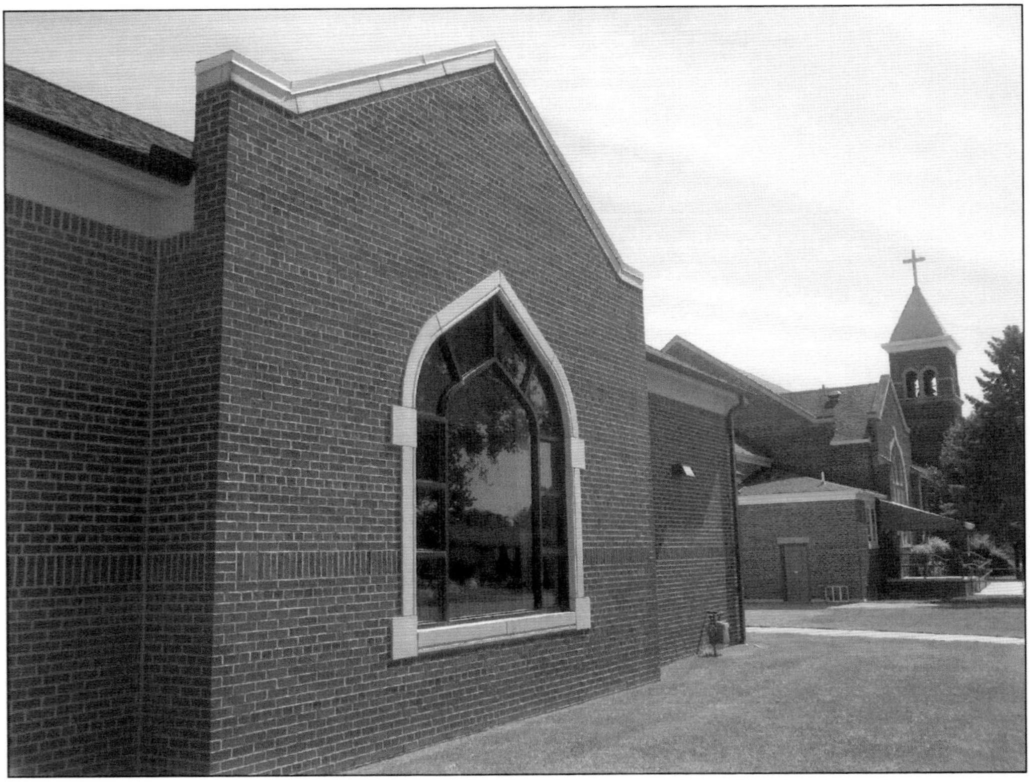

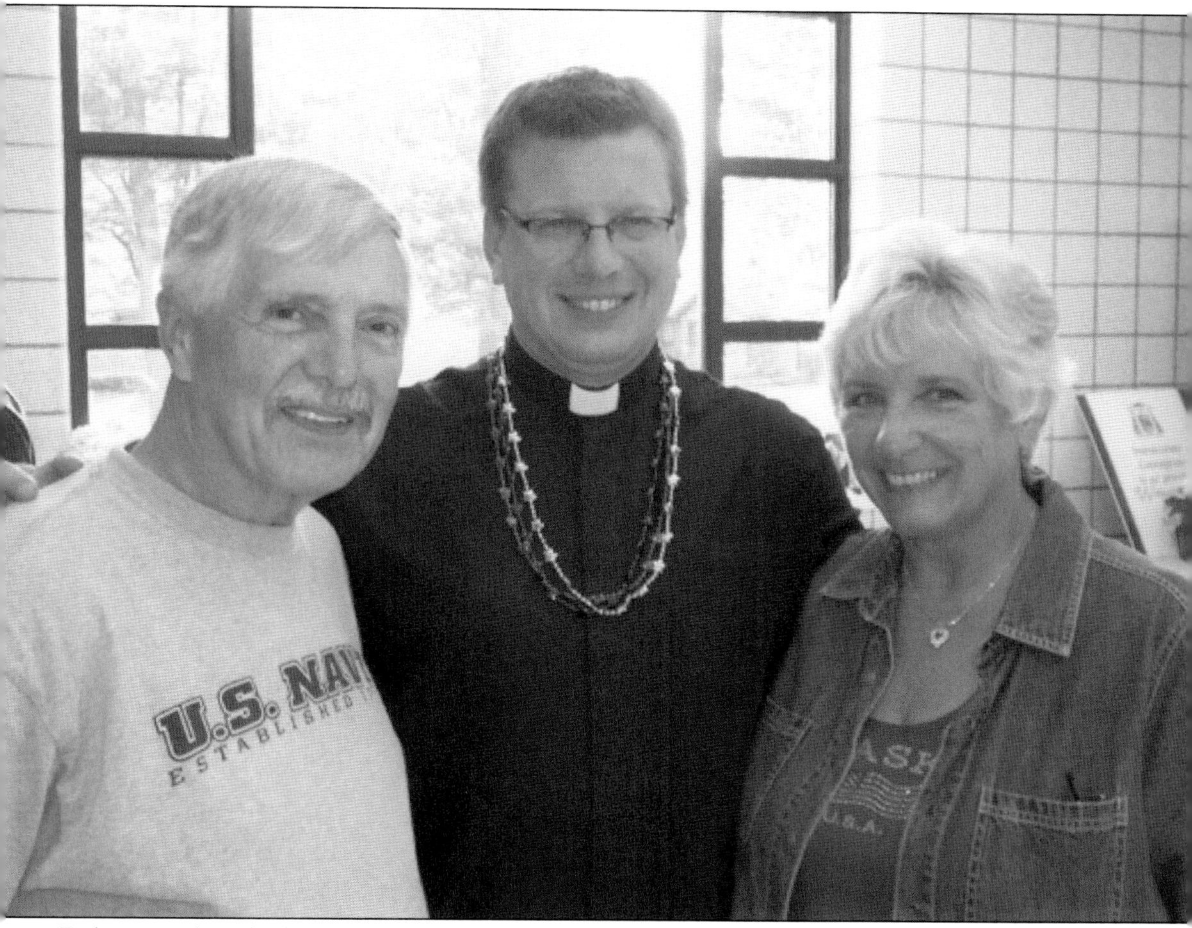

Father Tomek Maka (center) was appointed and served his first pastoral assignment from 2008 to 2012. He was born in Poland and became a US citizen in June 2011. Here, parishioners Norm and JoAnn Augustine help Father Tomek celebrate the occasion inside Burgard Hall with a luncheon. His biggest contribution to the parish was inspiring parishioners to pay off the debt for the new buildings, which was accomplished in just over three years.

From Age to Age you Gather a People

IC

160th Anniversary

Immaculate Conception Church, Ira Towship, MI

1853 ~ 2013

Current pastor Father Joe Esper was appointed on July 1, 2012. He oversees a growing and thriving church community with all the organizations of the church, including councils and commissions, committees, ministries, and the IC school. In 2013, the church made plans to celebrate its 160th anniversary with special events and a play that told its long history. A contest was held to create a new logo that would mark the anniversary date; all parishioners were invited to participate. Father Esper declared the winning entry (pictured), "From Age to Age you gather a People." In the long history of the church, approximately 30 former students of Immaculate Conception who became priests or sisters. It was Father David Burgard who so eloquently stated the endearing words that will last for ages: "And so the journey continues."

Three

SETTLEMENT OF AU LAC/ANCHORVILLE

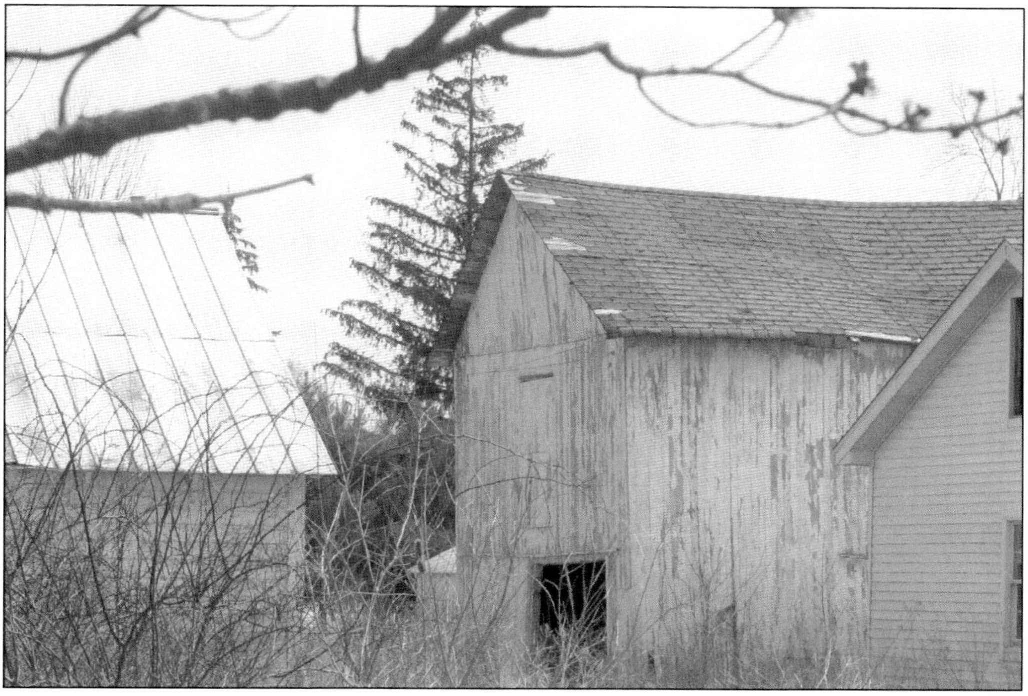

The discovery of some 700 French letters in the Savoyard family barn in Anchorville revealed the story of Jean Baptiste Tornay, one of the early Ira Township pioneers who came here in 1850 from (French speaking) Orsieres, Switzerland. Included in the cache found by Jim Savoyard were Tornay's official certificate of origin and passport documents.

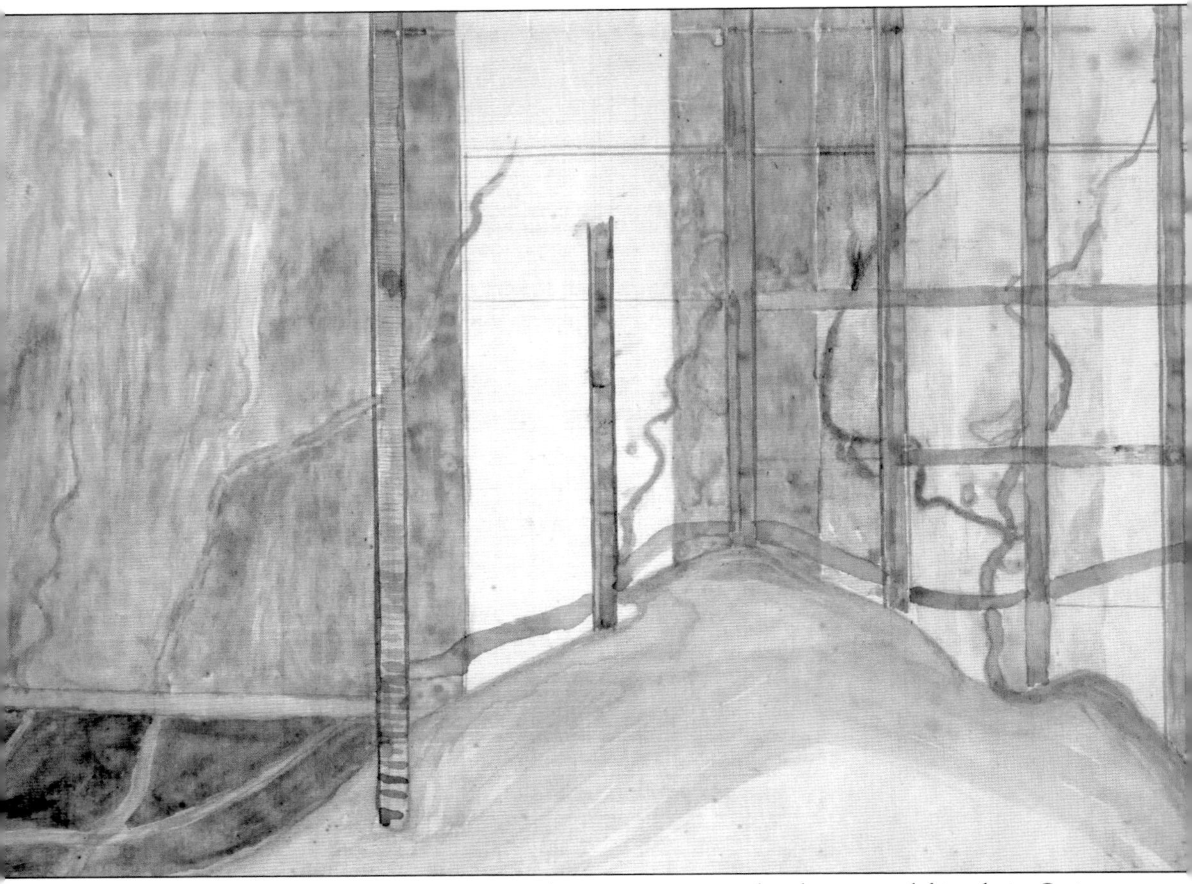

For over 20 years, Jean Baptiste Tornay kept in contact with relatives and friends in Orsieres, Switzerland, writing letters to his uncle Isadore Tornay, explaining to him the opportunities of purchasing land. Jean Baptiste had sketched a drawing of Anchor Bay (pictured) to illustrate to newcomers the sections of land and rivers and to show the proximity to Lake St. Clair. One of Isadore's sons, Joseph Nicolas Tornay, and his wife, Constance (Lovay), were convinced of a better life and planned their voyage to Ira Township very carefully. From 1850 to 1871, they wrote letters back and forth and, finally, in April 1871, when the conditions were right, they made the voyage. The letters tell the story of their journey. Jean Baptiste was also an agent who helped families with their passage to the United States. (Courtesy of Jim Savoyard.)

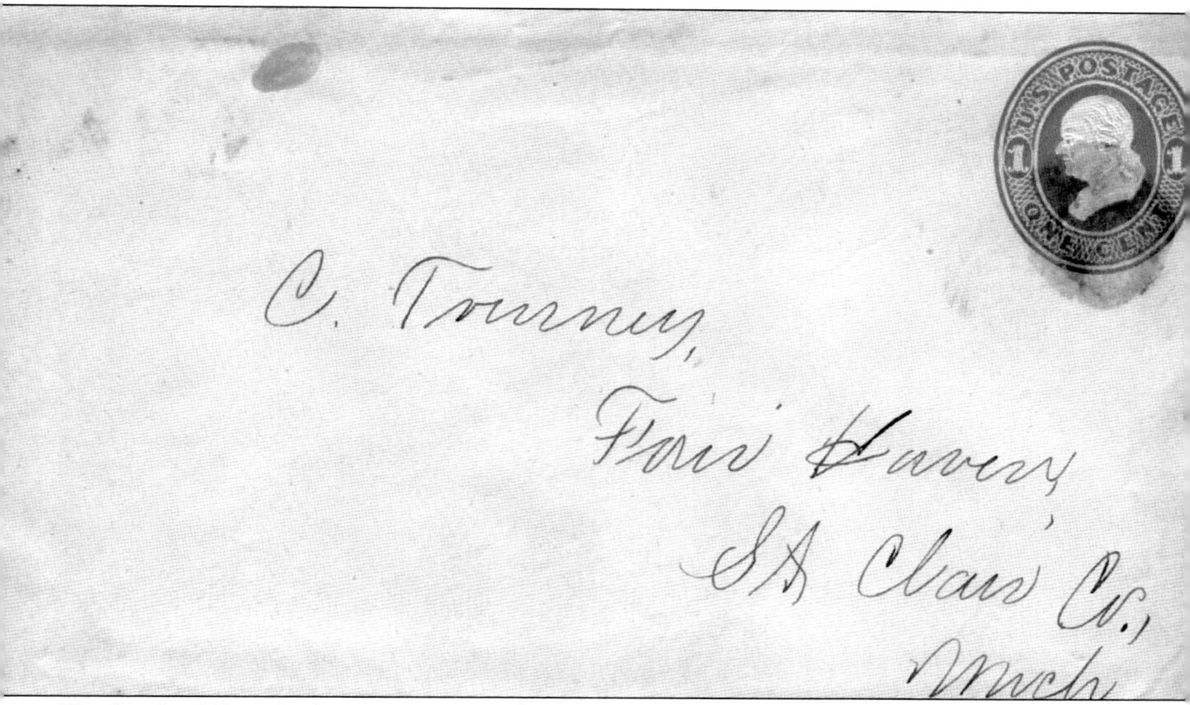

The family of 12 made the voyage six months apart, on two different ships. In a charming letter dated 1871, the eldest son, Sidoine, tells his mother, Constance, of his journey to America: "We embarked at Liverpool onto the ship on the 18th of April in the morning. We spent 13 days at sea, and even with 5 days of storms, I wasn't sick for one minute since we left, for 3 days we had to stay on the ship in New York because of a smallpox outbreak. We were well fed throughout the whole journey." They arrived at their uncle's house in Anchorville on May 8 at 8:00 in the evening. Sidoine proclaimed to his mother, "we had the best journey in the world." (Courtesy of Jim Savoyard.)

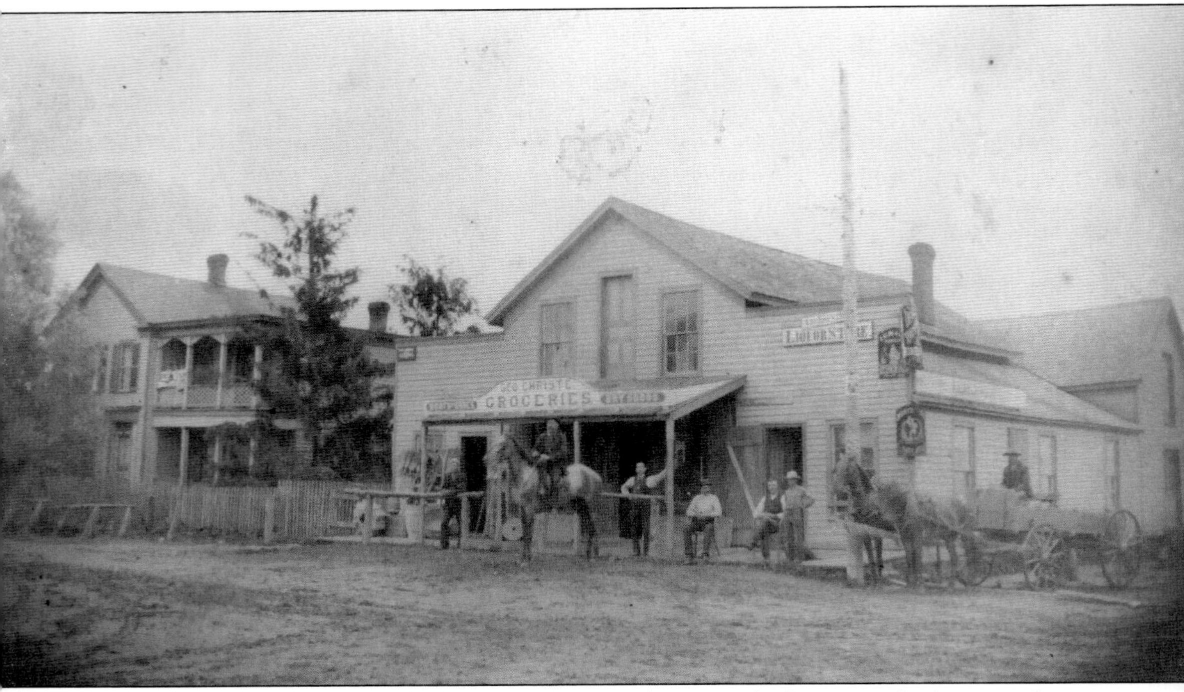

In 1835, two years before statehood, a large general store and saloon were built across the street from the Immaculate Conception Catholic Church. A one-story wooden building, it was the center of commerce for farmers for miles around. This property had once been part of the Swan Creek Indian Reserve; after the removal of the Swan, the area began to flourish economically.

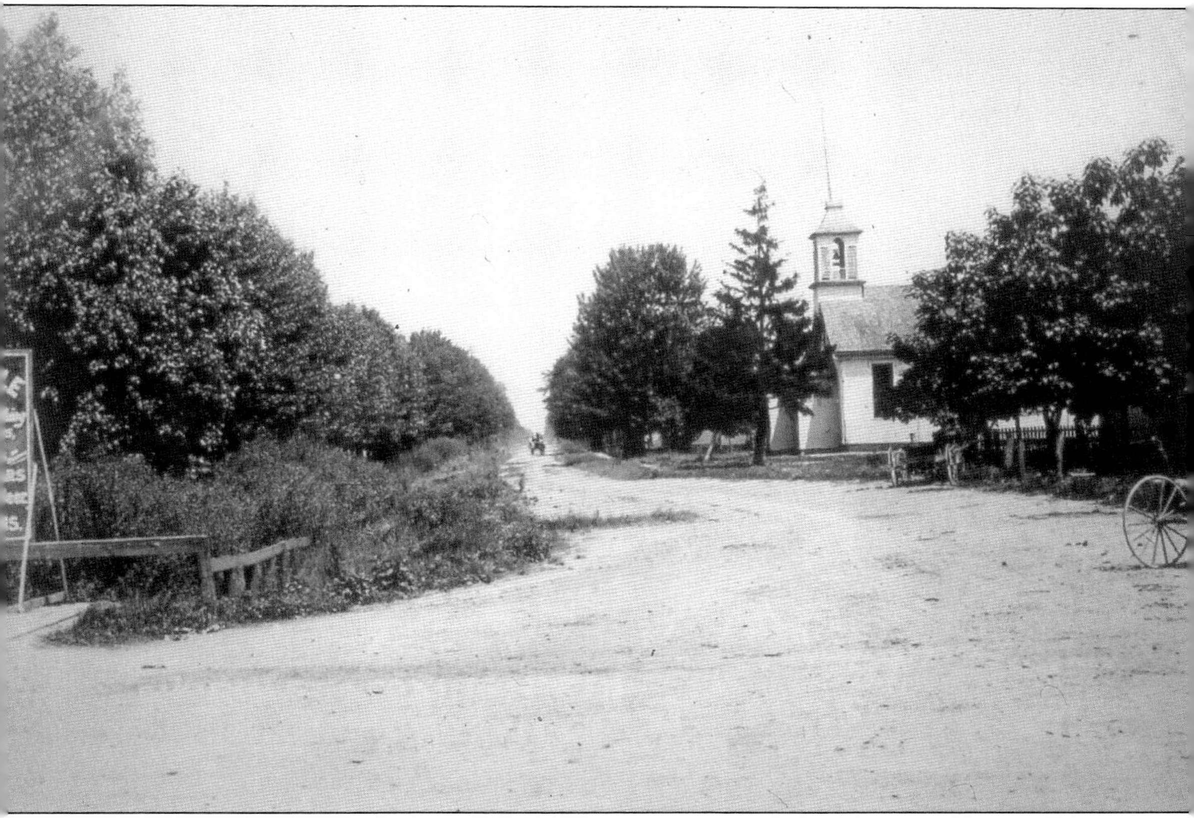

This photograph looks north on Church Road, where directly across M-29 from the Anchorville General Store, the Sacred Heart Institute School can be seen on the right. A parked horse and buggy can be seen alongside the Immaculate Conception Church, as well as another approaching on Church Road. The roads were dirt, which made travel difficult in the spring and on rainy days when they turned to mud. On the left is a sign advertising the Anchorville Hotel's amenities.

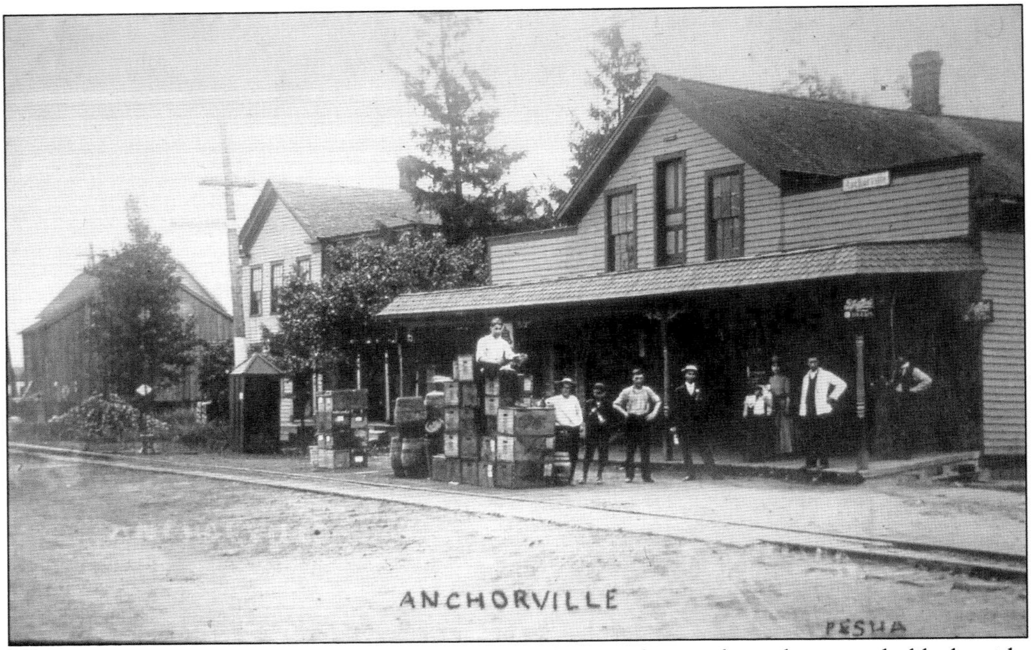

By 1850, the Anchorville area included several general stores, three or four saloons, and a blacksmith. The first general store built its own dock and described it as "one of the busiest ports north of Detroit." In 1859, the owner was Henry Johr; he expanded the business by having a warehouse constructed. It can be seen down the track, just past the store.

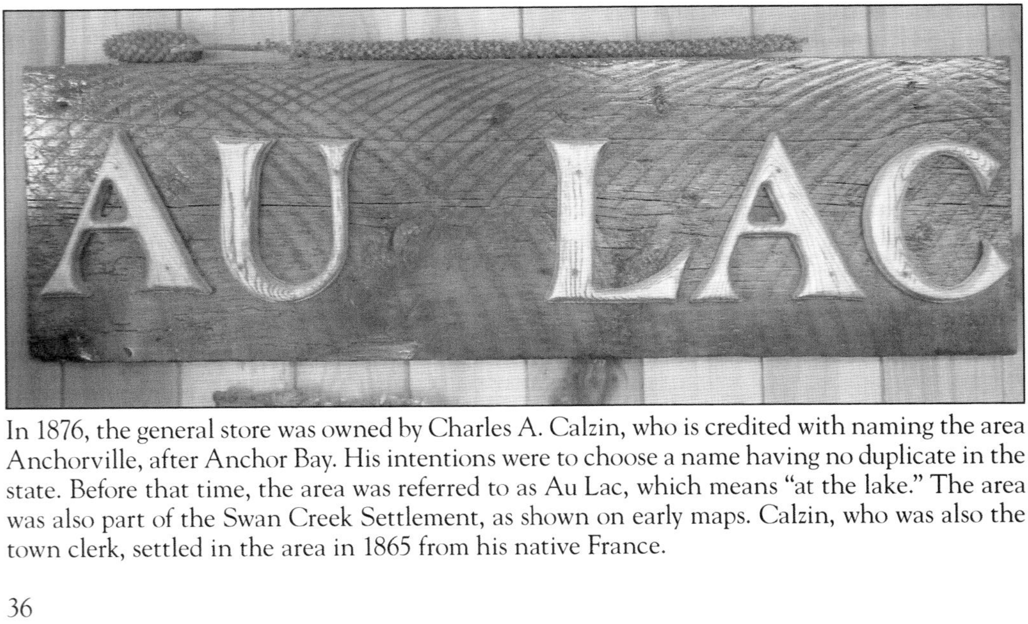

In 1876, the general store was owned by Charles A. Calzin, who is credited with naming the area Anchorville, after Anchor Bay. His intentions were to choose a name having no duplicate in the state. Before that time, the area was referred to as Au Lac, which means "at the lake." The area was also part of the Swan Creek Settlement, as shown on early maps. Calzin, who was also the town clerk, settled in the area in 1865 from his native France.

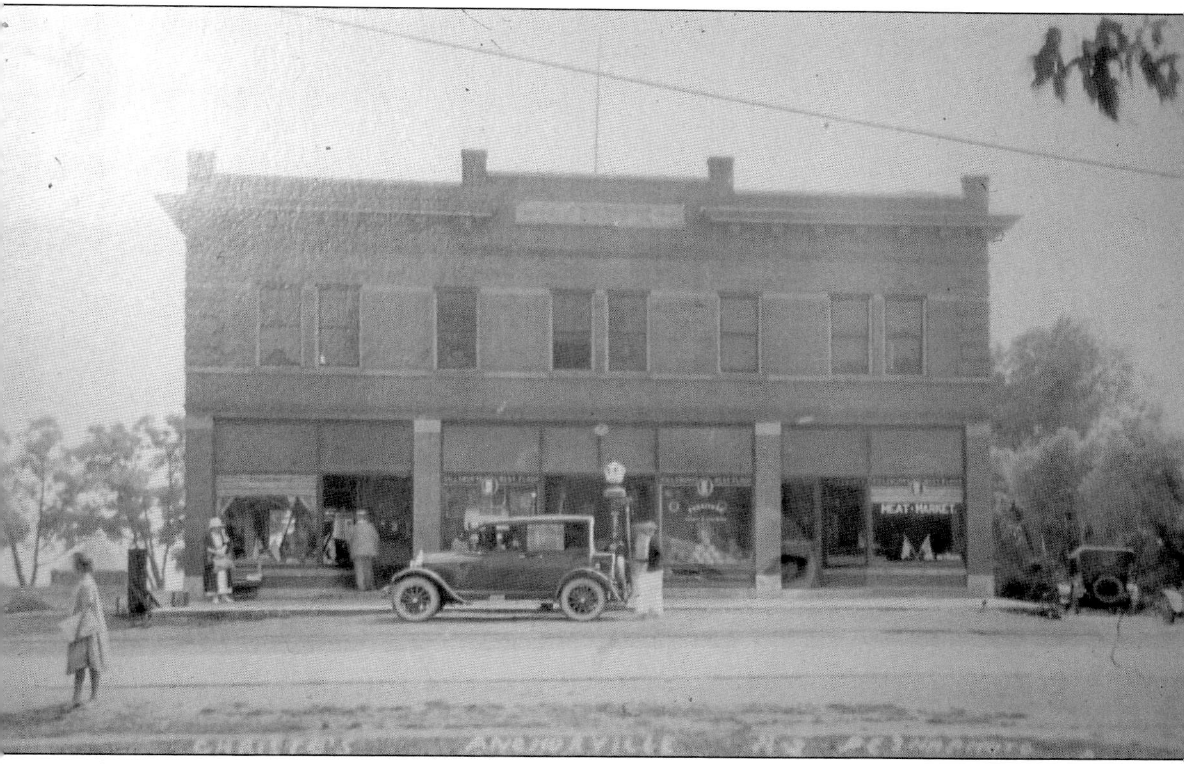

In the 1880s, the Christie family began its long connection with the store. A.J. Christie was the first store owner and a postmaster. The Christies continued to serve as postmaster from 1885 to 1940. By this time, the store had two stories and continued to sell groceries and general goods including shoes, boots, and furniture. It also served the public as a saloon, with Adolph Eckhout as a partner.

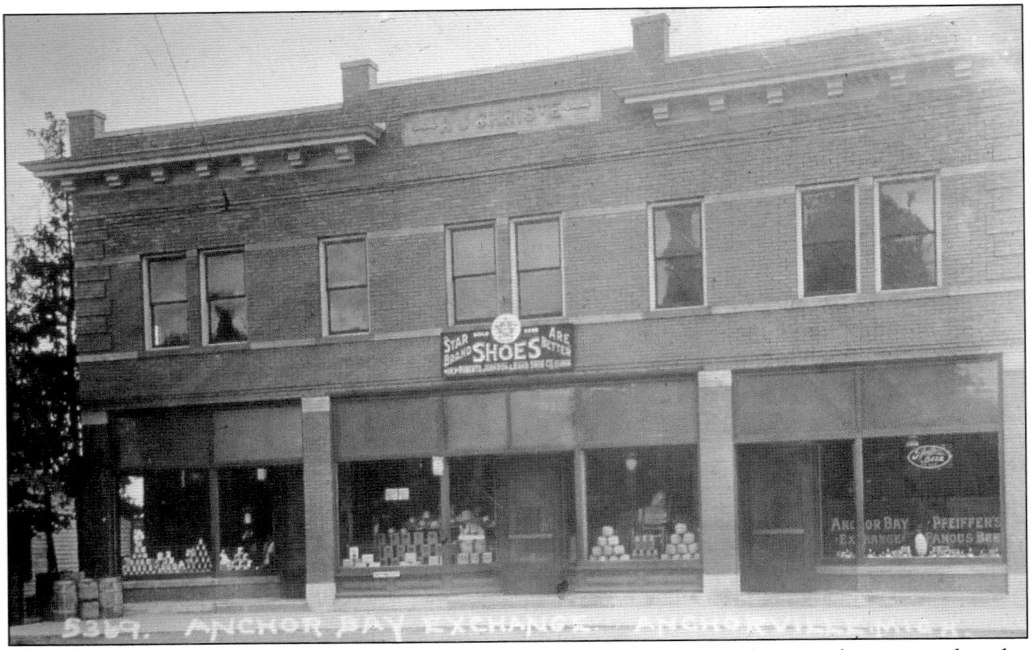

The store continued through the years, although the dock was allowed to weather away after the interurban railroad began in the 1900s. Rail transportation caused the demise of much of the shipping to the area; by 1920, the dock was mostly a memory and a few spiles in the water.

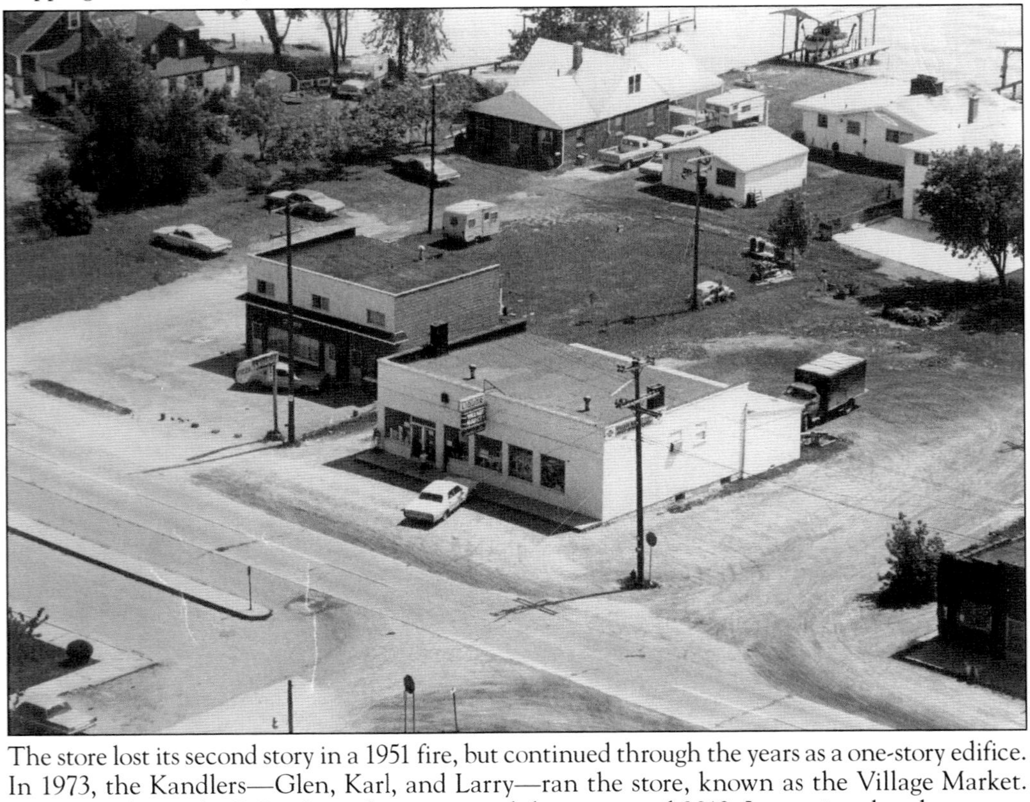

The store lost its second story in a 1951 fire, but continued through the years as a one-story edifice. In 1973, the Kandlers—Glen, Karl, and Larry—ran the store, known as the Village Market. Following them, the D Brothers chain operated the store until 2012. It remains closed.

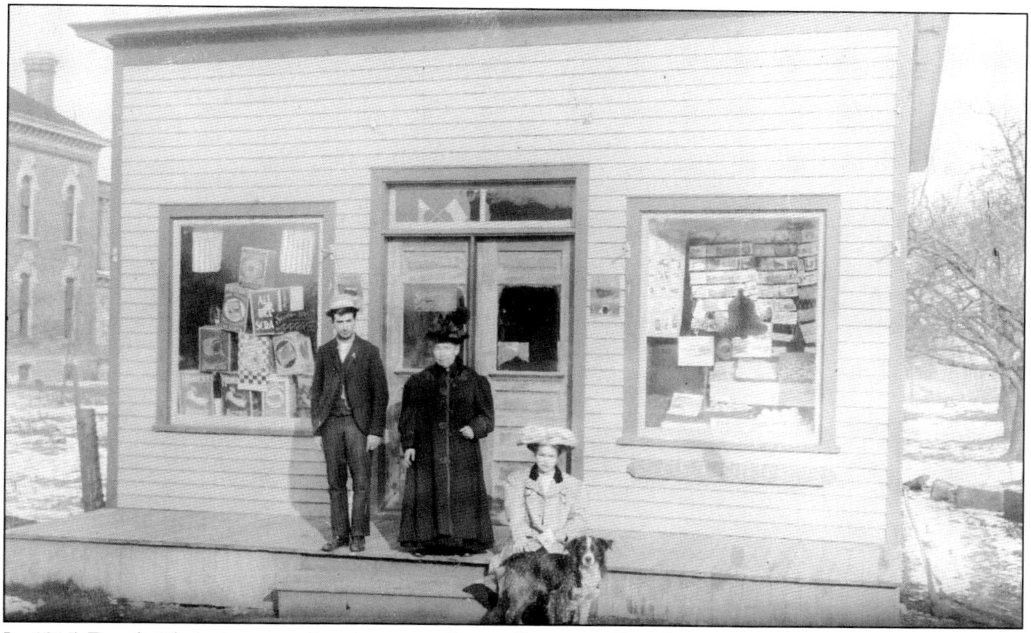

In 1915, Frank Christie opened and operated a small store, selling his wares of tobacco, confectionery, stationery, and postcards. It was also an ice-cream parlor. Shown in the above photograph are Frank, his mother, his sister, and their dog Carlo. The store was located on M-29 east of Immaculate Conception Church in Anchorville. It became a stop for the Detroit Interurban Railroad. After Prohibition ended and alcohol became legal, the store was renamed Christie's Tavern. Cold beer was now legally enjoyed. Throughout the 1950s, neighbor kids went there for penny candy and soda pop. It was a convenient stop for locals.

Frank Christie

Confectionery, Tobacco and Cigars, Stationery and Post Cards

ICE CREAM PARLOR IN CONNECTION

Magazines, Books and Toilet Articles
A Specialty

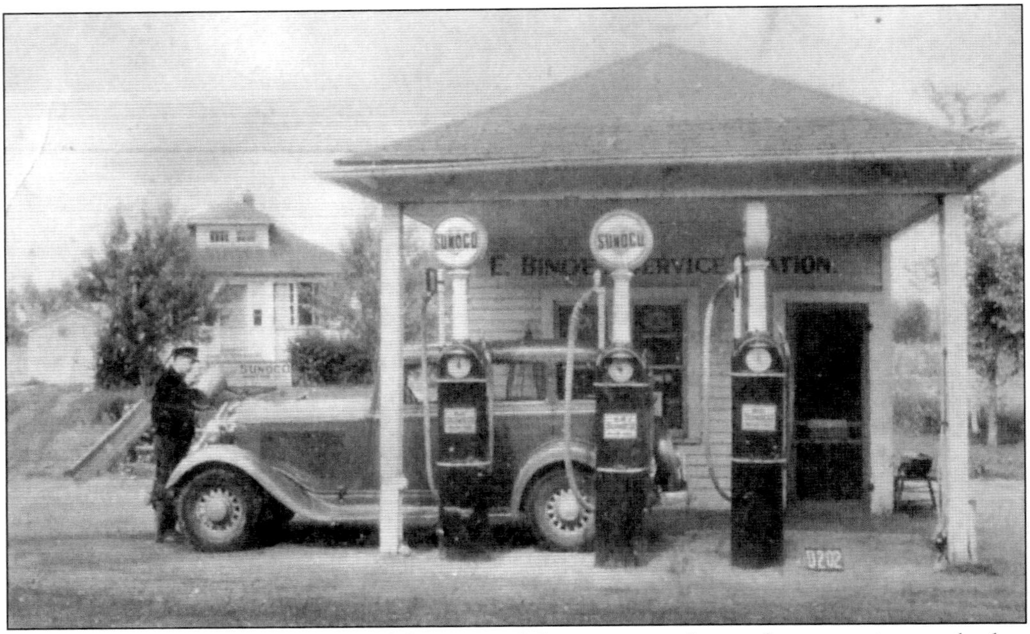

As the production and popularity of the automobile grew, a need arose for gas stations and other facilities associated with cars. Ed Binge, a homeowner and entrepreneur, opened a Sunoco service station in the 1930s. It was located about a quarter mile east of downtown Anchorville along the shoreline on Dixie Highway (M-29). The above photograph illustrates the look of the era's automobiles and gas pumps. This station serviced a number of the local residents and vacationers who drove along Dixie Highway. The below photograph shows the home of the Binge family. (Both, courtesy of Dennis Furtah.)

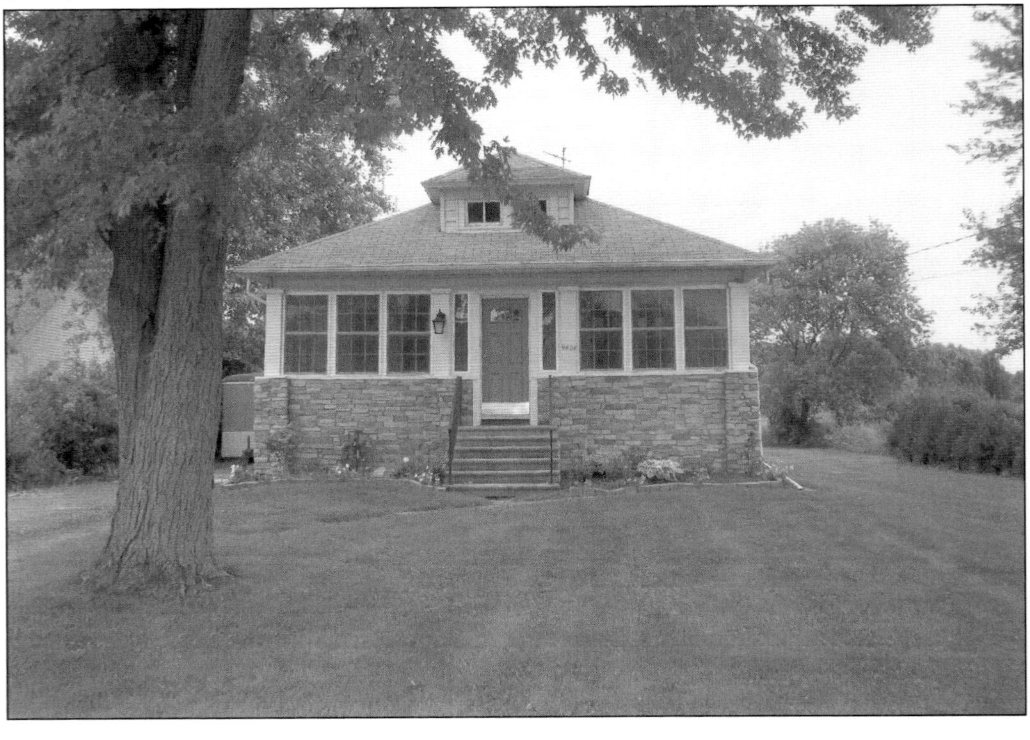

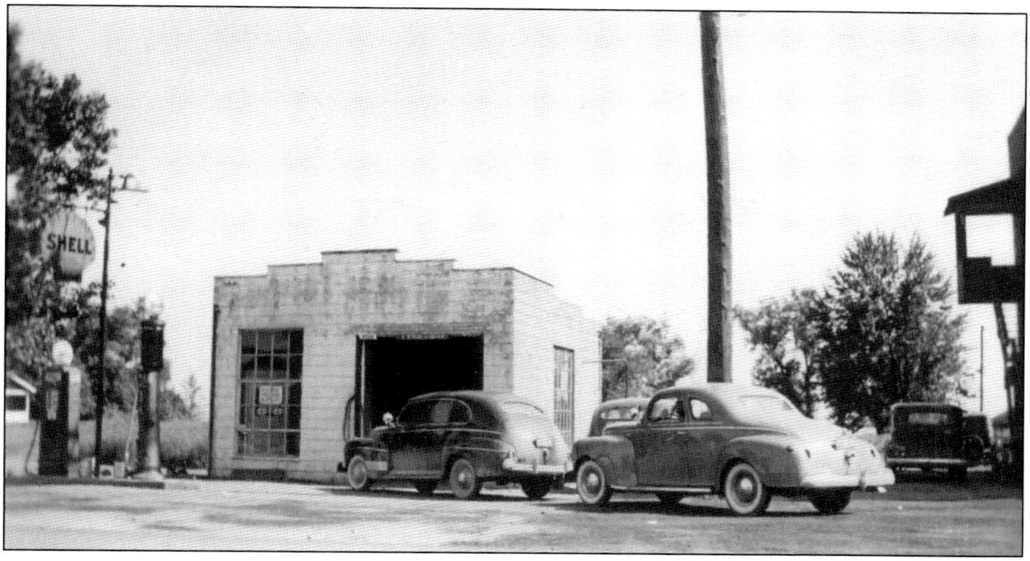

In 1957, Donald and Betty Wheeler moved their family from Utica, Michigan, to Anchorville and built a home behind the Village Market on Lake St. Clair. They purchased the property where the old Shell gas station stood along M-29 (above), tore down the existing building in 1960, and built a new two-story structure. The top floor was made into apartments. The Wheelers included a full-service Texaco gas station and a restaurant serving fresh donuts, breakfast, and lunch. The business also included a bait-and-tackle shop and 40 newly built ice shanties that rented out for $5 a day. Don's son Jeff took the customers out to their shanty in a 1937 Chevy Jetty. For a fee of $5, Jeff would use a chainsaw to cut a hole in the ice for the fishermen. During the winter months, the ice could be up to three feet thick! (Both, courtesy of Dawn Juska.)

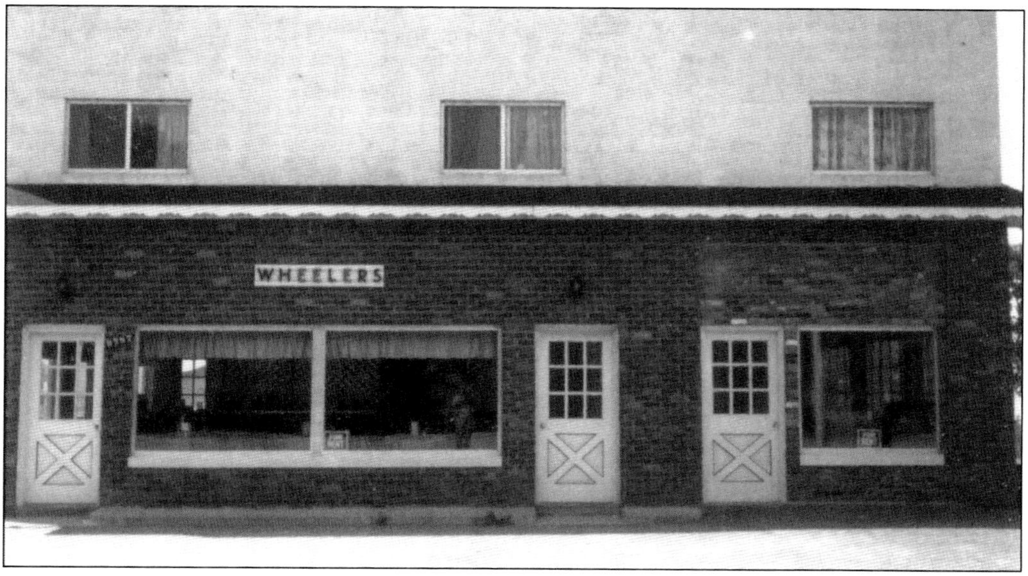

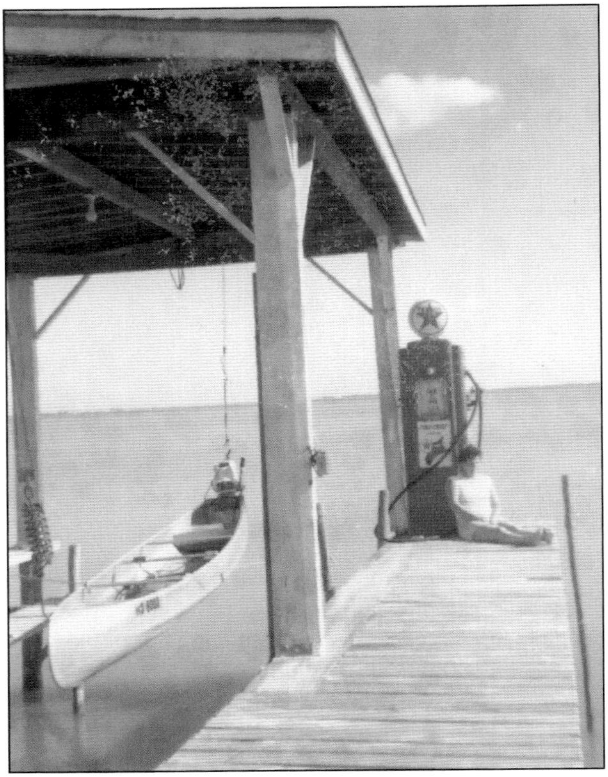

A catering service for the shanty renters was available. Don's daughter Dawn made the food that was delivered by Jeff. The bait room sold night crawlers and minnows. Playing the 5¢ pinball machine in the store was a favorite pastime for the kids in the neighborhood. Summer boaters were serviced by a Texaco gas pump located on the lakefront at the end of the dock (left). Winter brought another economy to the businesses of Ira. There were at least four official places that rented fish shanties along the shoreline on Dixie Highway (M-29): Bowers Boat Livery, Wheelers, Tips Place, and Joswick's. Additionally, hundreds of privately owned shanties dotted the bay, which had at least four or five places where a car could access the lake. Wheelers closed in 1965, and today, Del Barba Insurance Company (below) operates an agency at that location. (Both, courtesy of Dawn Juska.)

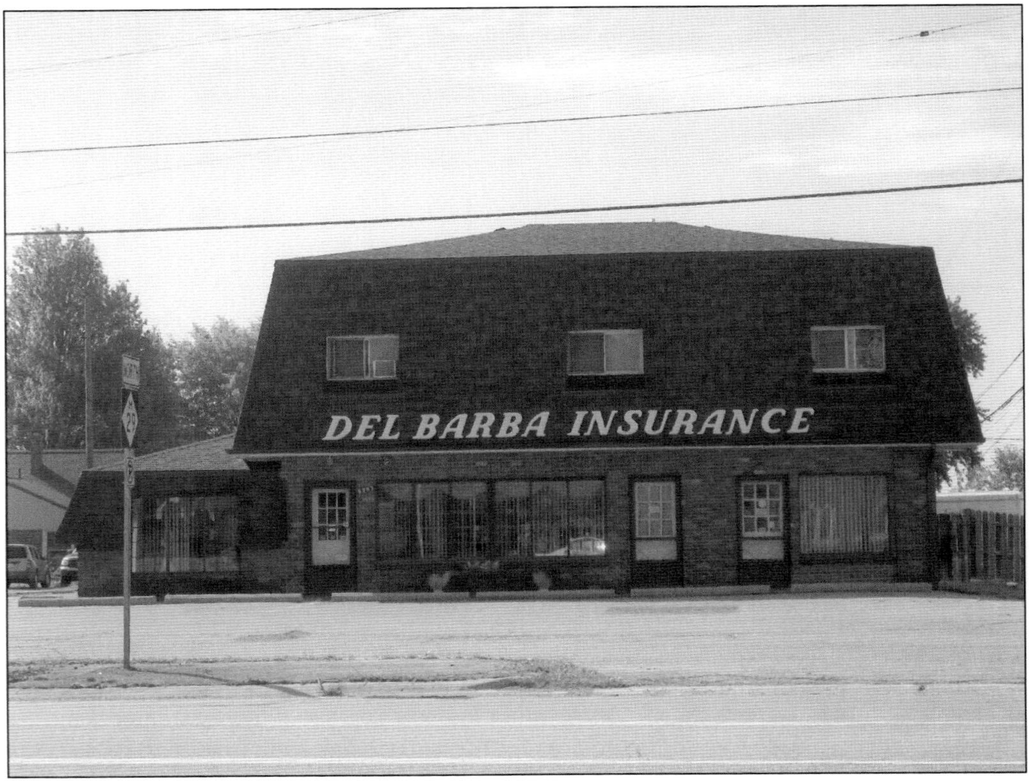

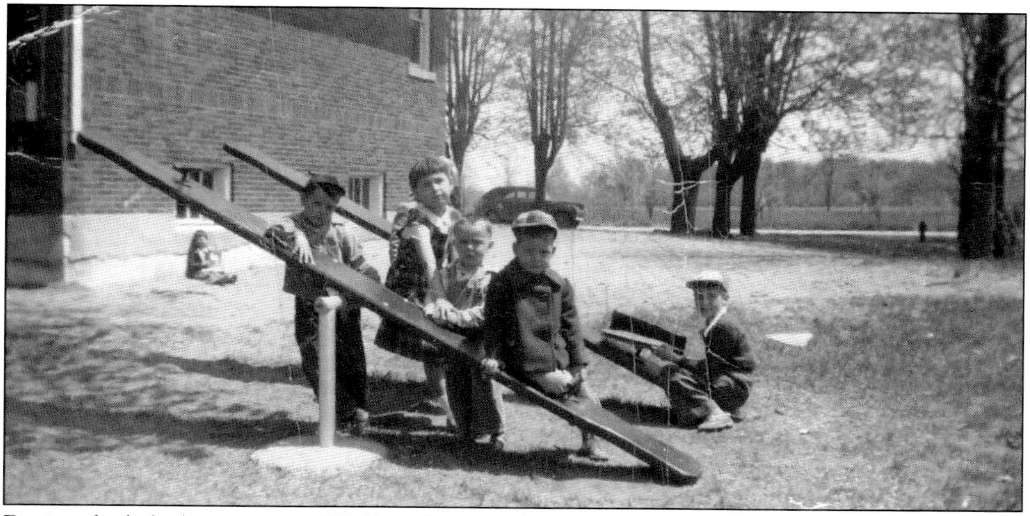

During the baby boom years of 1940 to about 1955, a generation of kids from Anchorville (around 40) grew up in a small-town atmosphere close to Immaculate Conception Church and School and the Bloom School. The post office, the Village Market, Christie's Tavern, and Wheeler's variety store and the Indian Trail that ran along Short Cut Road were their domain. They became friends and, in most cases, were related (cousins, brothers, and sisters). Don Furtah (below, sitting on the ground) was one of the oldest and most creative of the group that would become known as the Anchorvillains. It was the era of early mornings and long nights, when their mothers would open the front door and call out their names, saying, "Time to come home!" (Both, courtesy of Stacia Rivard.)

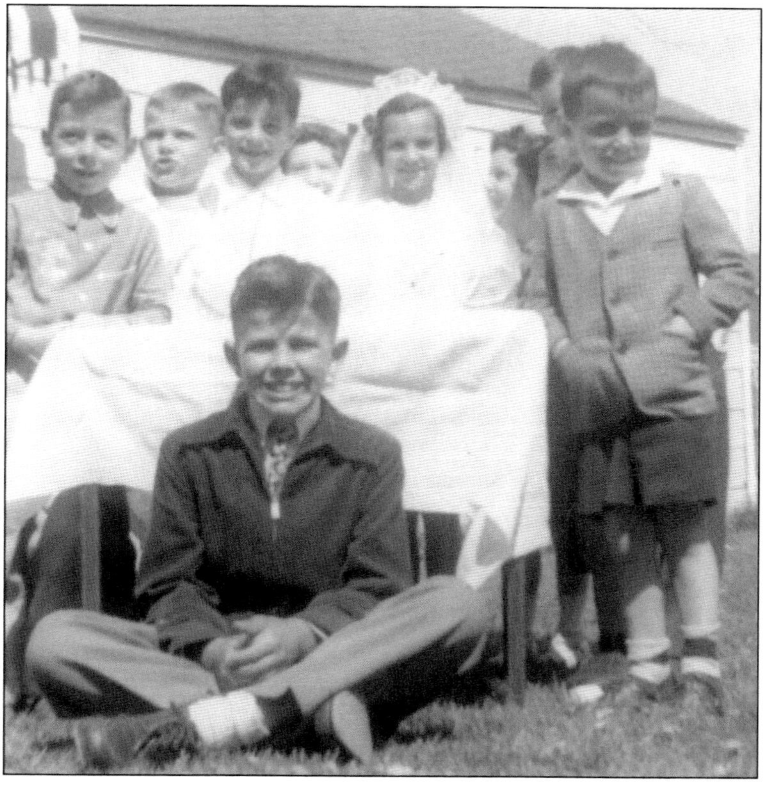

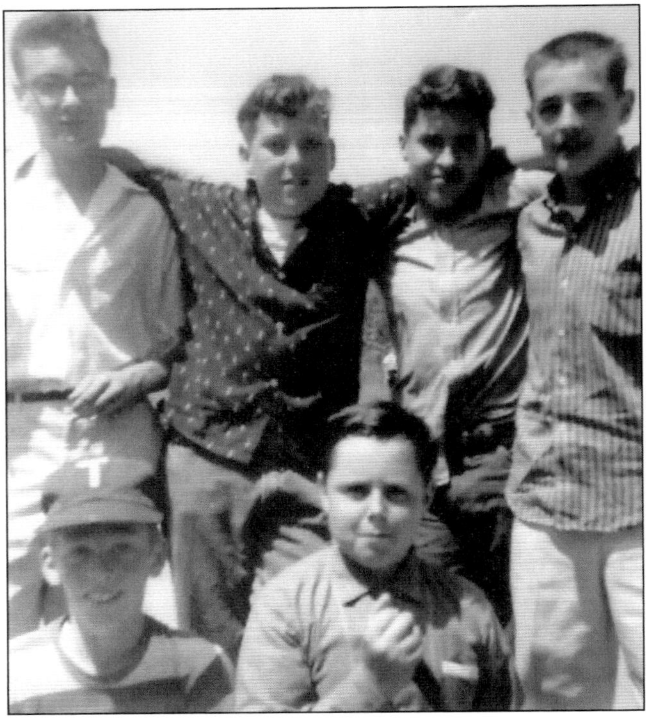

The innocent mischief the Anchorville kids got into included water-balloon fights, firecracker displays, Halloween pranks, and toilet paper stretched out across Church Road. At the intersection of Short Cut and Church Road, where they would gather, sat two cement structures known to them as the "Blocks." They threw stones at a streetlight on the corner. One night, someone hit the light, and there was darkness as everyone ran home! No one knows who threw the stone that put the light out. Before Ira Little League baseball was organized, George Hack put together teams that competed in the Blue Water District, playing games at Stockers Field, located at the west end of Short Cut Road. (Left, courtesy of Muriel Dee; below, courtesy of David Furtah.)

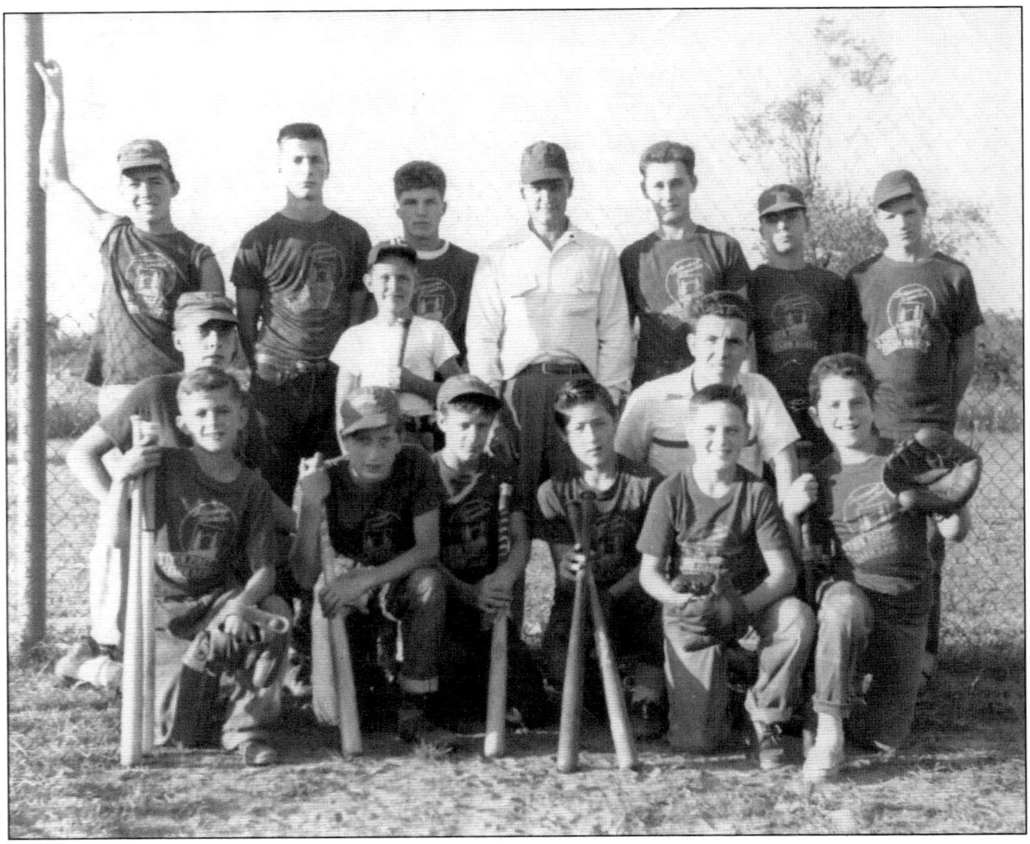

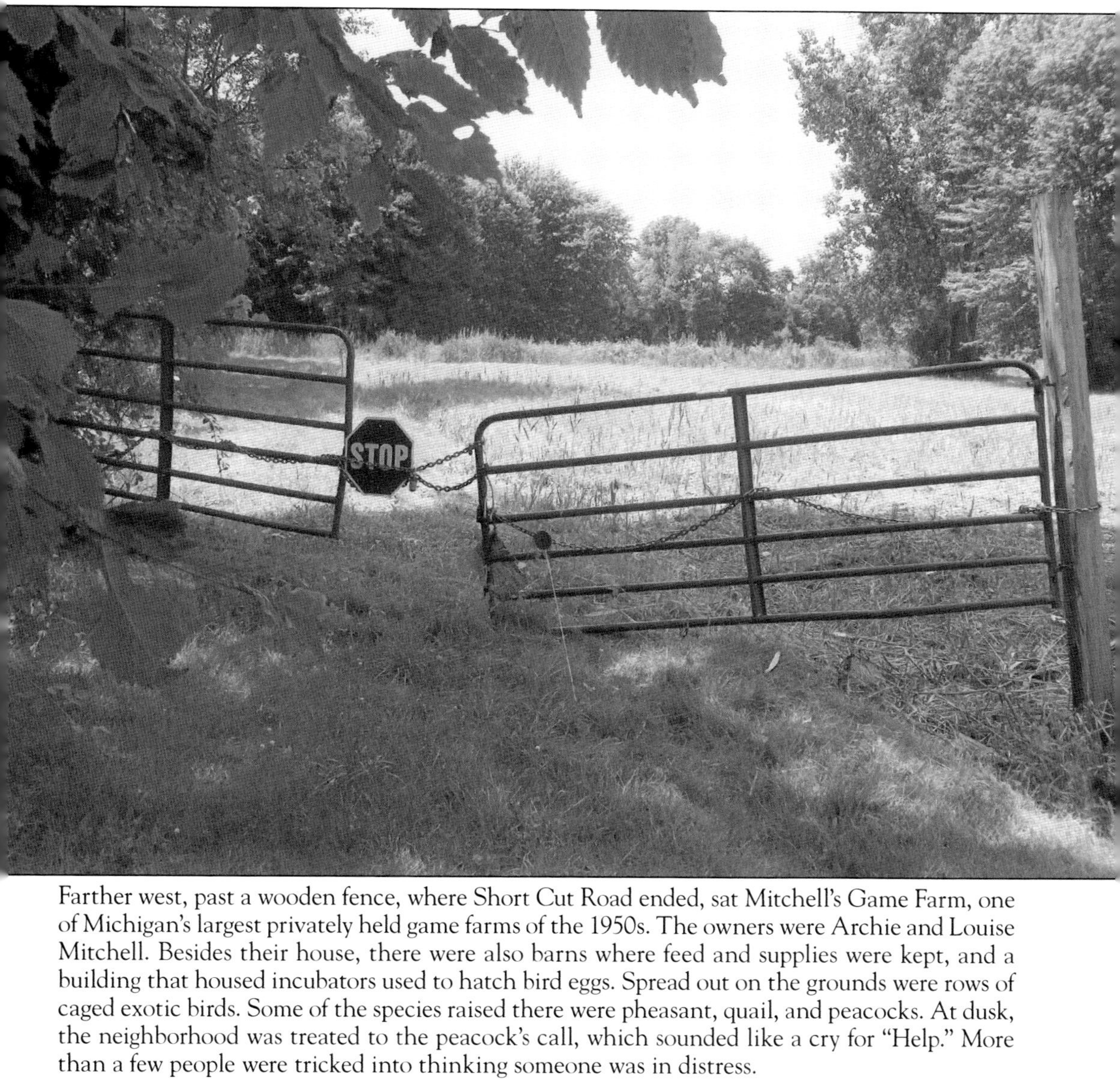

Farther west, past a wooden fence, where Short Cut Road ended, sat Mitchell's Game Farm, one of Michigan's largest privately held game farms of the 1950s. The owners were Archie and Louise Mitchell. Besides their house, there were also barns where feed and supplies were kept, and a building that housed incubators used to hatch bird eggs. Spread out on the grounds were rows of caged exotic birds. Some of the species raised there were pheasant, quail, and peacocks. At dusk, the neighborhood was treated to the peacock's call, which sounded like a cry for "Help." More than a few people were tricked into thinking someone was in distress.

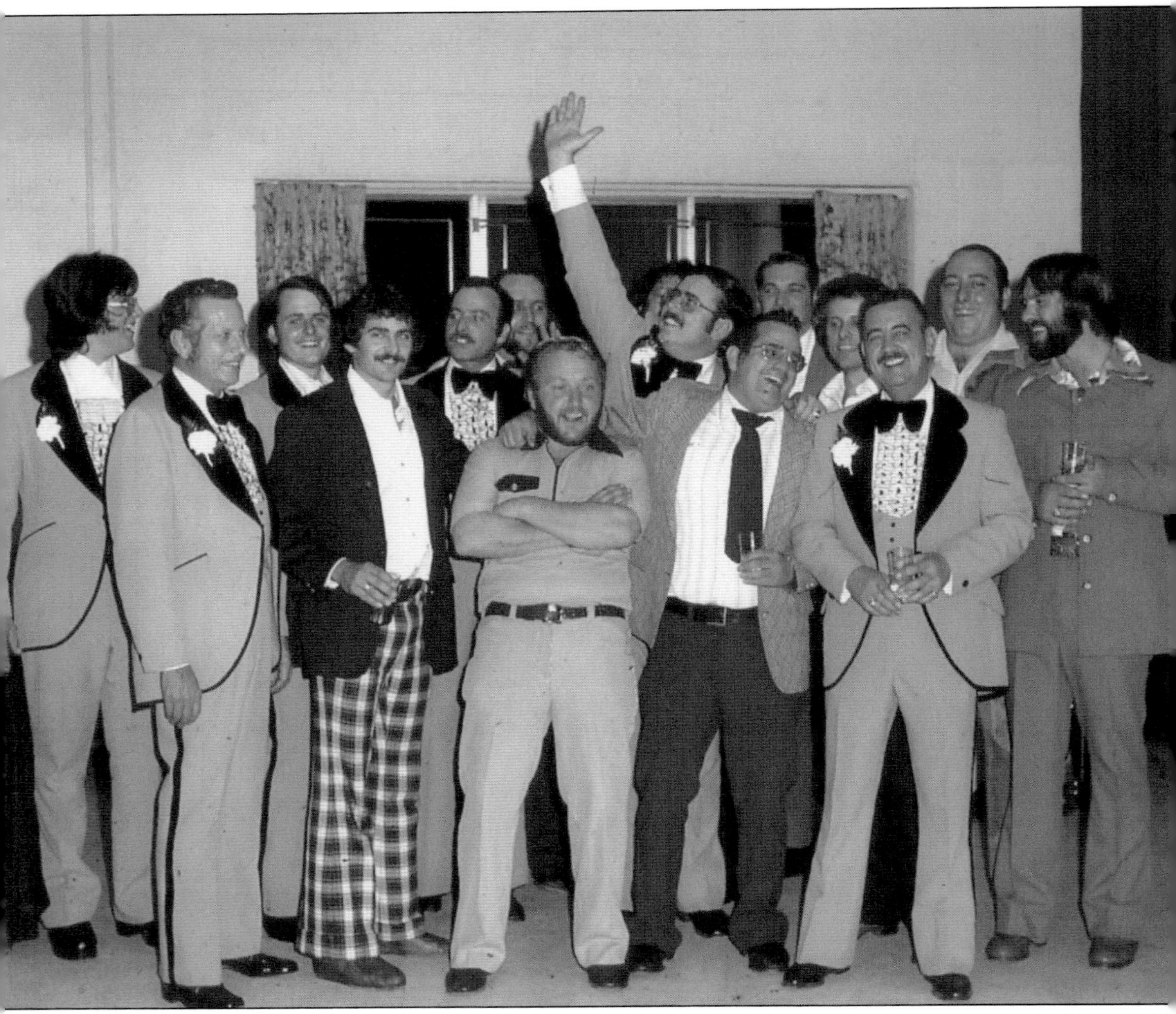

For 50¢ an hour, most of the kids took a summer job working on Mitchell's farm, which was walking distance from their homes. Newspaper delivery was another source of income; the routes took them down Dixie Highway along Lake St. Clair and covered most of Ira Township. It was not only a way to make money, but also a way to meet and make friends and was a life experience worth remembering. Summer and winter activities involved packing peanut-butter sandwiches in waxed paper, milk in an old olive jar, and heading out to some woods for the entire day. Ice-fishing was also a great time to get away for the day, along with fishing down behind the Village Market. The Anchorvillains grew up in a time that was peaceful and carefree, and that produced memories to last a lifetime. In the 1970s, at a Furtah family wedding, the group reunited and posed for this photograph. (Courtesy of Dennis Furtah.)

Four

SETTLEMENT OF SWAN CREEK/FAIR HAVEN

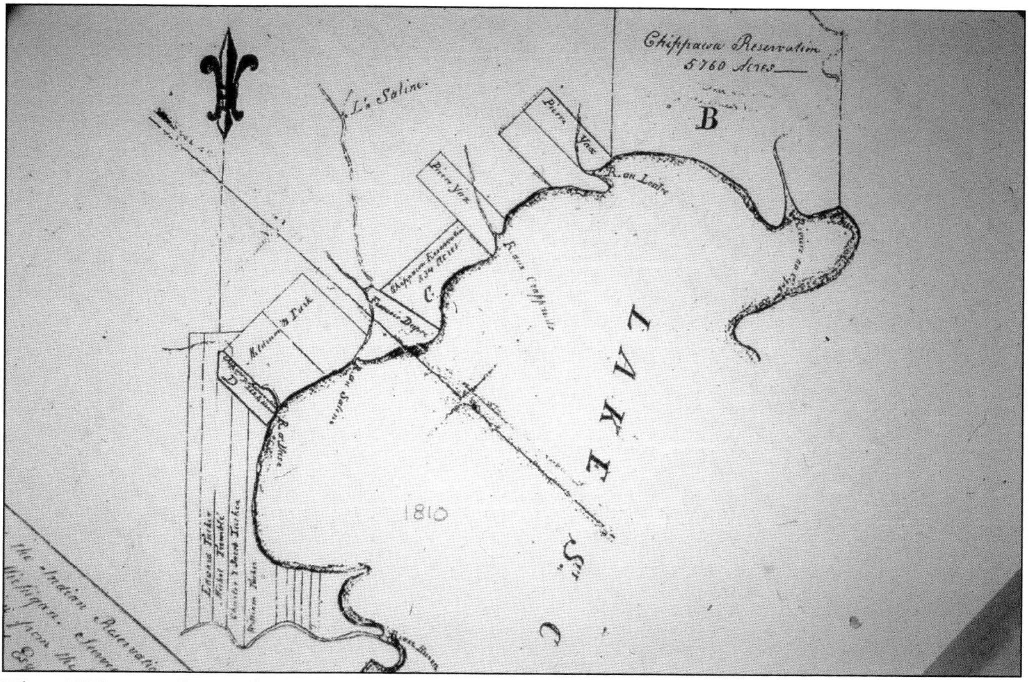

This 1810 map shows the reservation of the Swan Creek Settlement, located at the mouth of the Swan Creek. The reservation was established by the 1807 treaty with the Chippewa Indians. The largest of three reservations bordering Lake St. Clair, this reservation on Anchor Bay was later to become Ira Township.

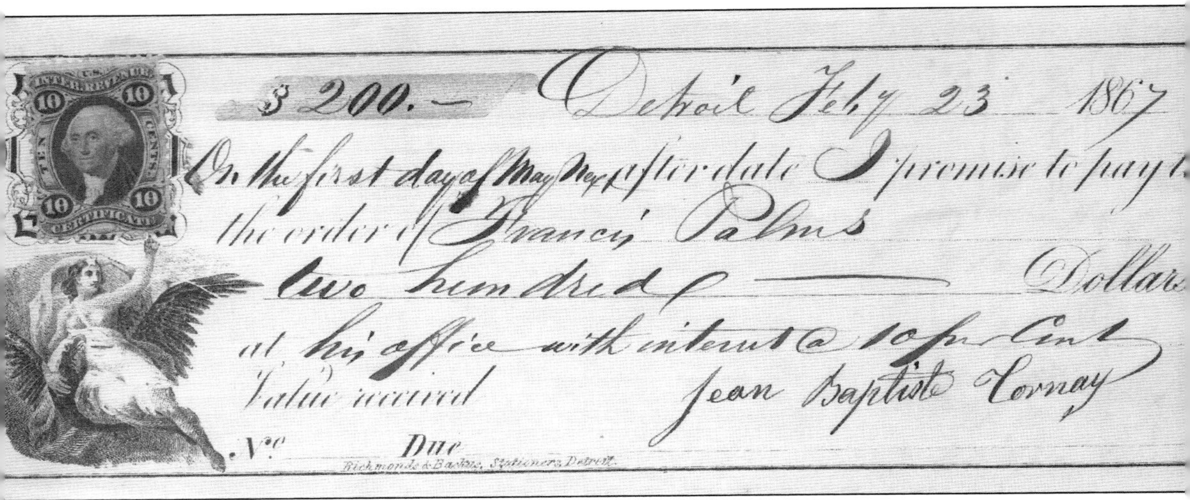

$ 200.— Detroit Feby 23 1867

On the first day of May next after date I promise to pay to the order of Francis Palms

two hundred — Dollars

at his office with interest @ 10 per Cent

Value received Jean Baptiste Tornay

No. Due

Richmond & Backus, Stationers, Detroit.

Francis Palms was one of the largest landholders in Michigan. He was gifted a vast tract of land from a Pottawatomie Indian chief, Chief Lerner, and bought more tracts as they became available upon the release of the Indian Reserve lands. Palms married the chief's daughter, and Palms Road, a major thoroughfare in the township, was named for him. He was also the namesake of the Francis Palms building in Detroit, which houses the Fox and Fillmore Theatres. As a landowner and businessman, Palms oversaw a great deal of early Ira Township's development. In a letter dated October 27, 1854, sent to Jean Baptiste Tornay, Palms requests a response to the query regarding the purchase of a windmill for Mr. Pottier and Mr. Racine. In the letter, Palms wrote that his clients "had seen several windmills, but they will wait a few more days to make a decision." Apparently, the response was slow in coming, as his letter includes the following: "Please have the goodness to send me a response that I can send to New York. The post departs 3 times a week from Baltimore on Monday, Wednesday, and Friday at 10 o'clock in the morning." (Courtesy of Jim Savoyard.)

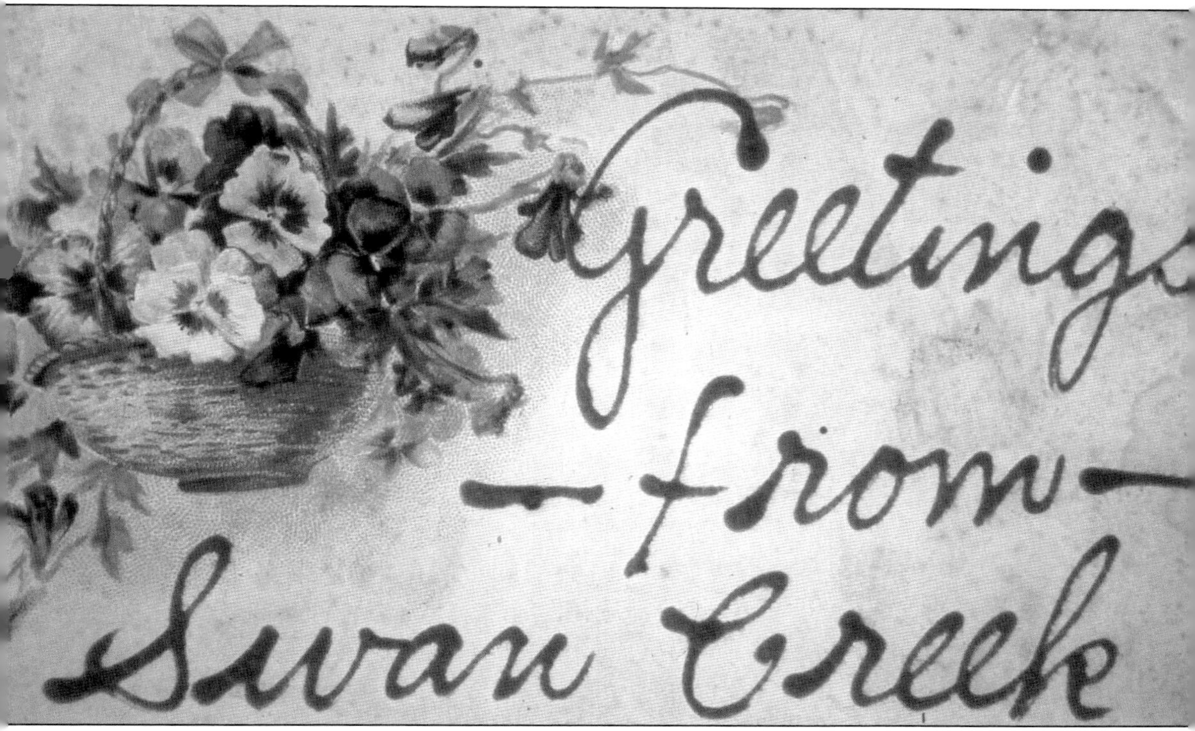

Federal postal records indicate a post office called Swan Creek starting on October 17, 1859, with Thomas C. Delano as the first postmaster. On February 11, 1862, it was renamed Fair Haven for its favored location on the bay. Ira Township's first schoolteacher was Crockett McElroy, who, at only 22 years of age, also became supervisor of Ira Township. He was known as the "boy supervisor." He opened a general store across the street from Immaculate Conception Church and constructed a large dock there, which made Anchorville a major lake port for a number of years.

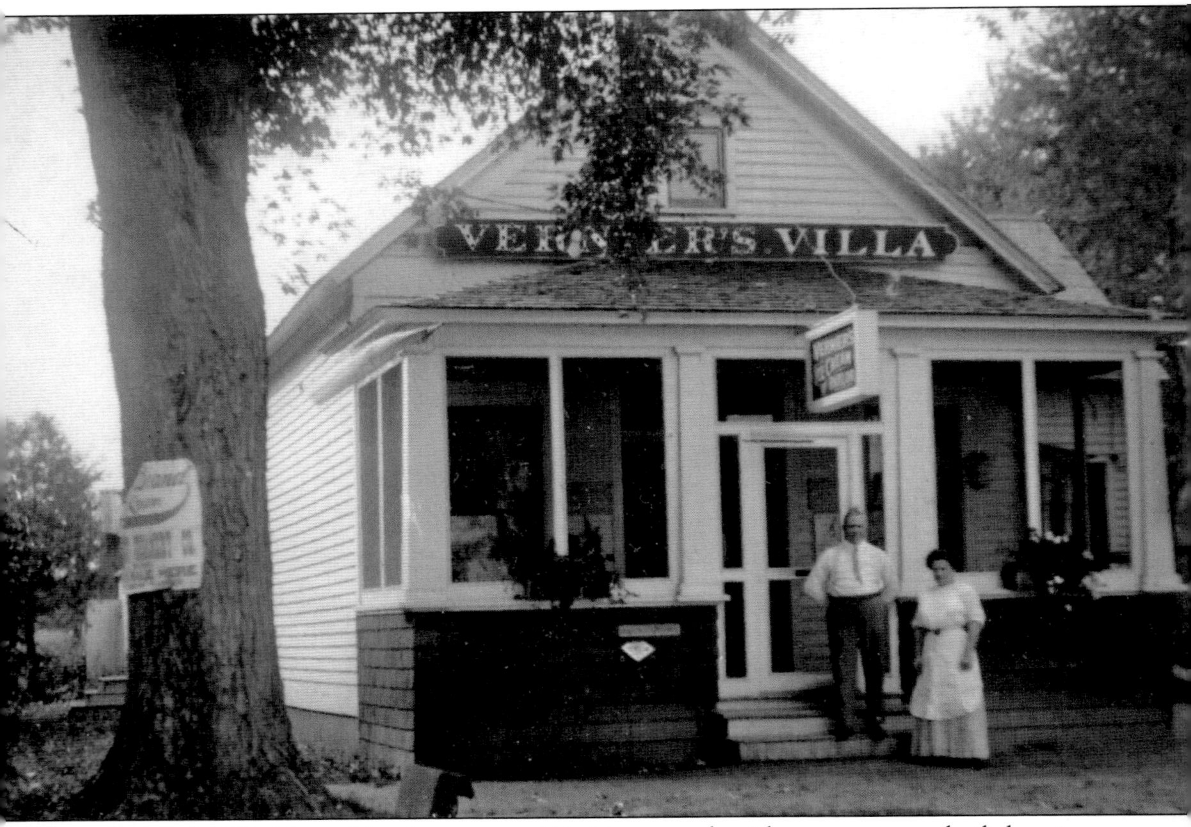

Around 1870, Victor Vernier came to Fair Haven and, with two partners, built housing on Waterworks Drive and Long Island Court. While its details are lost to history, this establishment, called "Vernier's Villa," was most likely the first business operated by the entrepreneurial Vernier family in Fair Haven. Based on the storefront sign and poster on the tree in the photograph, it was an ice-cream parlor. It was in operation sometime between 1870 and 1896.

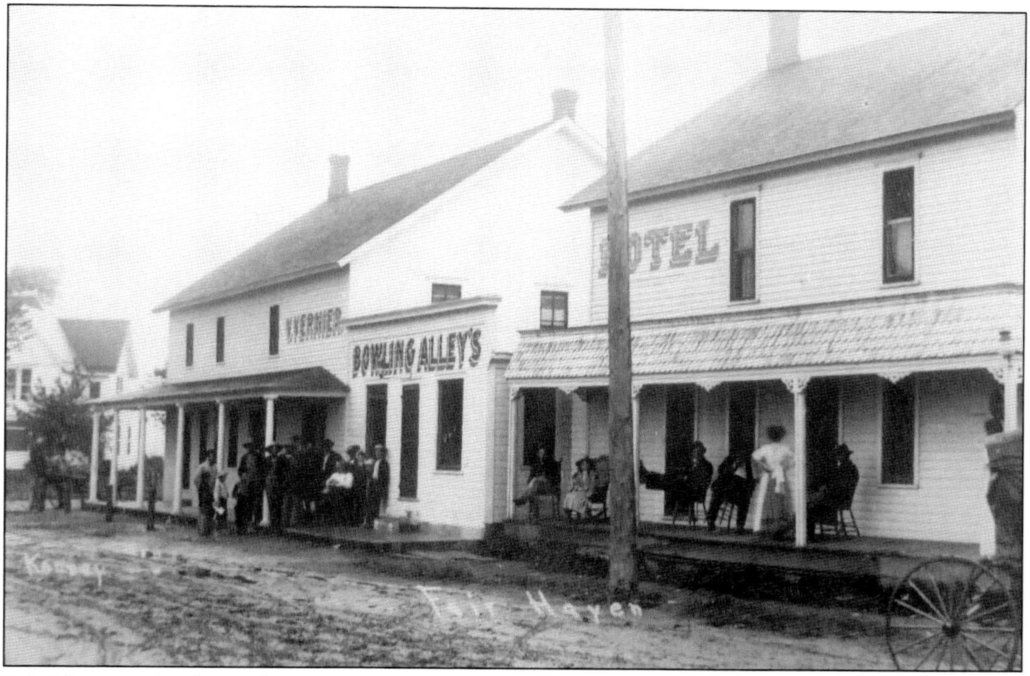

Fair Haven gained popularity as a tourist spot, and in 1896, Victor Vernier built a combination restaurant, hotel, and bowling alley. In 1914, the bowling alley was torn down and replaced with a two-story brick structure. One of Fair Haven's most distinguished landmarks, the restaurant was a popular eating and gathering place well into the 2000s. Shown below is the Vernier Hotel as it grew in prominence. Descendants of Victor Vernier continued to run the establishment. Leo Vernier Sr. was one of Ira Township's longest-serving supervisors (1960–1972), as well as his grandson Leo Vernier Jr. Great-granddaughter Lynn (Vernier) Prudhomme was the last family member to operate the business known as Vernier's.

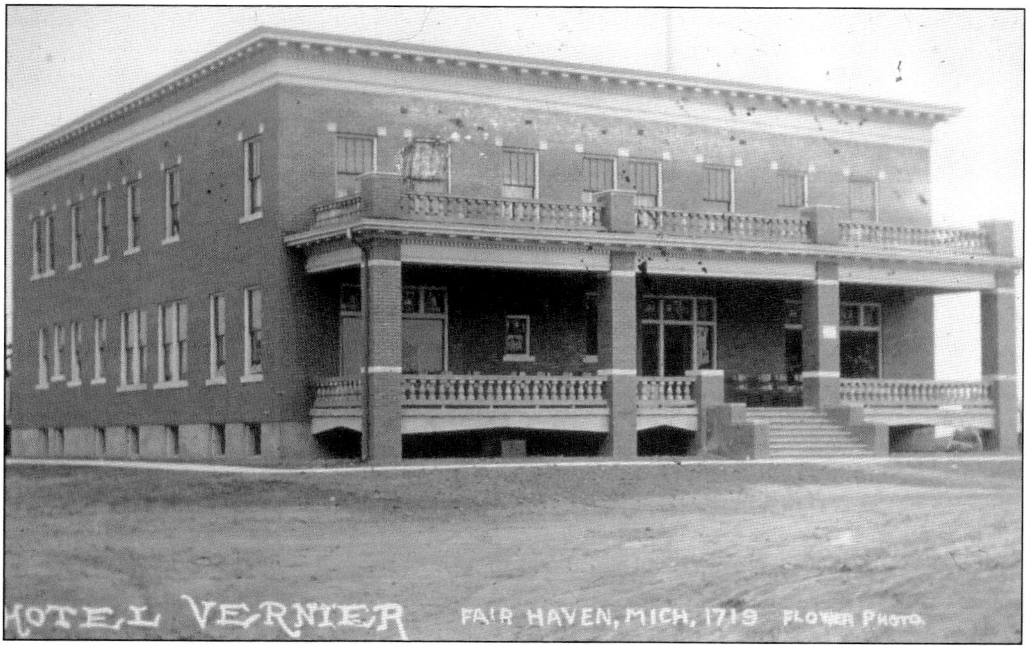

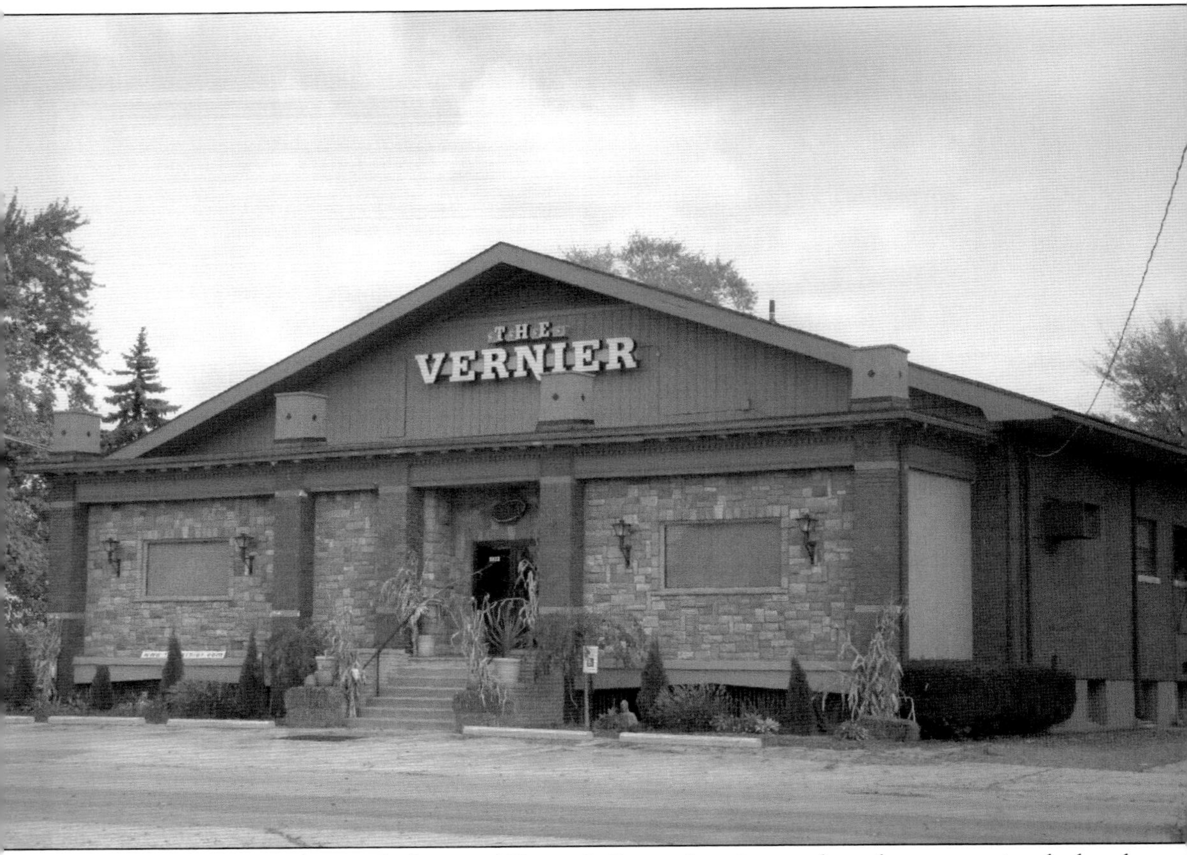

In 1976, a massive fire nearly destroyed Vernier's. But, with assistance from the community, the hotel was rebuilt as a one-story restaurant and bar. It was built "brick by brick during one of Michigan's coldest winters," as noted in the 1990 publication *The Heritage of Ira—A Sesquicentennial History*. In late 1926, three men were killed during a fierce gun battle between two gangs apparently fighting over local liquor rights. One of the gangs involved was the infamous Purple Gang. This Detroit-based gang was quite technically advanced (they used walkie-talkies) and was active in the Anchor Bay area during the years of Prohibition. When they needed "tech support," they came to see August "Mr. Jake" Jaikey, a television and radio repairman and a resident of the Vernier Hotel. On the morning after the shootout, children on their walk to school witnessed the bodies being carried out to a hearse. Bullet holes from this long-ago gunfight are still visible near the restaurant's bar. Still standing on Vernier Road near busy M-29 and the Swan Creek, the now-vacant building serves as a testimonial to the vibrancy and color of an earlier era.

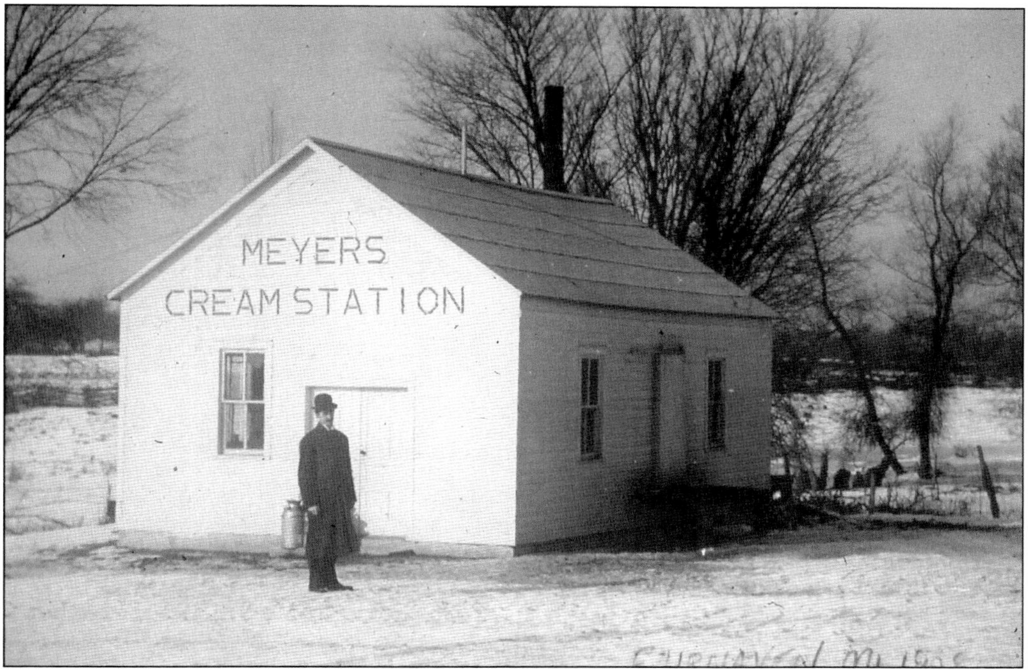

Fred Meyer built this cream station in the early 1900s, because local farmers had no place to store their extra milk. After the milk was separated here, the cream was taken to the creamery in Chesterfield Township on Gratiot near 23 Mile Road. Eventually, most of the creameries in the area were bought by the Detroit Creamery. Meyer's farm was located on Short Cut Road.

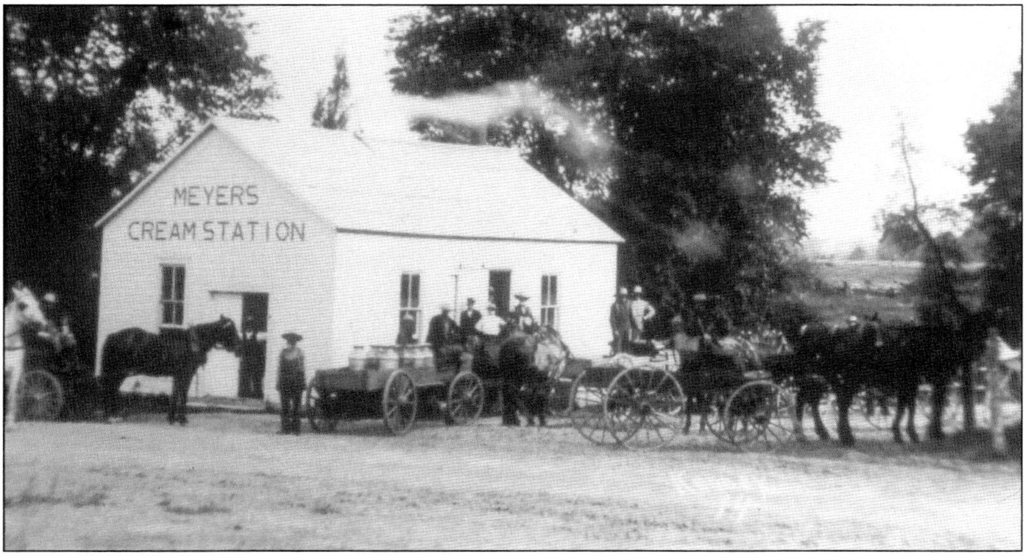

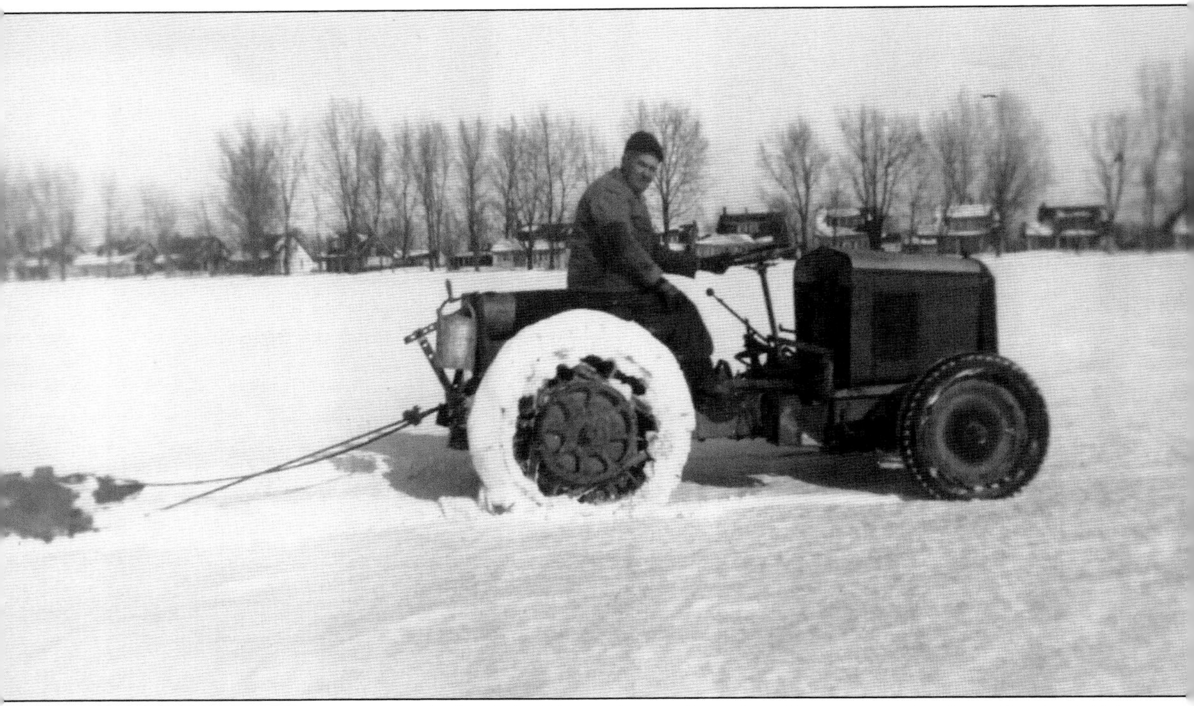

Like many Ira residents, Joseph "Joe" DeMars, shown here hauling ice on Anchor Bay in 1944, was an entrepreneur. In his lifetime, he was a farmer, a mechanic, a notary public, and a sailor on the Great Lakes. He moved his house from near Palms Road, south down M-29 for over a mile using hewn tree trunks as rollers. From his new location, he dug a canal out to the bay to create and run a boat livery in early Fair Haven. In the summer, he operated a "sand sucker," a machine that removed sand from the bay, which he sold. (Obviously, this was before the days of the Environmental Protection Agency.) In winter, he and other locals cut blocks of ice from the bay. The ice was sold in warmer months to residents and tourists alike. Joseph and Louise (Rose) DeMars had ten children, nine of whom lived to adulthood.

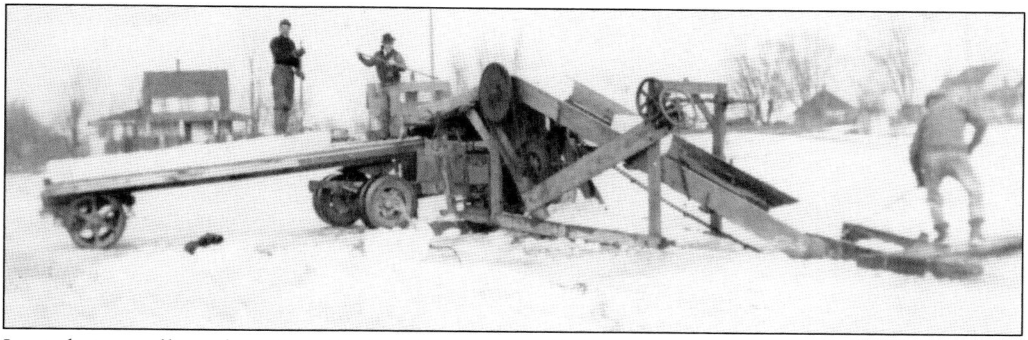

Ice is being collected on Bouvier Bay in the early 1940s, using a machine that Joseph DeMars helped to engineer. The blocks of ice were lifted from the surface of the bay and aligned on a flatbed wagon. Ice would be brought for storage to the ice house. Located on M-29 by Palms Road, it was owned by father and son Theodore "Ted" and Charles "Charlie" Deimel. Pictured here are Elwin Vigneron (left), Joseph DeMars (center), and an unidentified person.

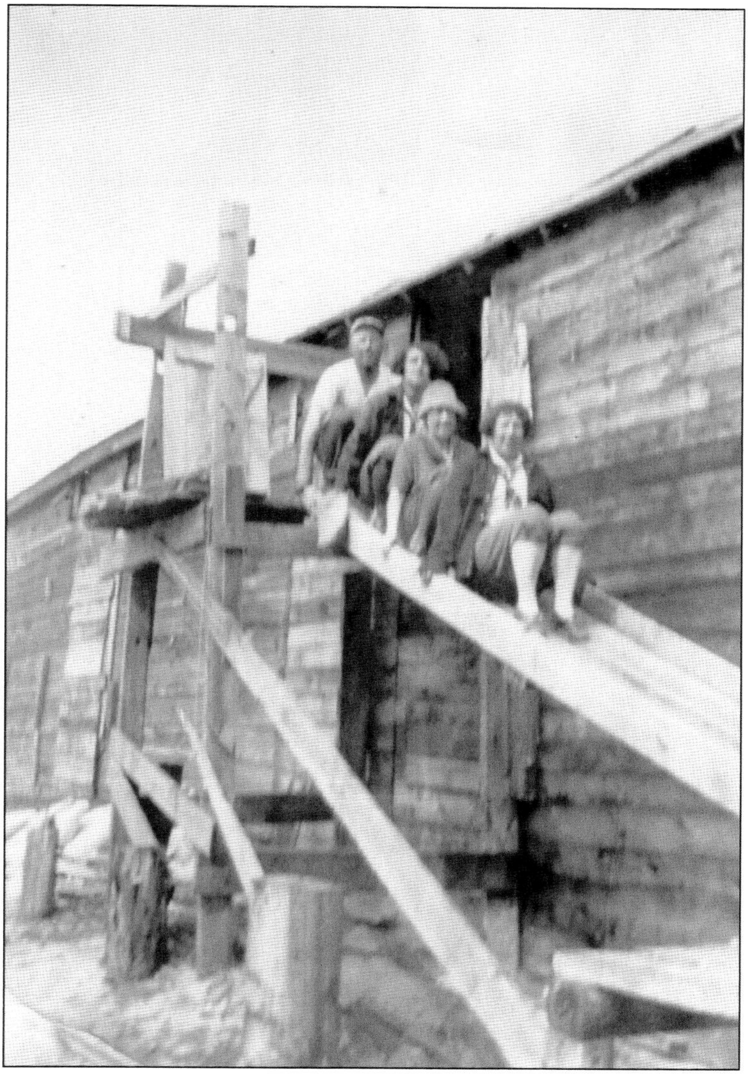

Pictured on the ice slide are, from left to right, Charles Deimel, Justine (DeMars) Evoy, Jeanette (DeMars) Deimel, and Gertrude (DeMars) Stoner. The icehouse was a wooden structure lined with corkwood, above and below its foundation, for insulation. Floorboards were slatted to allow drainage. Ice blocks were packed with sawdust to prevent refreezing. Once stacked, everything was covered with canvas, giving the icehouse a uniquely "wet" smell. Ice was sold for a penny a pound.

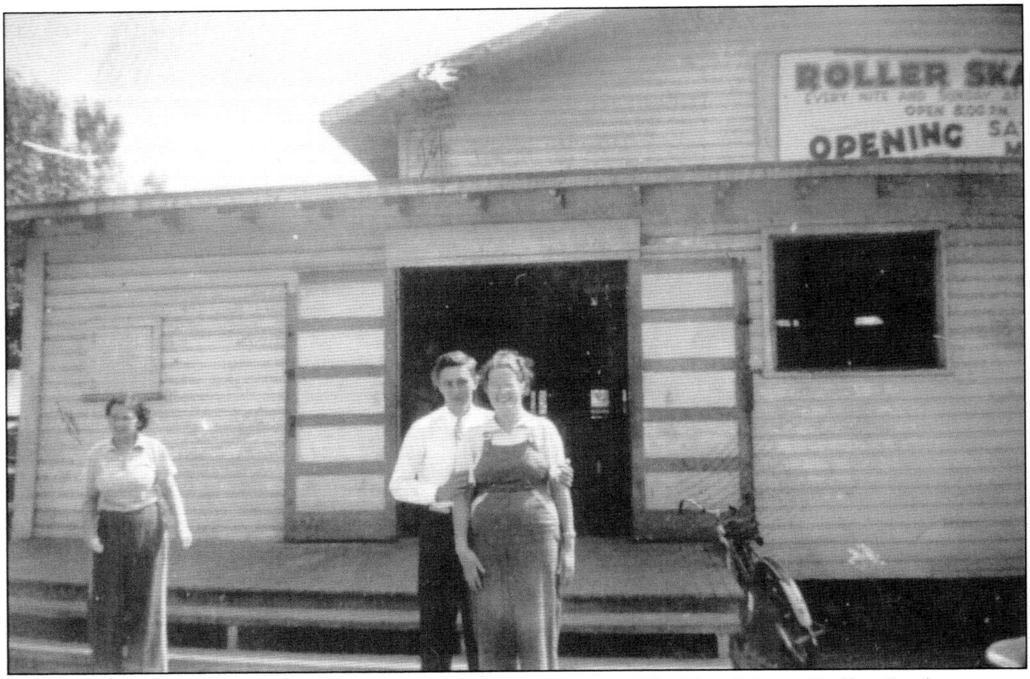

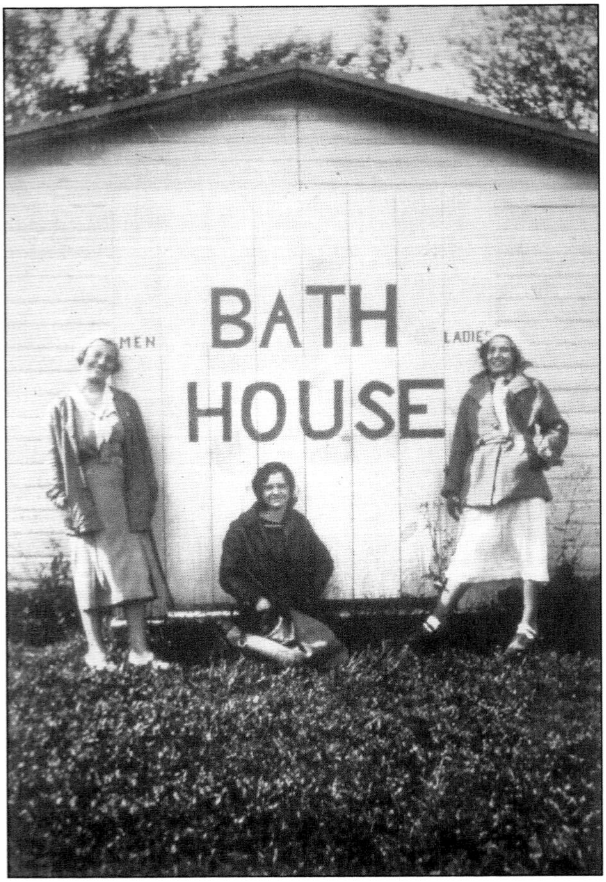

The Fair Haven Roller Rink was a popular spot for Ira residents year-round. It was especially popular during the summer resort months. Here, owner Mickey Dunn poses with his floor manager, Madeline DeMars. During its peak season, the rink was so populated with skaters that it was impossible to see the floor for all of the skates on it.

Several public bathhouses were in operation in Ira during the 1920s. They provided a place to pause for refreshment and renewal for summer resort visitors. The service and accommodations of these bathhouses were a necessary part in the transition from daytime boating and fishing activities to evening fun at the roller rink or in the dance halls.

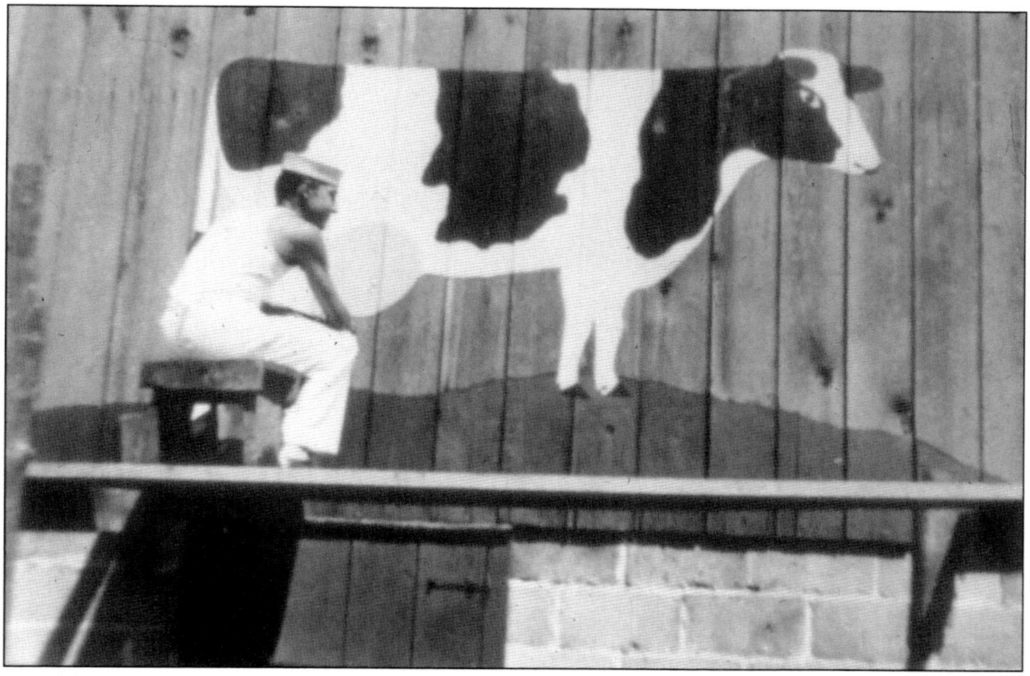

Harold Miller pretends to milk a Holstein cow he painted on Hammer's barn, located on the corner of Swan Creek and Broadbridge Roads. Miller, who painted the cow in the 1920s, used a photograph of a cow found in the old *Farm Journal* as his model.

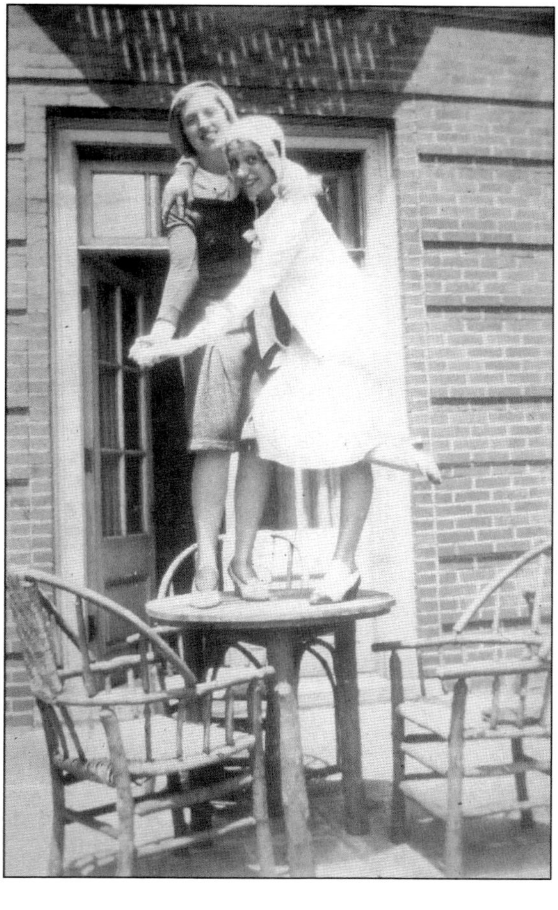

Shown here are two flappers in the Roaring Twenties. This was a new breed of young women who wore short skirts, bobbed their hair, and flaunted their disdain for what was then considered acceptable behavior. Flappers were seen as brash for wearing excessive makeup, smoking, and driving automobiles. These unidentified women at a cottage in Fair Haven are a good example of the fun-loving era.

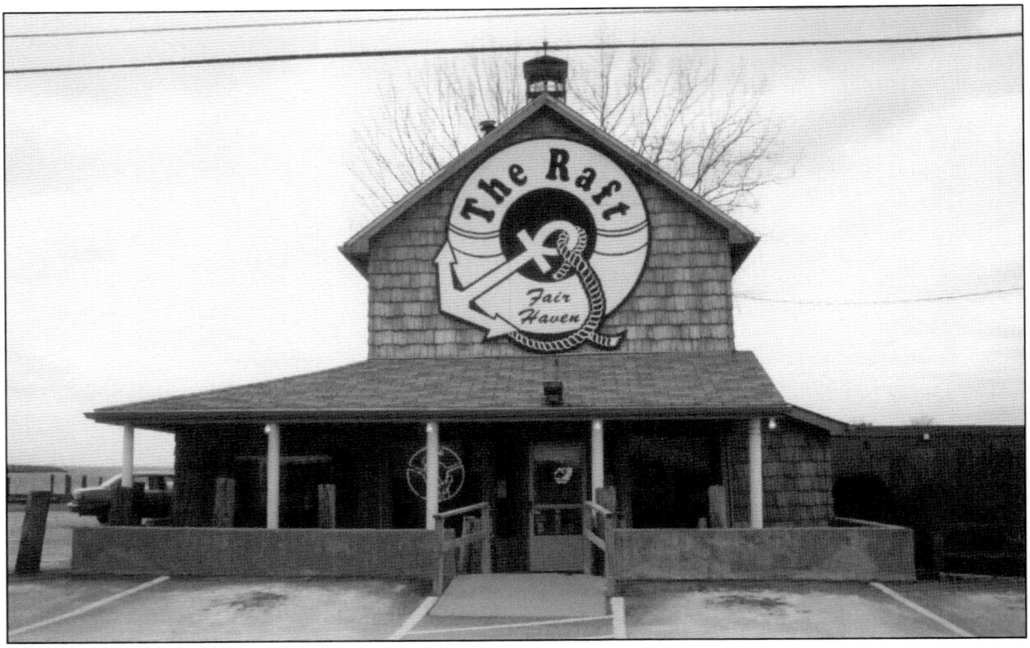

The Raft has long been a favorite restaurant in Ira Township, pleasing palates with its Raftburger for many generations. The Raftburger is not something baked around a raft. Actually, the Raft name only dates to 1976, although the building had its start around 1910. Reputedly a barn at first, by the time of the interurban railroad's heyday in the 1920s, the building was used as a hotel and boat livery. The front building was an ice-cream parlor and lunchroom for hotel guests and the public. In the 1930s, the building housed Well's Boats, where fishing tackle and bait were sold. In the summer, boats could be rented; in the winter, visitors could rent an ice shanty.

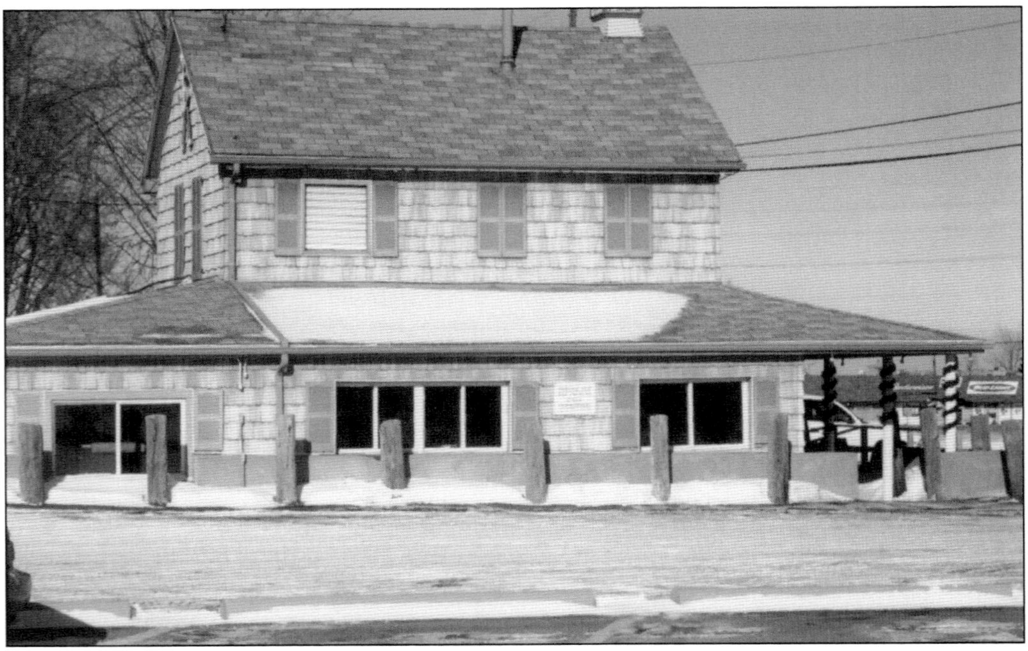

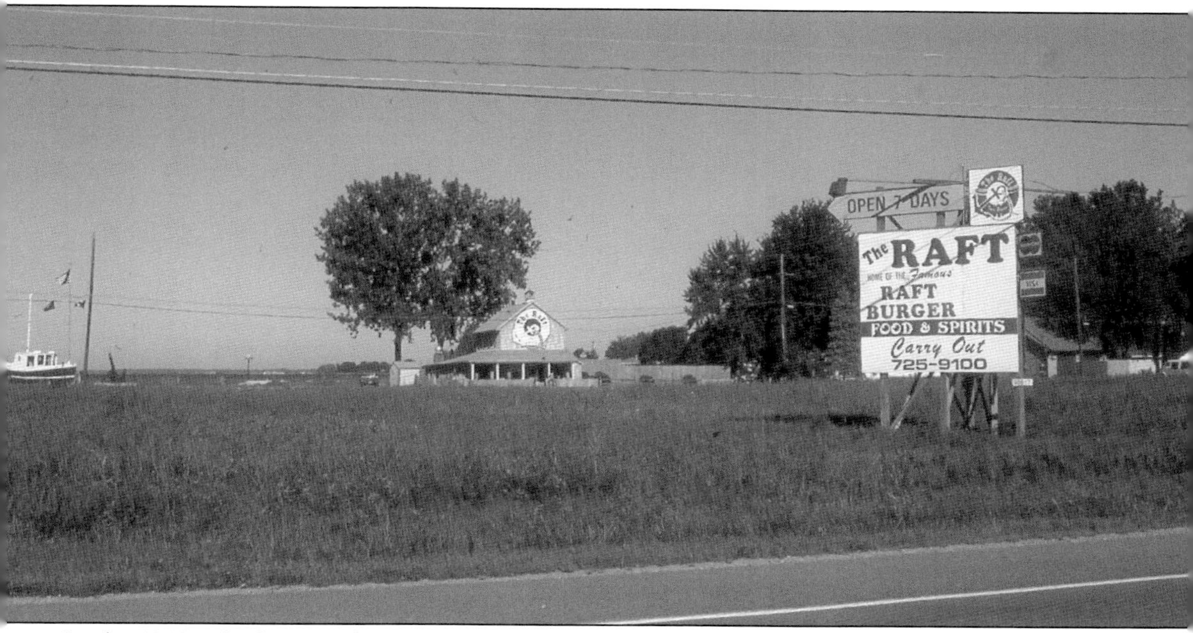

In the 1940s, the business became Herm's, named after new owner Herm Whitford. He had a lunchroom and bar, sold bait, and rented boats and shanties. In other words, it was business as usual. Herm's new slant was that it rented apartments in the back, often to vacationers who wanted to be by the bay. In following years, it was briefly called Schneider's, and then for nine years it was named Bob and Dee's. It was then purchased by Howard Chartrand, who renamed it the Raft. It is under this name that the establishment is known for its burgers and chili. This 100-year-old building continues to be the purveyor of Raftburgers. Hold the onions!

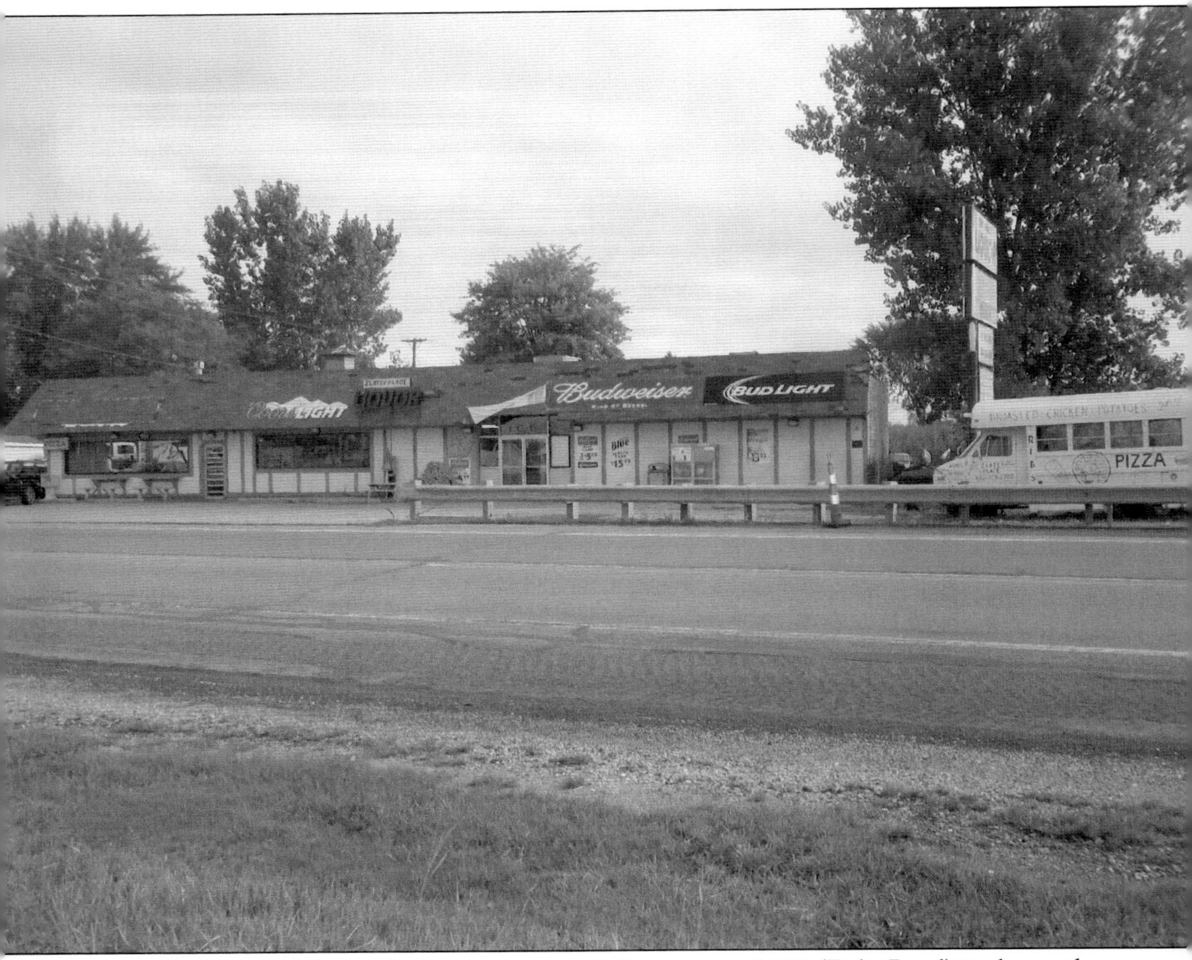

The locals named this early shopping center at the curve on M-29 (Dyke Road) in the southeast border of the township for Ernie Copeland. The beginning of the corner started with Copeland renting a hot dog stand from Herb Meyer. From there, he moved the stand to the Copeland Corners location in 1928, where a building was erected. After Prohibition, Copeland got a liquor license to sell beer and wine and added restaurant space. He also began to sell groceries and added a gas station. Later on, he also sold radios and other appliances. He and his wife lived in an apartment above the store. Copeland eventually converted his Copeland Corners grocery store into a Chrysler-Plymouth car agency and showroom. In 1936, he sold his other businesses and moved his automobile company to Mount Clemens.

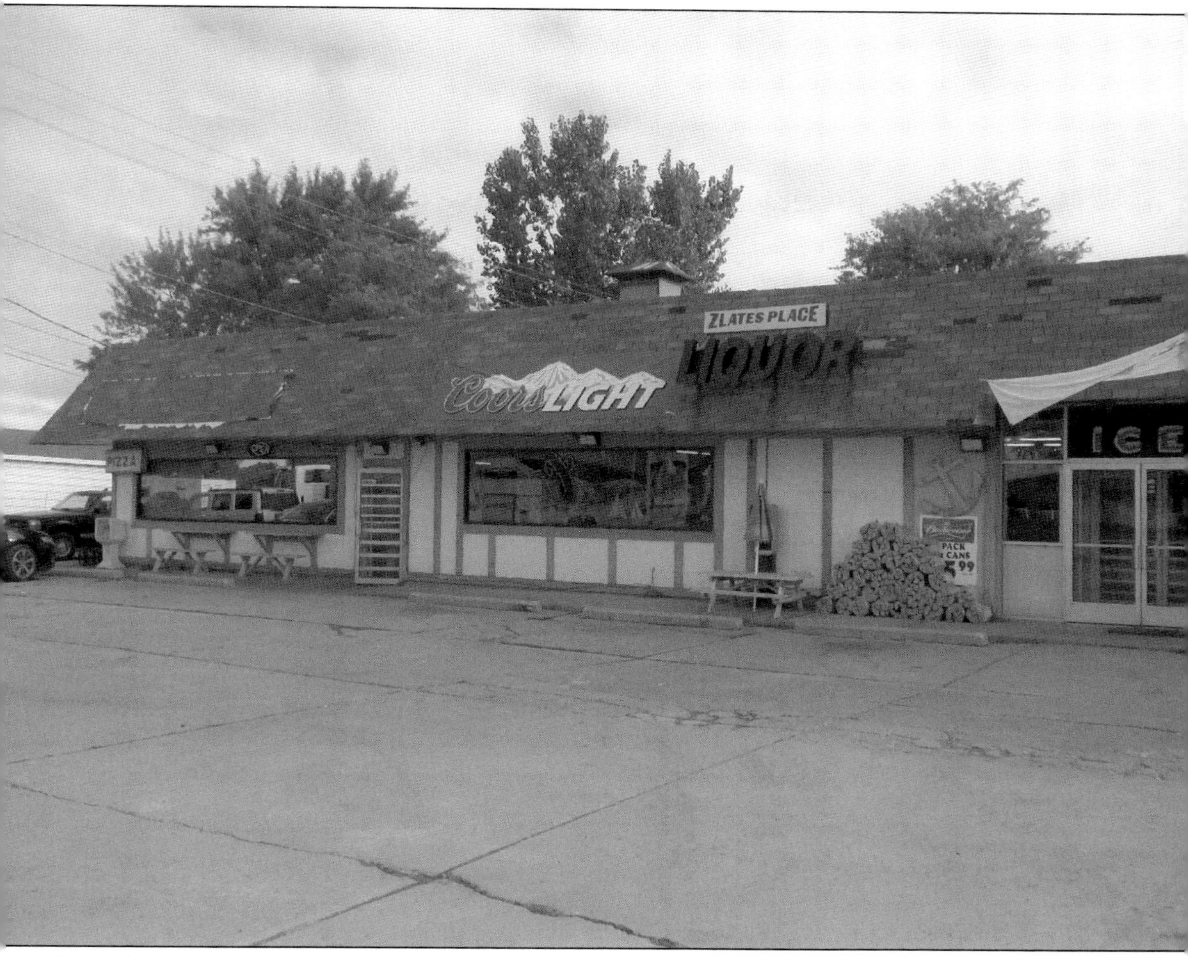

Many businesses have found a home at Copeland Corners over the years. A gas station and auto repair business called Lakeshore Service operated there until 1962. Other establishments included an auto electric business and Roman's Grocery, which operated from the 1950s until 1966. John Rowling's real-estate office gave way to PDQ Printing and One-Hour Photo, which opened at Copeland Corners in 1977 and ran for about 20 years. Around 1969, Norm Groesbeck operated a marine supply store at the corner. He sold boats, motors, trailers, all manner of marine supplies, and snowmobiles. Grocery and take-out food sales continued with the arrival of Zlate's Place in 1956. Owner Frank Sunday also ran a plumbing and heating business. Beacon Hardware operated there from 1956 to 1977 under proprietors Helen and Martin Barnes, then for an additional few years under new owners George and Sarah Baker. Life continues at Copeland Corners, which now is neighbored by Bouvier Bridge Marina.

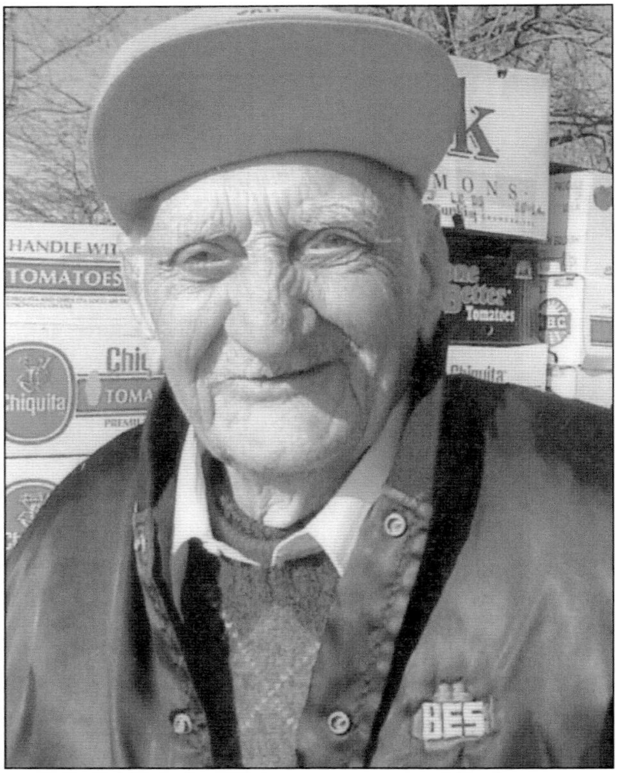

Potatoes-Joe roadside produce stand, located about one mile east of downtown Anchorville on Dixie Highway (M-29), has been a popular summer stop since the 1960s. Owner and operator Joe Paquette worked for years alongside his father, Cornelius (left), who passed away on Christmas Day 2004 at the age of 90. The Paquette family, among the early settlers to Ira Township, have become part of the heritage of Ira. Some of the produce that Joe sells, he grows himself. The rest is hauled from the Detroit Eastern Market. Every May, Joe sets up his stand and displays fresh tomatoes, melons, peaches, apples, green peppers, onions, and yellow and white seasonal combination corn. Below, Joe stands with his father, Cornelius, in front of their produce stand. (Both, courtesy of Joe Paquette.)

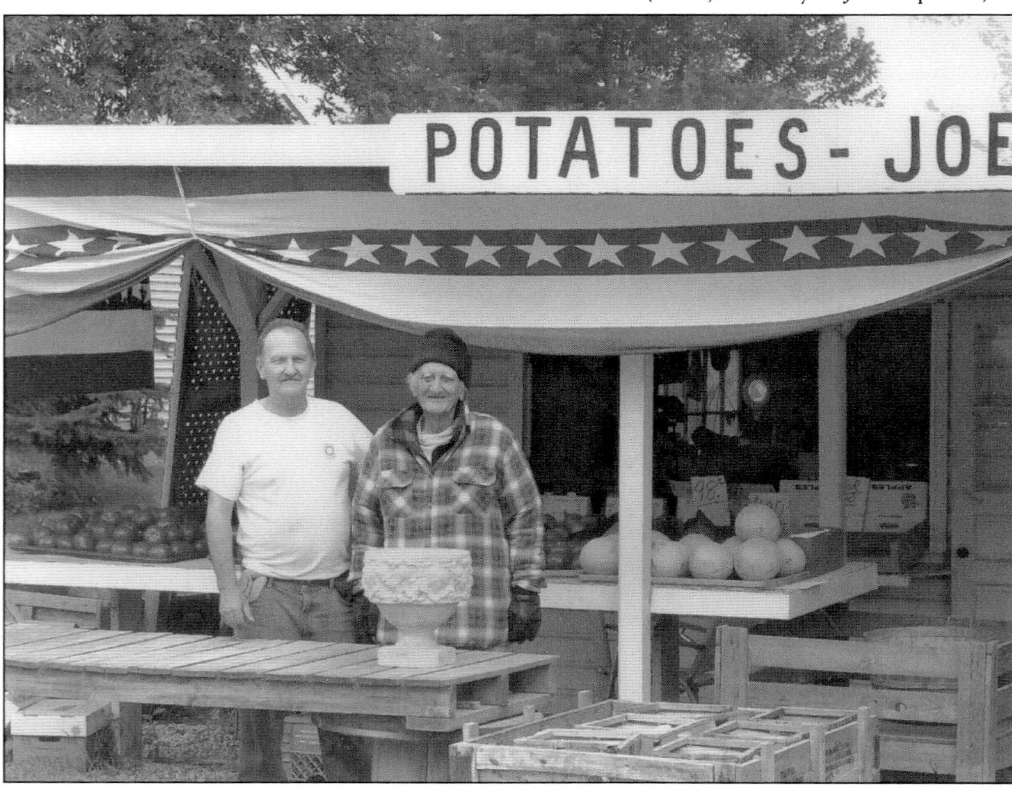

Five

Development of Ira Township

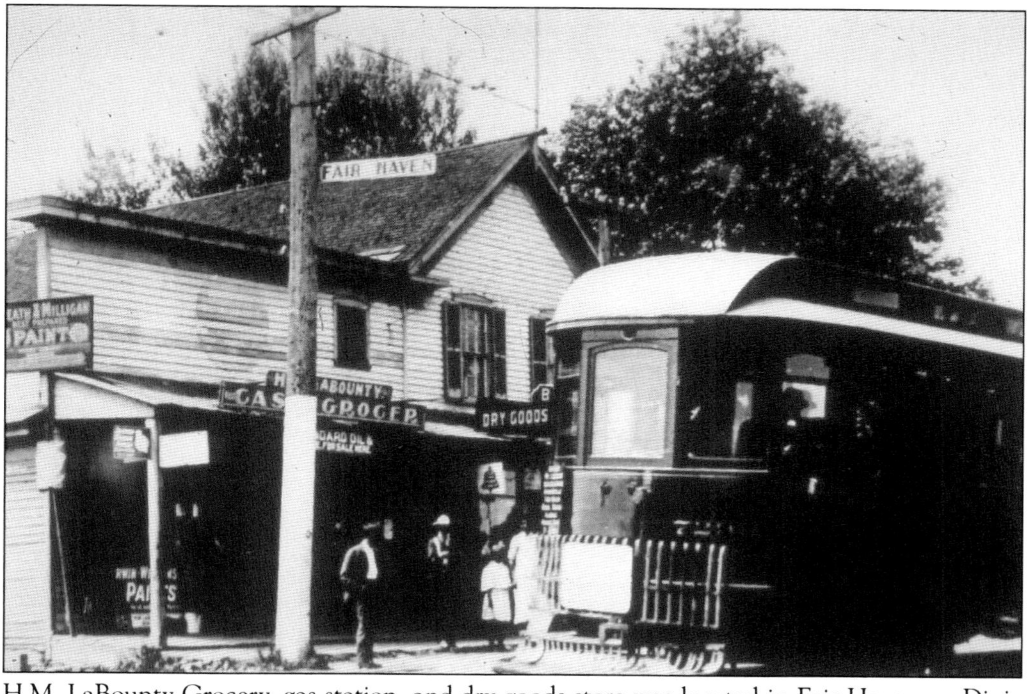

H.M. LaBounty Grocery, gas station, and dry goods store was located in Fair Haven on Dixie Highway (M-29). As seen here, it was also a stop for the interurban railroad. A closer look reveals a Bell sign, indicating telephone service for public use. Note how close the tracks were to the storefront, with little concern for personal safety. (Courtesy of Bond Schnoor.)

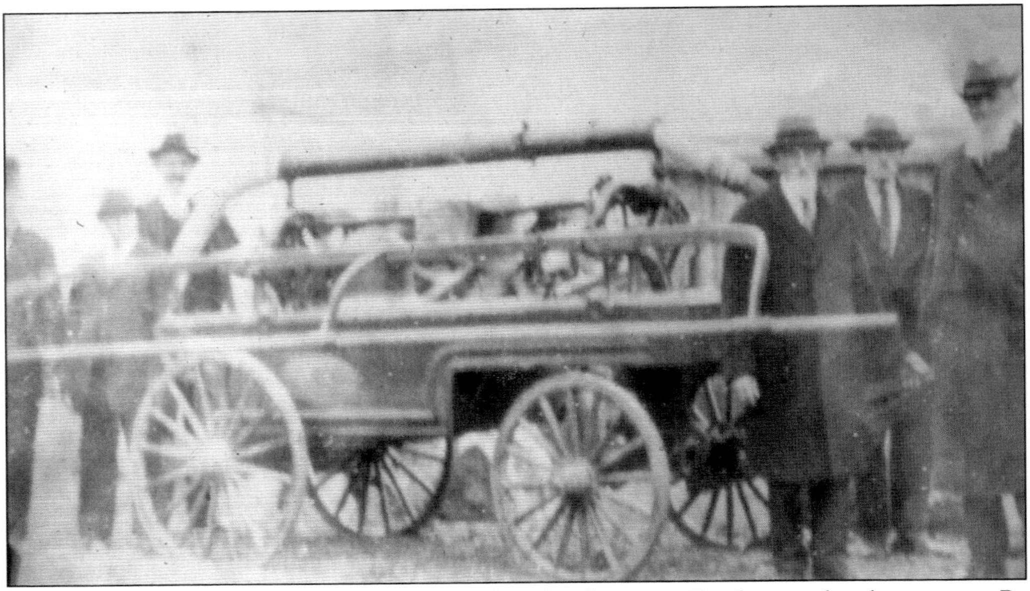

Since the founding of Ira Township in 1837, there has been an all-volunteer fire department. By the 1990s, with the use of more technical equipment, it is now a paid, on-call department. In the early days, bucket brigades were formed using three-gallon leather buckets filled with water. Townspeople would form lines, filling the buckets from a well, pond, or lake, and passing them to the source of the fire. Women and children would pass back the empty buckets to be refilled. This method of fighting fires usually resulted in failure. In the 1920s, an old hand-pumper (above) used by the New Baltimore fire department was the first piece of equipment purchased by the Ira fire department. The old hand-pumper was replaced in 1928 by a gas-driven REO pumper (below). (Both, courtesy of Ira Township Fire Department.)

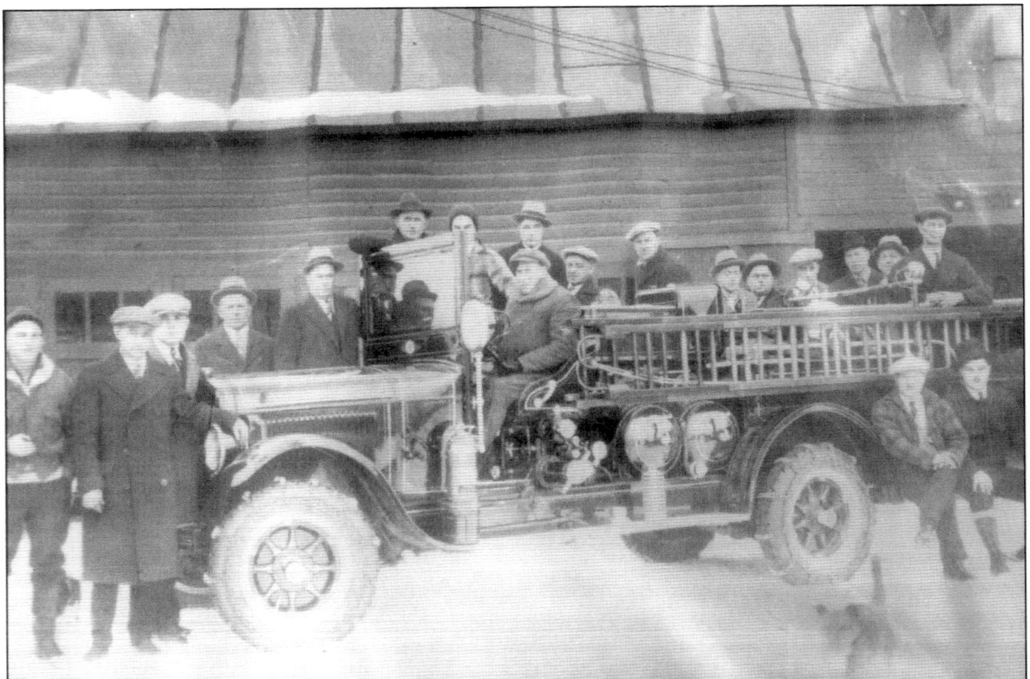

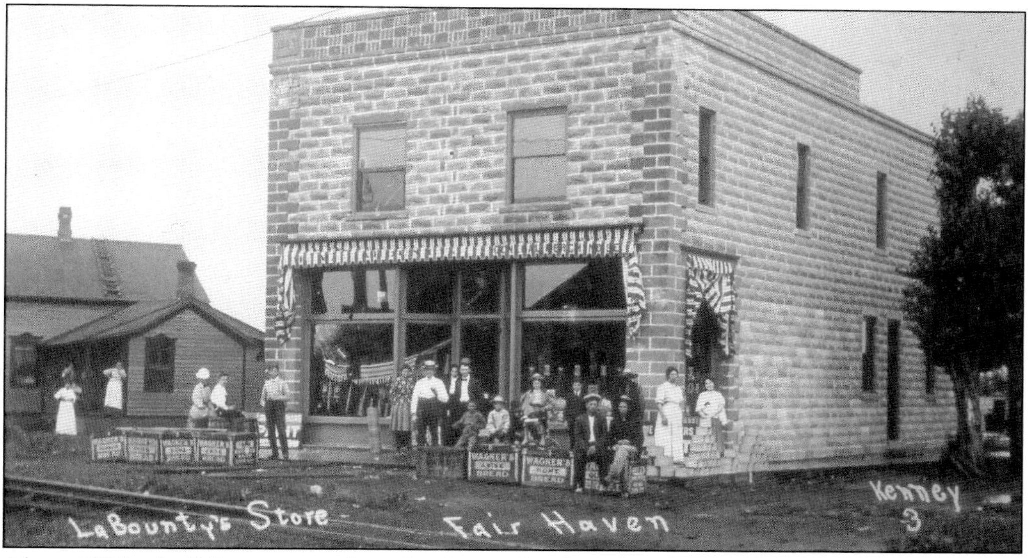

About 1930, a building was purchased to house the firefighting equipment. Located on M-29 in Fair Haven and built in 1907, it housed the H.M. LaBounty General Store and the Fair Haven Post Office (above) for many years. Prior to becoming the fire hall, it was Huebner's restaurant and then a repair shop. The fire hall was the social center for 25 years. Shown below in 1965 are some of the fire department volunteers. They are, from left to right, Frank Marino, Chester Thompson Sr., George Thompson, Leo Vernier Sr., Joe Furtah, Bill Stuler, and Earl Phillips. In 1971, a new fire hall was built on Meldrum Road in Fair Haven. During the 1970s, a five-speed diesel Mack pumper was purchased. It could pump 1,000 gallons of water per minute, which significantly increased the success rate for fighting fires.

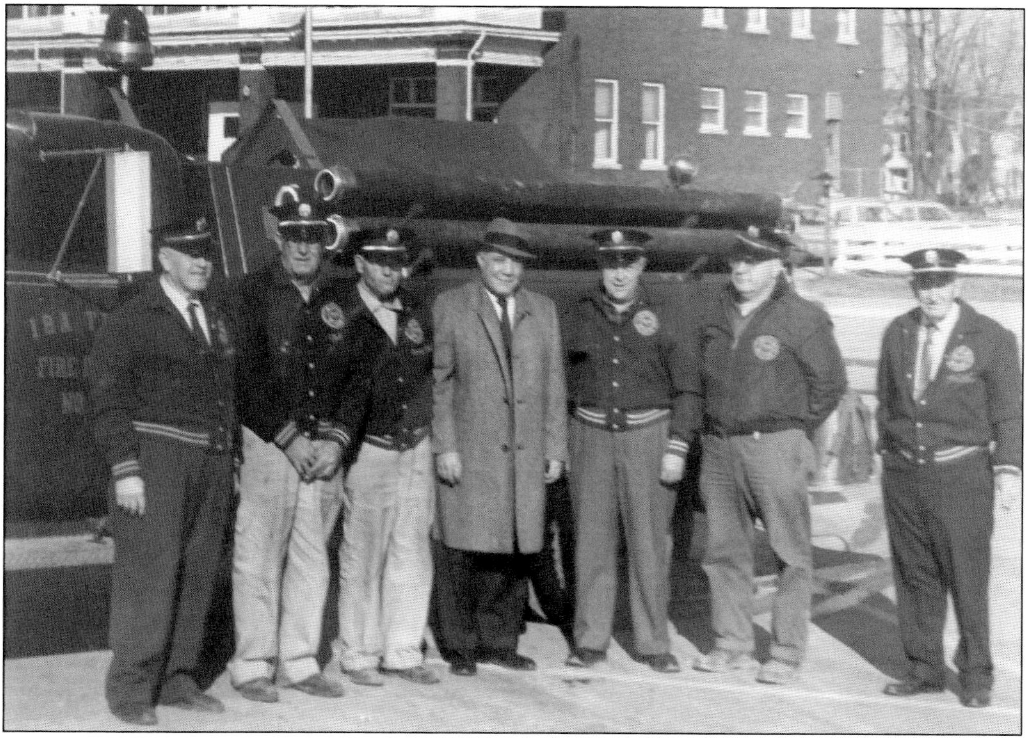

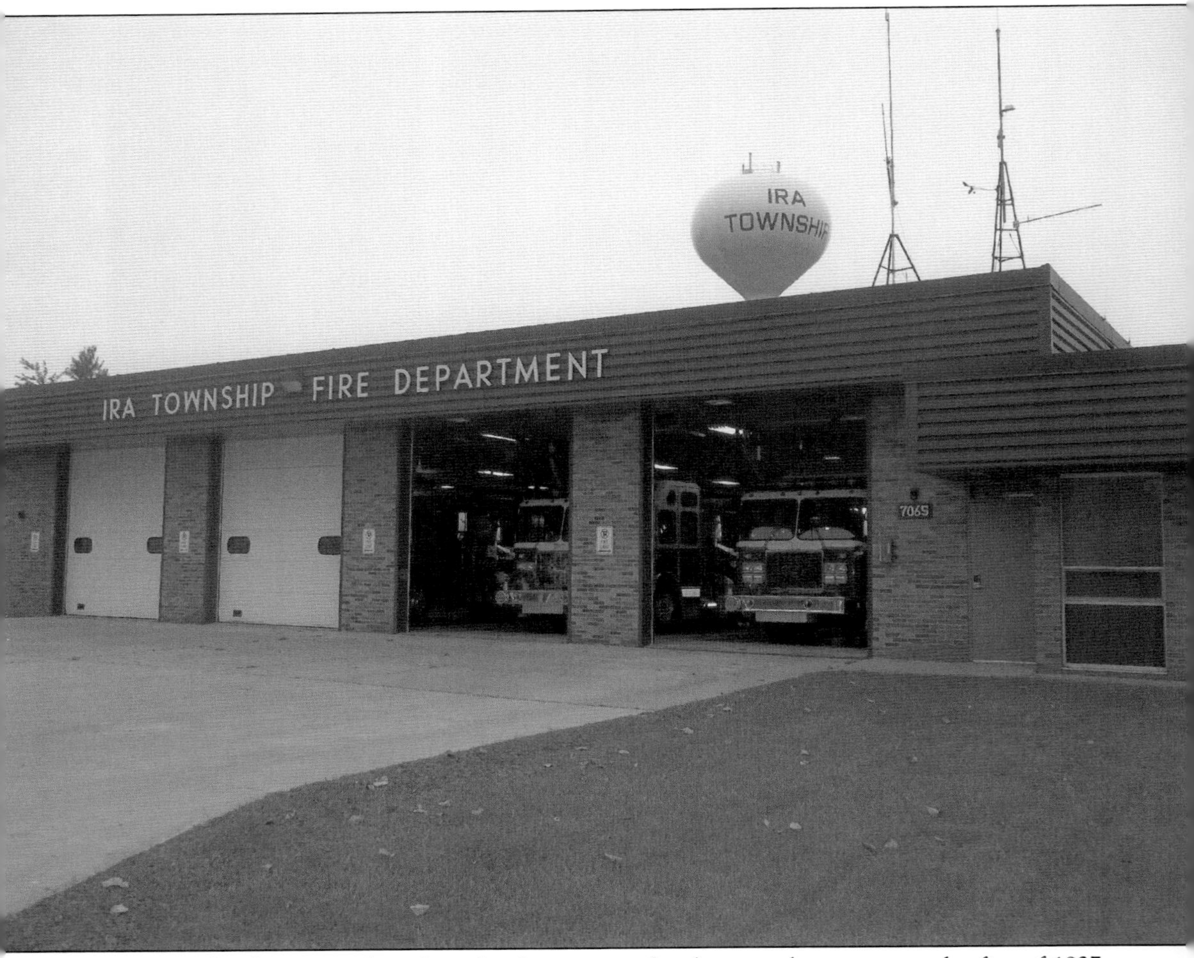

Among the disastrous fires that the department fought over the years was the fire of 1937 at the Daybreak Inn on M-29 near Bethuy Road. The two-story hotel and restaurant was totally destroyed. A 1951 fire caused by faulty wiring was a spectacular midnight blaze at the Village Market in Anchorville. In 1958, in frigid temperatures, a fire broke out at the Bayside Club in Anchorville. Because of the weather conditions, it ended in an unsuccessful attempt to save the building. An early morning blaze in April 1959 caused over $30,000 in damage to the Anchor Bay Inn on Dixie Highway in Anchorville. A 1961 fire at the Silver Saddle Riding Ranch, which firemen fought for over six hours, caused $45,000 in damage, including a silver saddle valued at $2,000. The Ira Township Fire Department (pictured) strives to react and do its best to save lives and property in the event of fire.

The fire department also has a fire-and-rescue unit that responds to calls in the winter months on Anchor Bay. Ice becomes unsafe, and foolhardy fishermen have to be rescued at the risk of firemen's lives. Each October, during National Fire Prevention Week, the department visits schools in the township to conduct surprise drills. In December each year, an election of officers is held, including for chief, assistant chief, captain, lieutenant, sergeant, treasurer, secretary, liaison officer, and chaplain. The below photograph, taken in 1985, shows officers and volunteers of the department. They are, from left to right, (first row) George Whiting, Stan Sommers, Terry Strong, Don Redman, Tom Henderson, and Jeff Walbecq; (second row) Tom Mack, Gary Robinson, Rev. Robinson, Jerry Burns, Skip Fehlmen, Angelo Mantini, and Andy Messina; (third row) Joe Furtah, Iner Erikson, Dick Tews, Chet Thompson, Jerry Tilly, and Victor Vernier. (Both, courtesy of Ira Township Fire Department.)

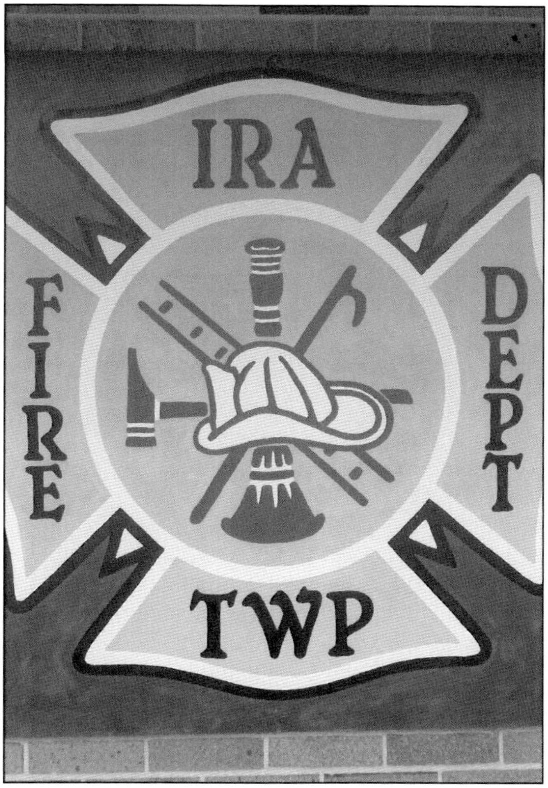

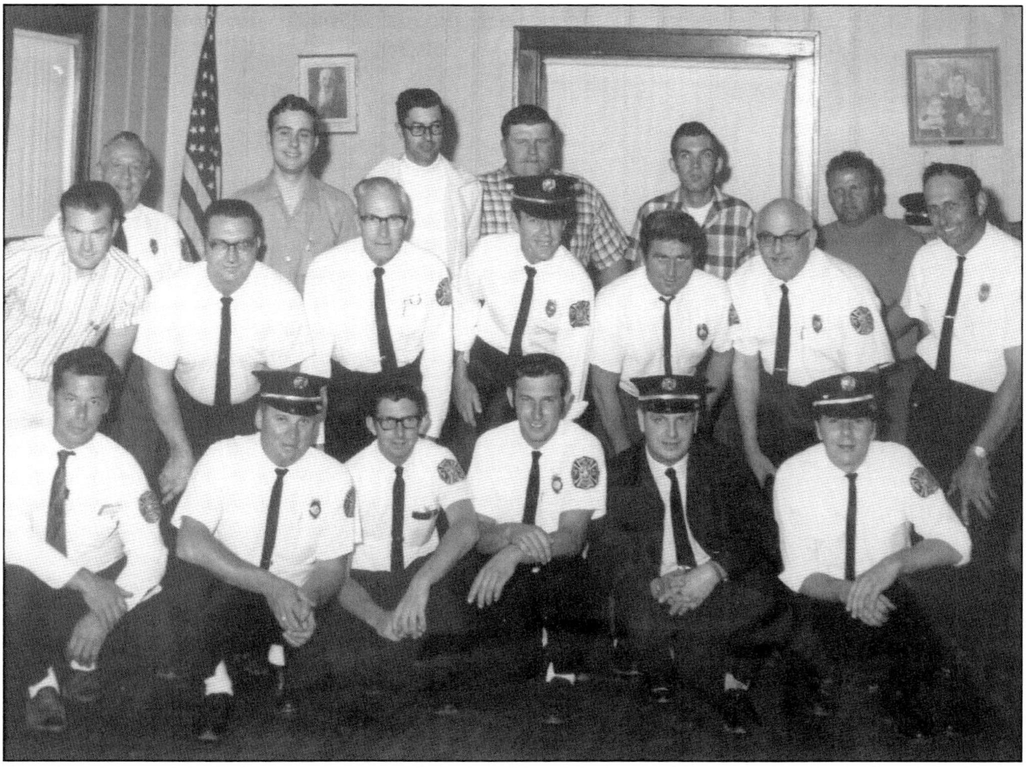

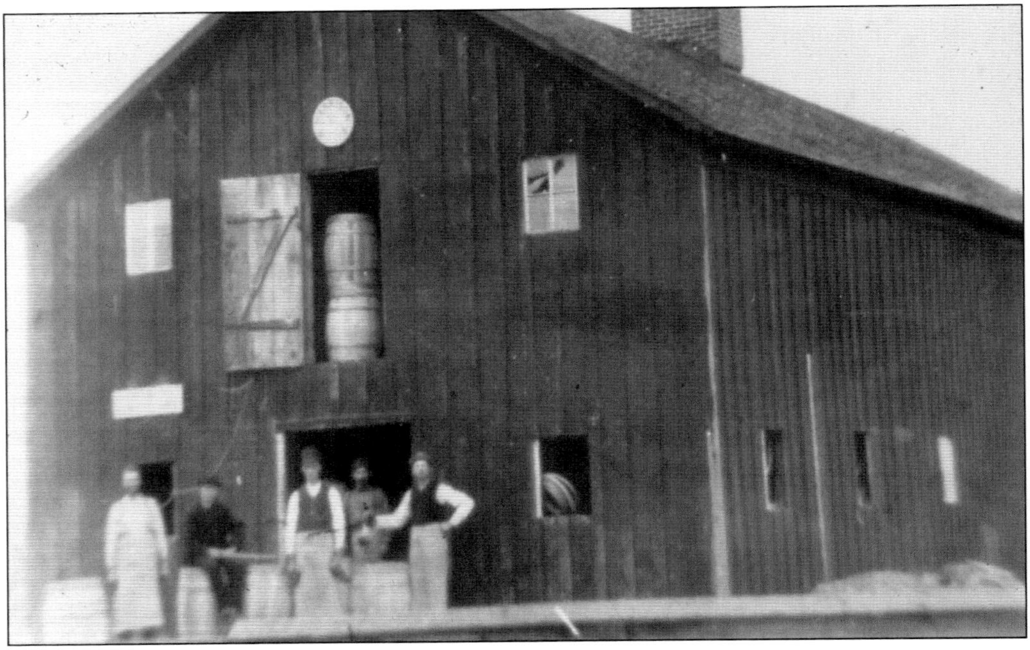

This cooper shop, where barrels were manufactured, was part of the H.C. Schnoor stave mill complex, located on eight acres on Dixie Highway (M-29), near today's DNR public boat access. The mill provided needed employment for local residents. Besides staves, hoops for ladies' skirts were also made at the stave mill. Schnoor operated here from the 1860s to the early 1900s. Shown above in 1898 are, from left to right, Emil Eppler, Joe Marcero, Chris Ruchman, Rob Shorkey, and Frank Dupont.

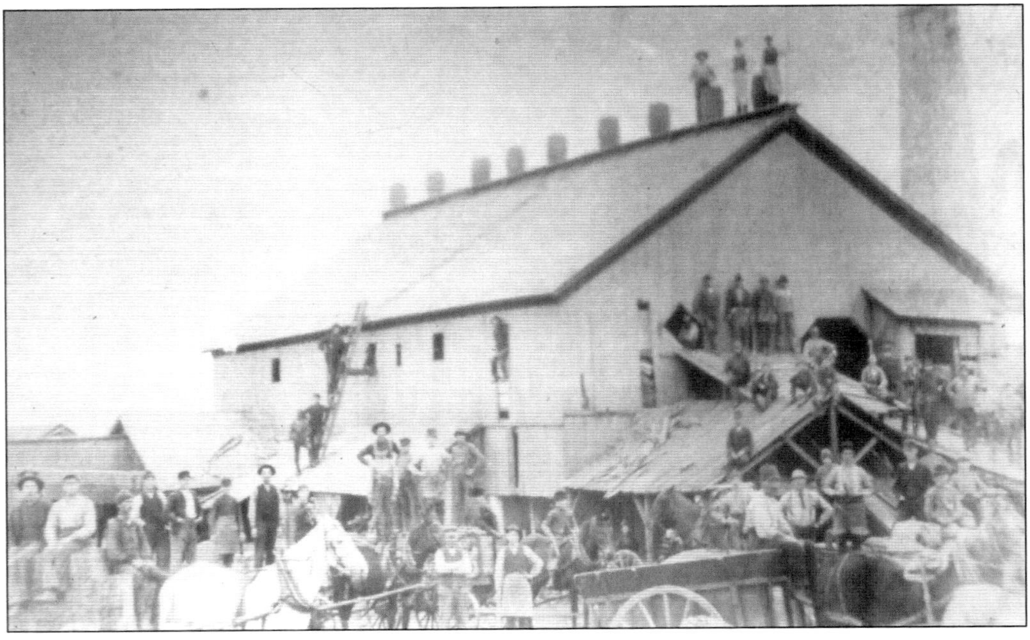

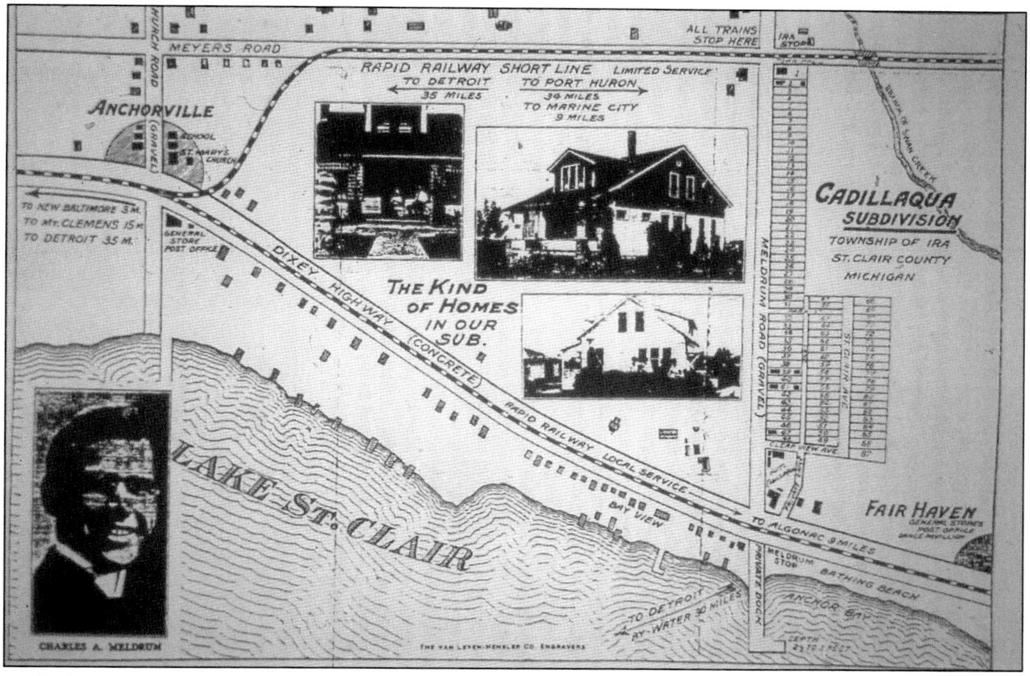

Called a civic-minded "promoter" by his daughter Phyliss Meldrum Horvath, Charles Meldrum, the owner of Hotel Cadillaqua, developed and promoted the Cadillaqua Subdivision on the east side of Meldrum Road between M-29 and Short Cut Road (then known as Meyer Road). With a 500-foot-long dock built into Anchor Bay by Meldrum at the end of Meldrum Road, he proclaimed, "this place should go on record as being one of the most healthful places in which to live." A member of one of the earliest families to call Ira Township home, James Meldrum was farming the land here by the 1830s. The 1915 postcard below shows a fishing trip from Hotel Cadillaqua. The well-dressed anglers show off their catch of the day.

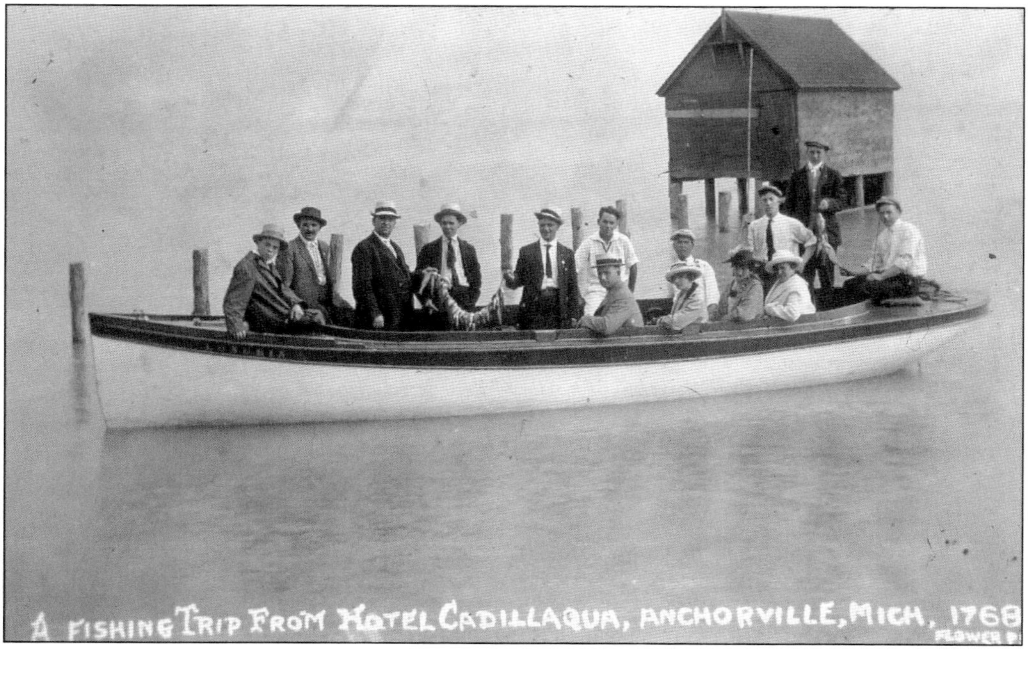

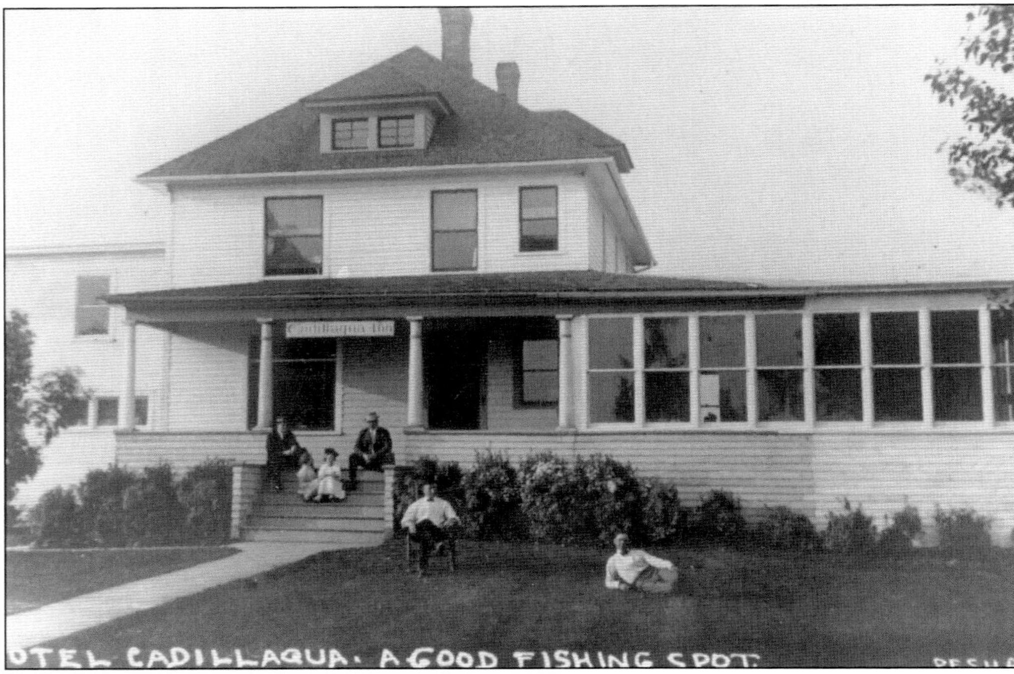

The Hotel Cadillaqua was a popular resort on the old electric interurban railroad (Detroit United Railway). It sat across M-29 with a view of Anchor Bay. The hotel was built by Charles Meldrum, a member of one of Ira's oldest families, at the corner of Meldrum Road and Dixie Highway. Meldrum added the wings and a bar by 1934. It was a good place to have wedding receptions, and was a great place to relax and enjoy beautiful Anchor Bay. With "beer on tap for 5¢ a glass. and a special plate of chicken, fish, frog, and steak for only 75¢, why go anywhere else? Sadly, the building was totally destroyed by fire in 1999.

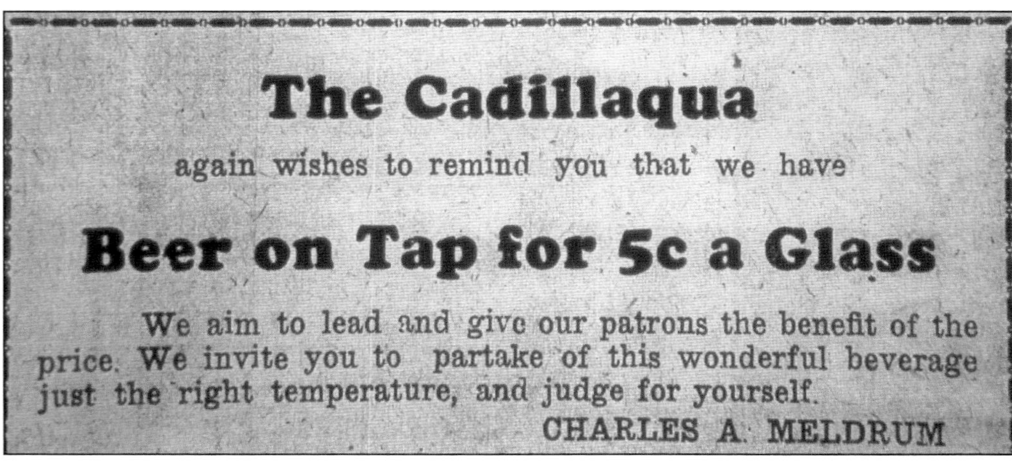

The Cadillaqua

again wishes to remind you that we have

Beer on Tap for 5c a Glass

We aim to lead and give our patrons the benefit of the price. We invite you to partake of this wonderful beverage just the right temperature, and judge for yourself.

CHARLES A. MELDRUM

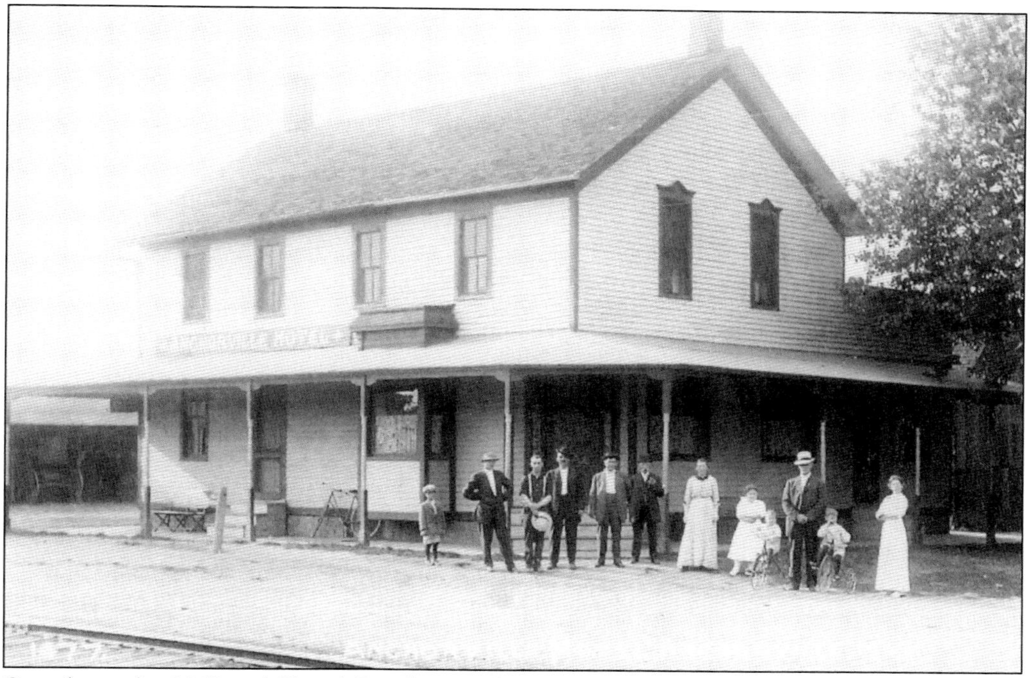

Once located at M-29 and Church Road, across from Immaculate Conception Church, Anchorville Hotel included a restaurant and saloon during its 1839–1945 history. A small livery was located behind the hotel, which was used in the winter months to stable the horses of those attending Sunday mass at Immaculate Conception Church. For the duration of the mass, the horses were covered with blankets to help keep them warm. Sometime after 1945, businessman George Hart purchased the corner lot and erected a brick building for a frozen food locker. He later converted it into the Three Little Pigs restaurant. It was sold to Jim Knapp and became known as Jim's Corner. Today, it operates as Bayside Dimitri's.

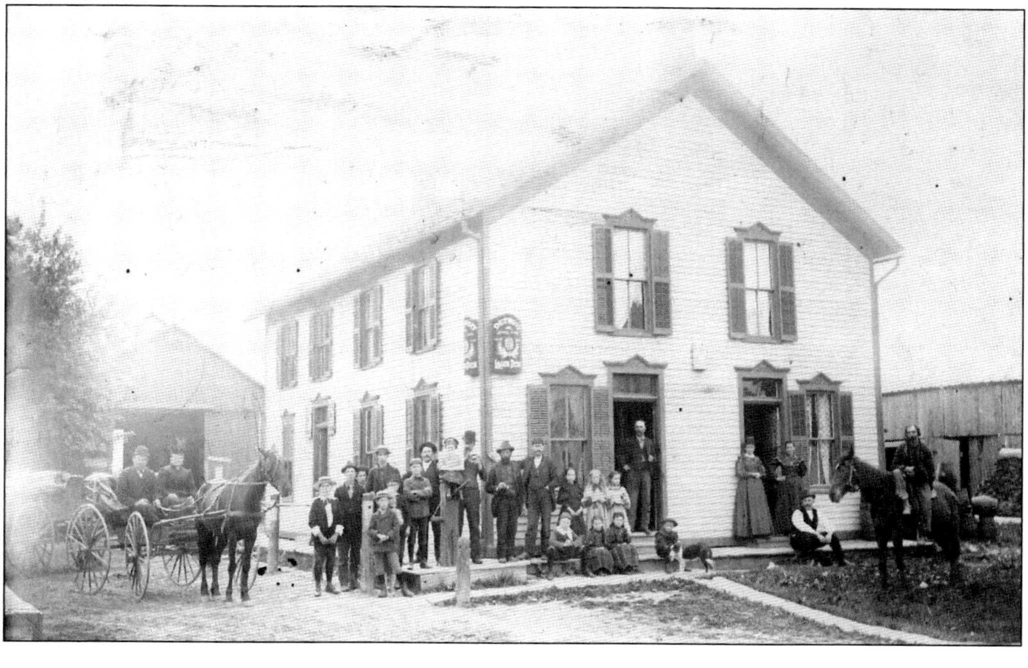

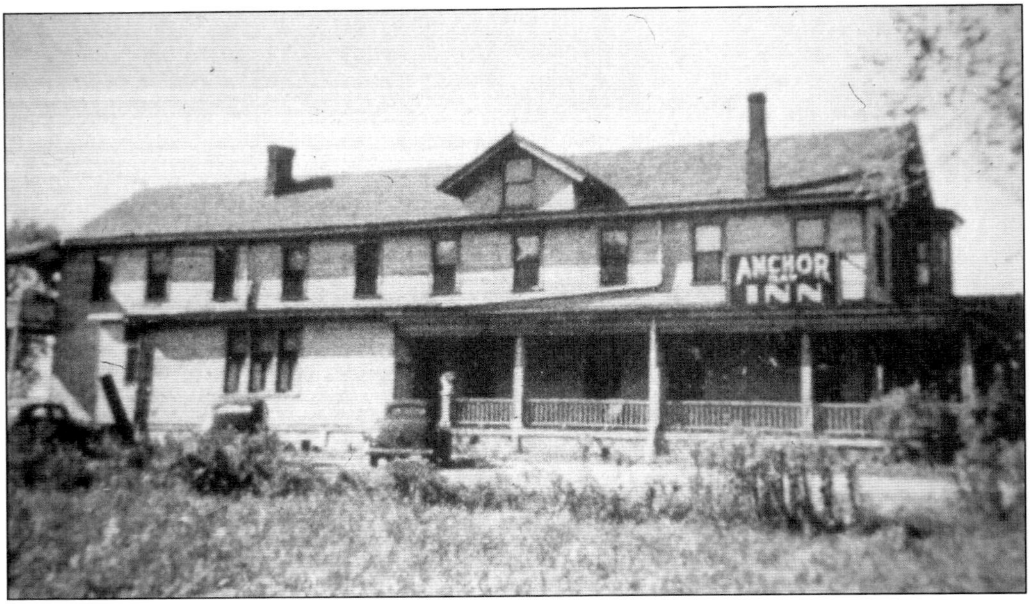

Shown above is the Anchor Bay Inn. This business on the bay has operated under several names, including Hohnhorst Hotel (below), Surf North, Tryst, and Tin Fish. At one time called Kapitski's, it provided a restaurant, bar, and overnight lodging upstairs for tourists, as it was just a step off of the interurban railroad tracks. Location also played into this establishment's role as a "blind pig" during Prohibition, because it was a good point for rumrunners bringing alcohol from Canada. With a destination on the north shore of Anchor Bay, the bootleggers could come straight across the lake to the inn, avoiding shoreline travel where they could be observed. Once docked, the cargo would be carried a mere 110 feet to reach M-29, a road that leads straight to the thirsty city of Detroit.

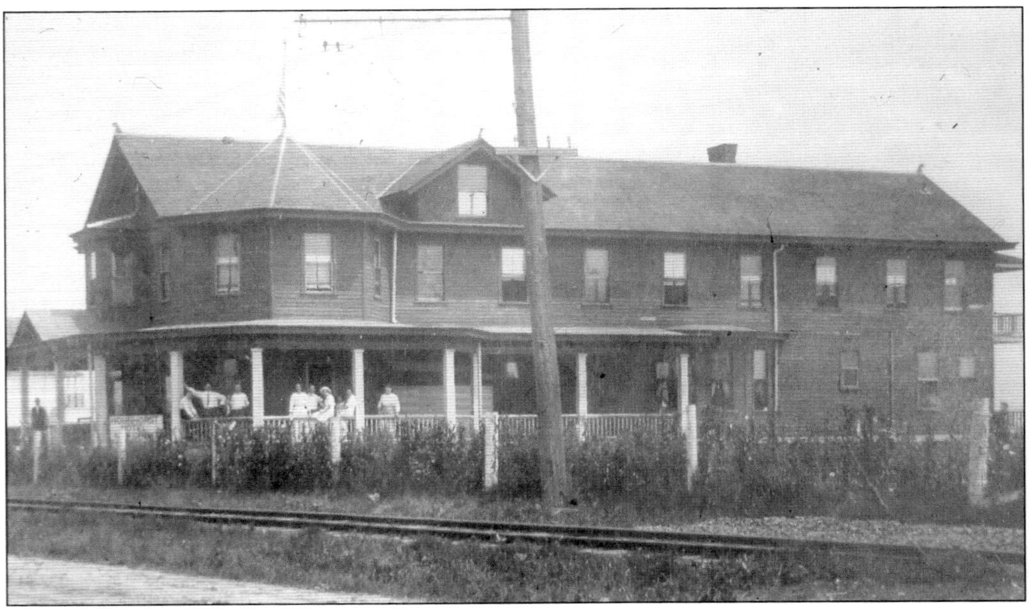

At right, Walter J. Torney stands next to his father's delivery truck in the 1920s. He helped with the family's butter and egg business. Julius and Mary Torney's 22-acre farm was located at the corner of Church and Short Cut Roads. Their families were among the early settlers in Ira Township, arriving with Julius when he was three from Orsieres, Switzerland, in 1871. Mary Marcero's family came from Canada in the 1840s. The couple's six children helped tend the farm, raise chickens, candle eggs, churn butter, tend the apple orchard, and split wood for the winter months. Torney & Sons trucks delivered their goods in Ira Township and from Port Huron to Detroit. Married in Immaculate Conception Church in 1899, Julius and Mary were lifelong parishioners. Besides farming, Julius cut hair at a barber station in the Vernier Hotel in Fair Haven.

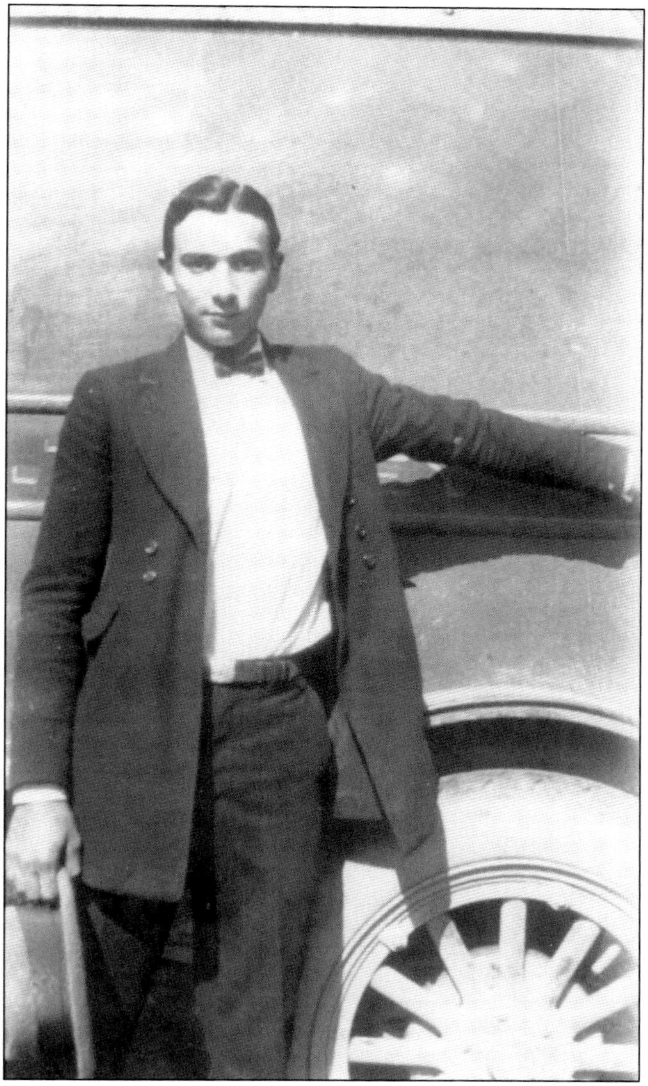

Anchorville, Mich.

J. L. TORNAY

DEALER IN

Fancy Eggs, Poultry and Groceries

ANCHORVILLE, MICH.

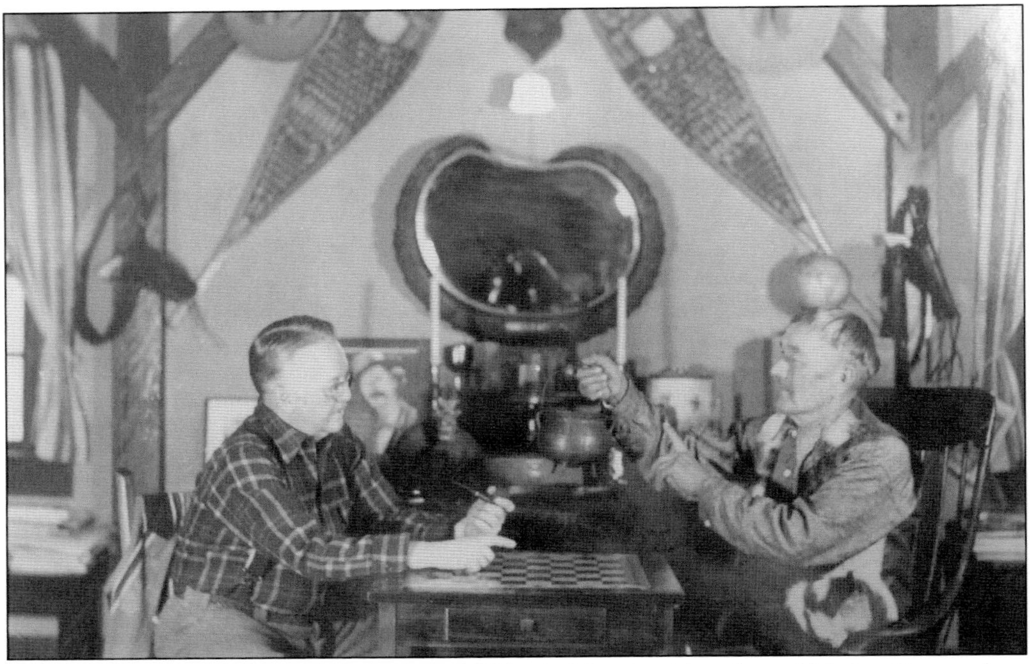

Gilbert E. "Square Deal" Miller (left) and Walpole Island resident Isaac Nehdee discuss plans to build Miller's Log Cabin Lodge and Bunk House on Long Island Court in Fair Haven. A businessman, Miller was co-owner of the Miller-Hoefer Company located in the Miller Building on 10 Miller Street in Detroit. The company dealt in jewelry, watches, and ephemera.

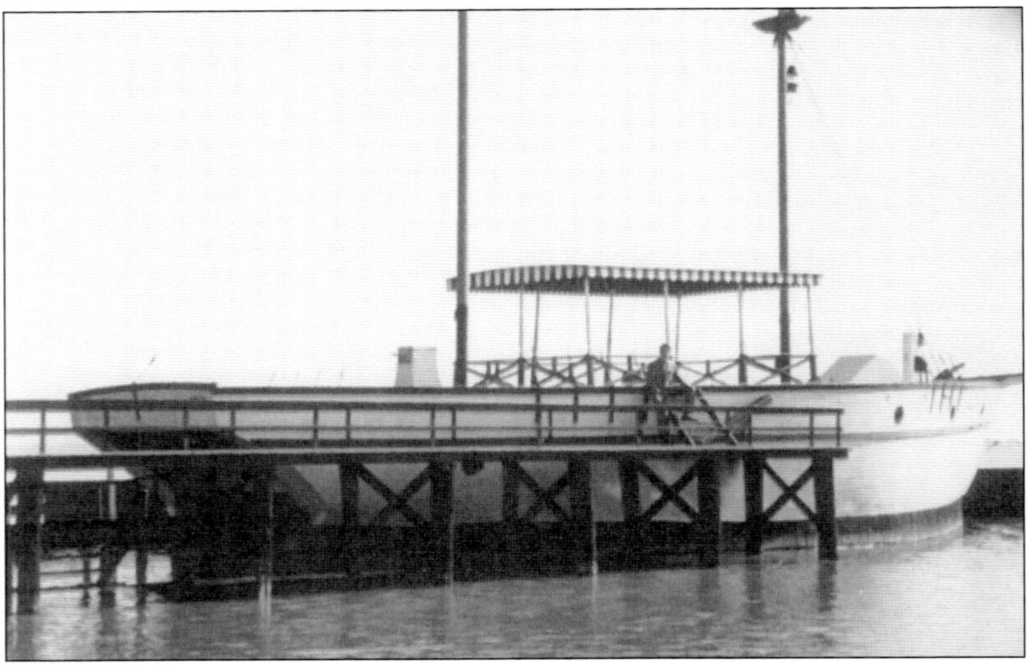

A known eccentric, "Square Deal" Miller may have been the only person to design and remodel an existing boat (he hollowed it out) into a boathouse to store another boat! This photograph shows the docked boathouse with its entrance at the stern for storage. Construction on both the lodge and the boathouse was carried out in the 1930s.

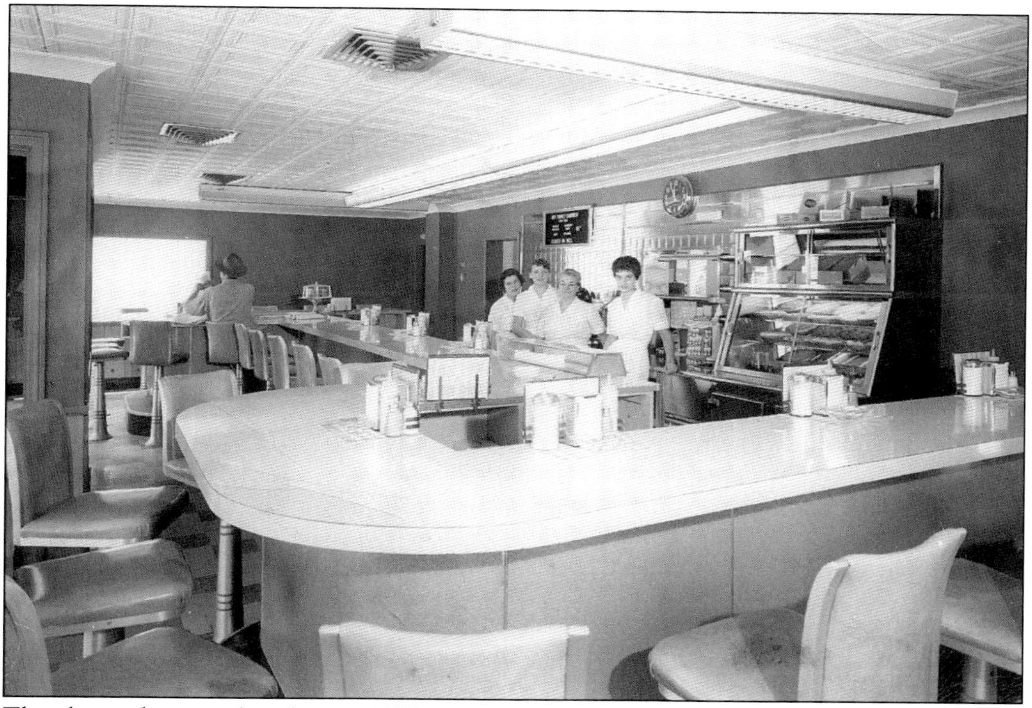

The above photograph, taken in 1955 at Dee Dee's, a Fair Haven eatery, looks as classic as a Hollywood movie scene. Pictured are, from left to right, Norm ?, Mabel Jones, Judy Carroll, Elsie Muhl, and Carolyn Vermullen. In 1990, Deborah DeGregorio, with the help of family, took over the restaurant (then Dixie Diner) and renamed it Buck's Fine Food. Due to business complications and resulting changes, DeGregorio reopened it as Buck's Dixie Diner in 2008. Upon reopening, lifelong resident and diner fan Mae Vernier congratulated the restaurateur, saying, "Thank you so much for waking Fair Haven back up." The below photograph shows the restaurant's interior in the 1970s.

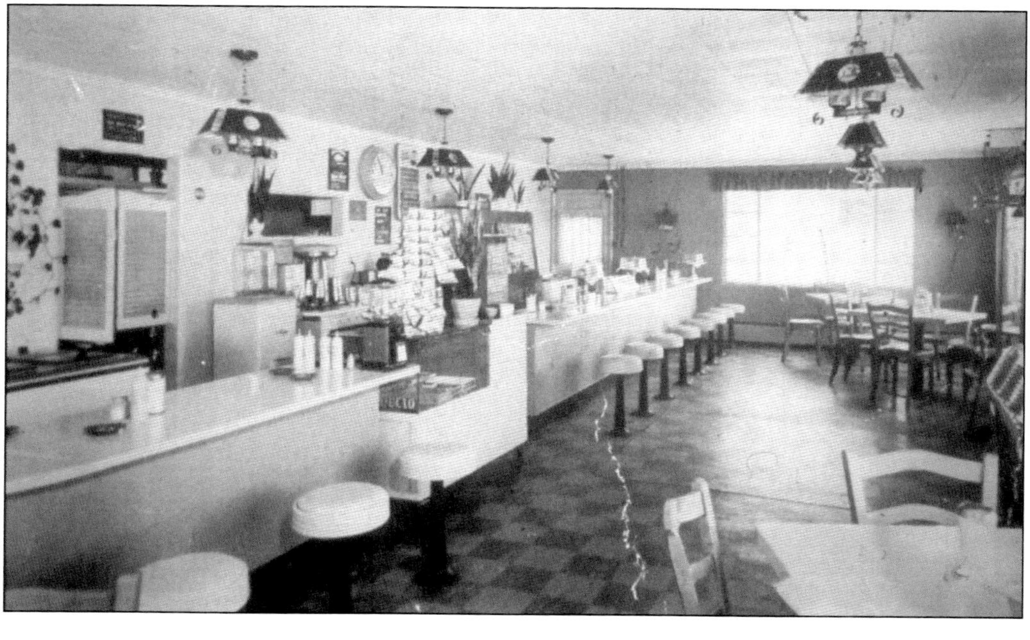

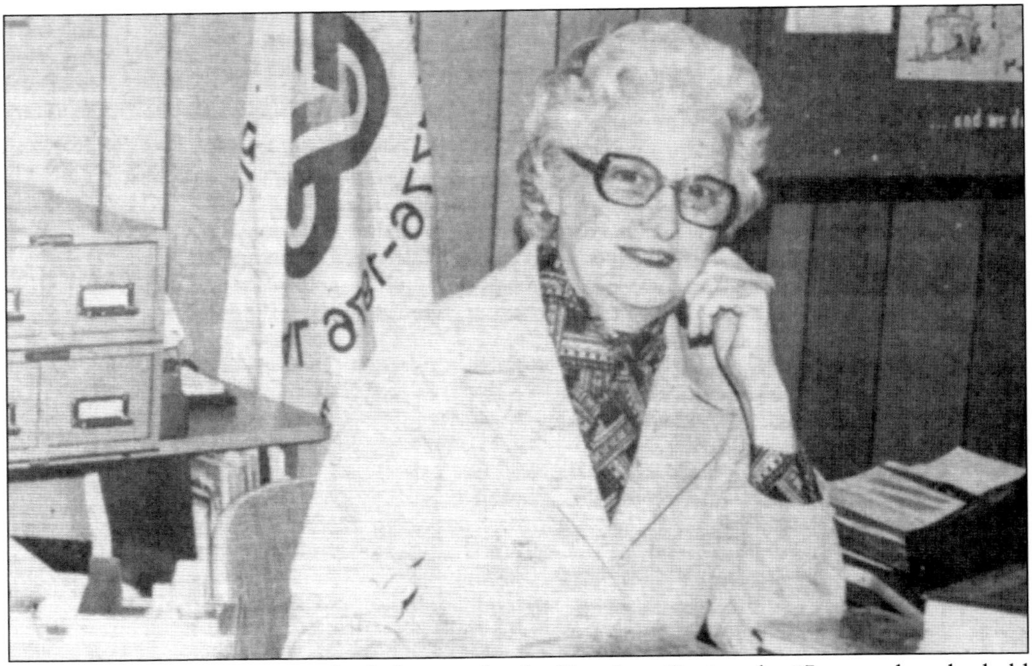

Phoebe Becker was Ira Township's first, and only, librarian. During the 17 years that she held that position, the library was actually a branch of the Blue Water Library Federation; it has since become part of the St. Clair County Library System. Becker retired in 1977. She summed up her years by saying, "To me it hasn't been work. It's been pleasure."

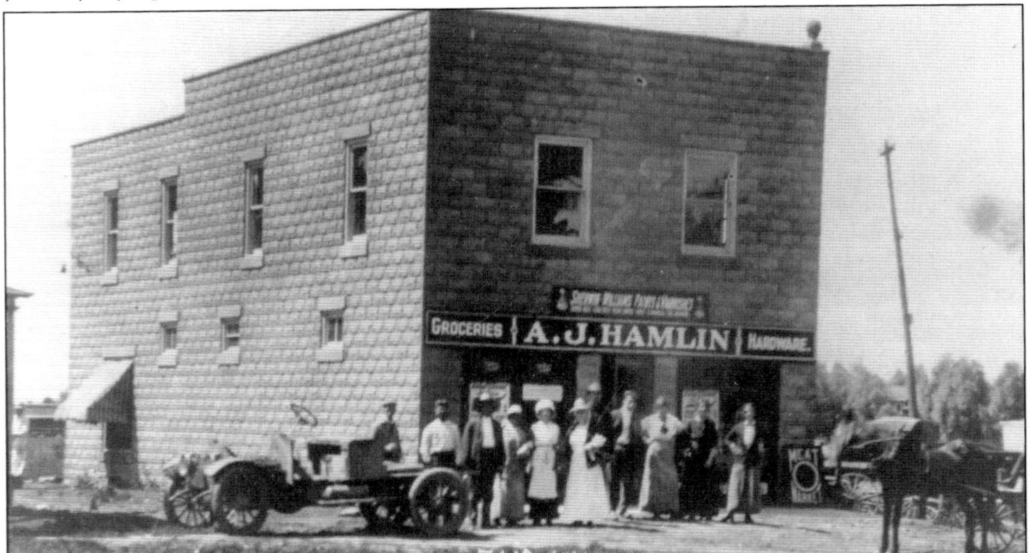

This 1907 building, located east of Swan Creek and between the "old" and "new " Dixie Highway, was originally the general store of H.M. LaBounty. Throughout its history, it was also several grocery stores. A.J. Hamlin operated one, and John Kandler owned it later. For 17 years, it was home to the Ira library. Briefly, it became an antique shop called the Cooperage. Sadly, this frontage has not been utilized for the past 30 years.

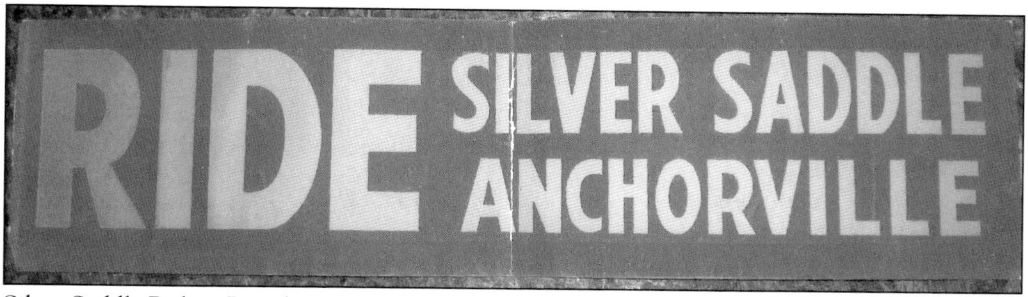

Silver Saddle Riding Ranch was opened in 1955 and was located on Meldrum Road just south of Marine City Highway in Anchorville. Owners Carl and Unis Remick came here from Montana, where Carl was employed as a working cowboy. Silver Saddle Ranch was on 60 acres of land. It had three or four barns and stables that housed up to 150 horses. Besides the rental horses, the ranch also boarded 30 privately owned horses. (Courtesy of Elaine Ehrhardt.)

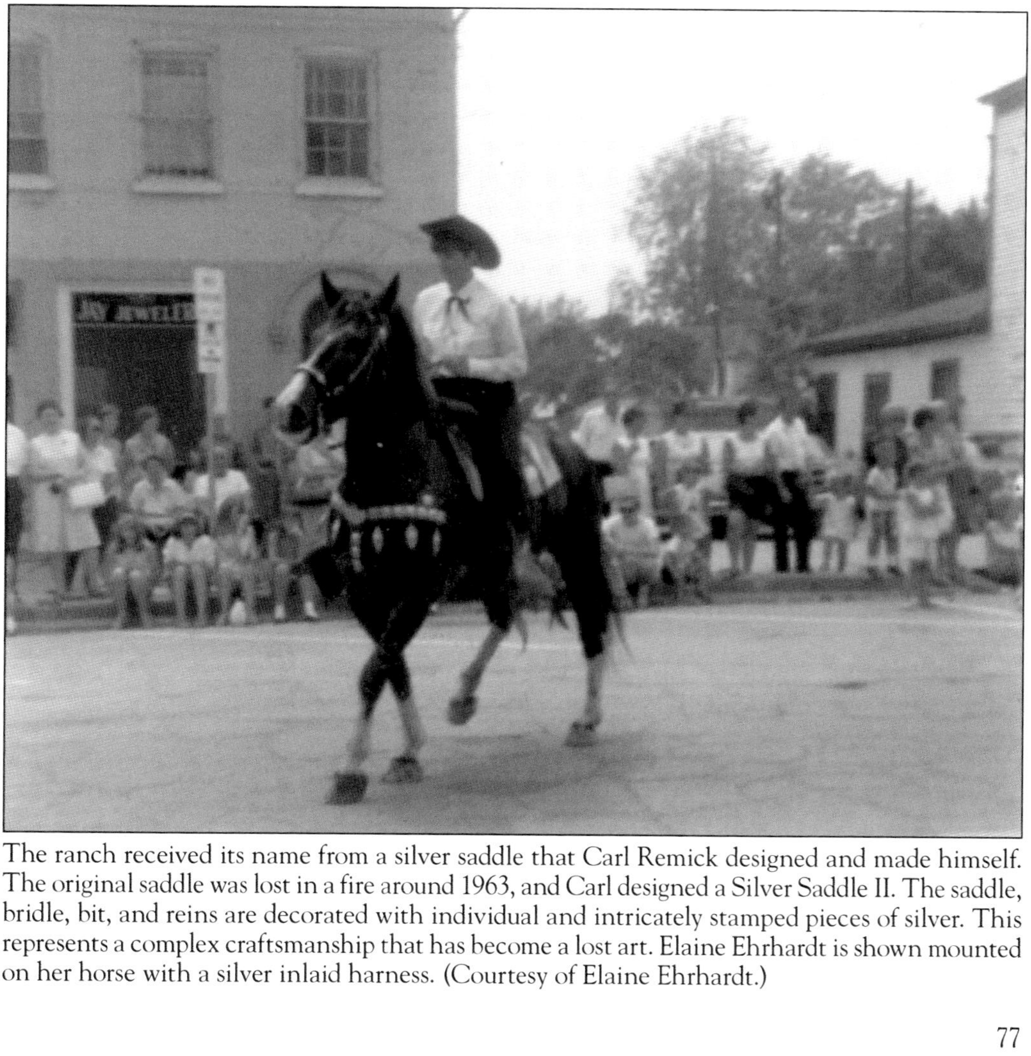

The ranch received its name from a silver saddle that Carl Remick designed and made himself. The original saddle was lost in a fire around 1963, and Carl designed a Silver Saddle II. The saddle, bridle, bit, and reins are decorated with individual and intricately stamped pieces of silver. This represents a complex craftsmanship that has become a lost art. Elaine Ehrhardt is shown mounted on her horse with a silver inlaid harness. (Courtesy of Elaine Ehrhardt.)

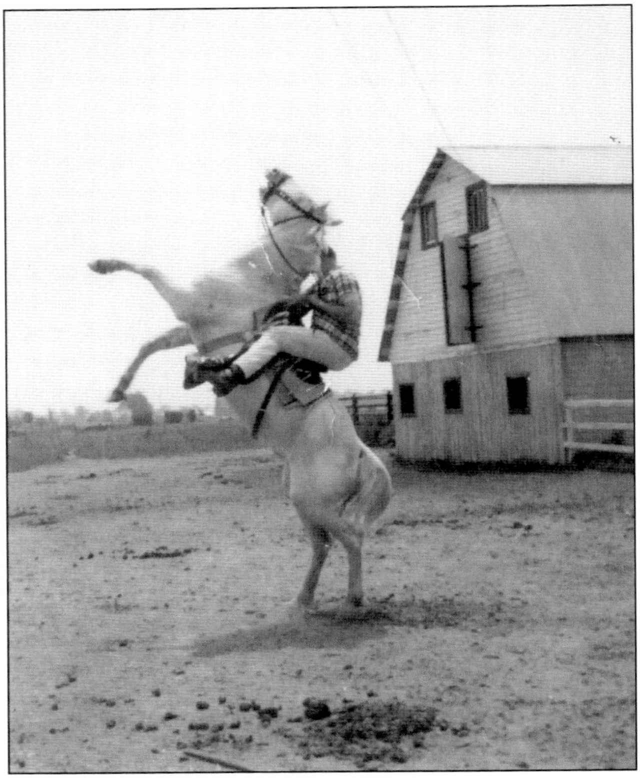

The excellent photograph at left, taken at the Silver Saddle Ranch, shows friend and neighbor Carl Ehrhardt rearing back his horse, Major. All the horses were given names; the ones purchased by Carl Remick usually already had names. Whiskey, Hondo, Cream Puff, Candy, Pop Corn, and Mr. Ed were just some of the colorful names. The riding ranch was opened to all who loved to go horseback riding. The fee to ride for an hour on weekdays was $3; on Sundays, it was $5. Kids of all ages and adults rode the horses along the ranch's well-established trails. Below, Carl Ehrhardt's wife, Elaine, stands next to the big and beautiful horse Mr. Dillon. Opening in 1955, Silver Saddle Ranch was sold about 1970 and operated for just a few more years as a riding stable. (Both, courtesy of Elaine Ehrhardt.)

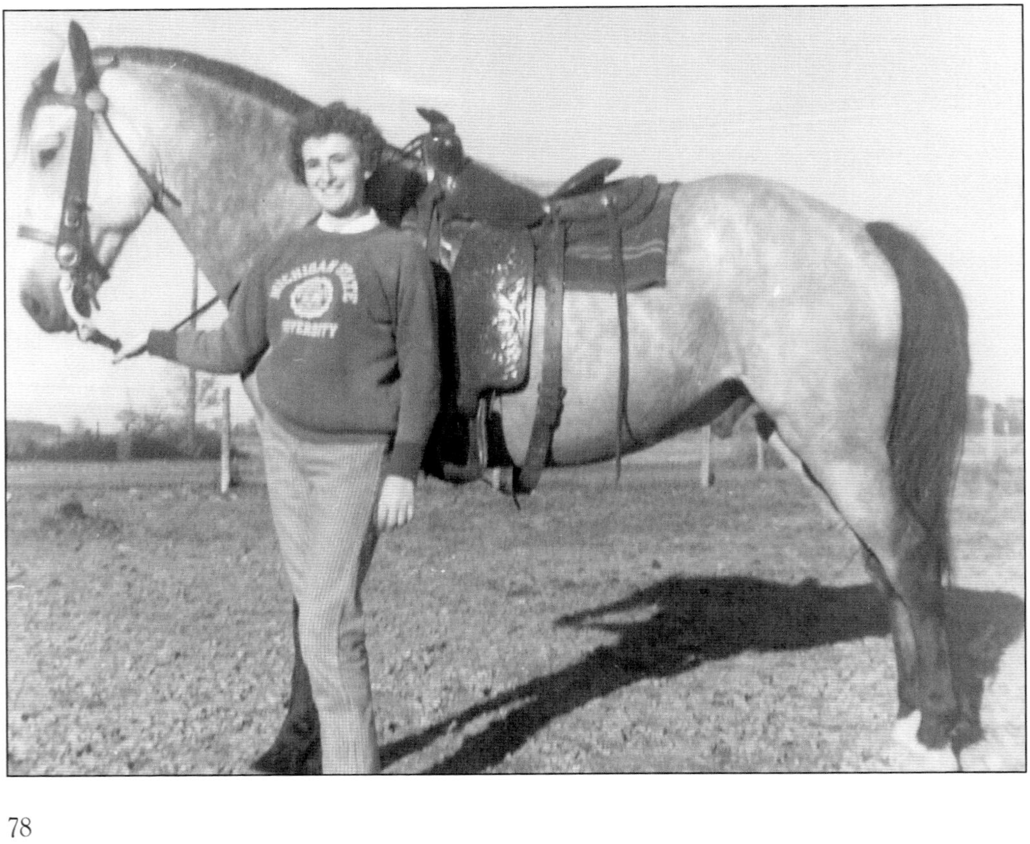

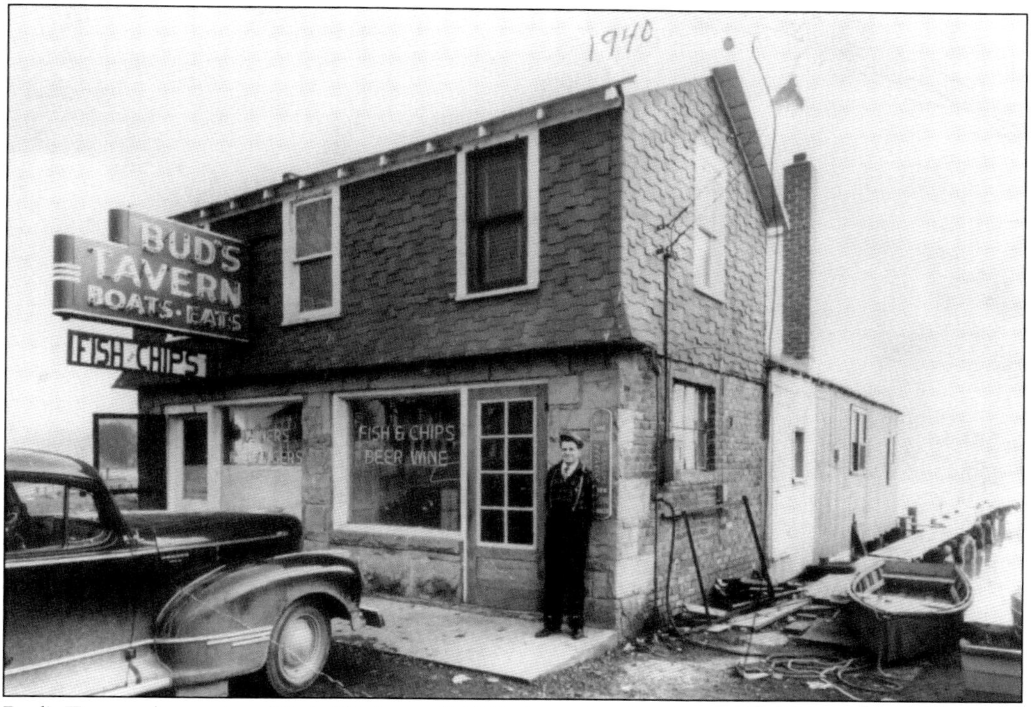

Bud's Tavern, located on Dixie Highway (M-29) along the shoreline of Lake St. Clair on Anchor Bay, had been a popular restaurant since 1940. Bud Goulet (pictured), owner and founder, came to Fair Haven with his wife, Bernice, during the Depression. They started out by opening up a lunchroom just west of the present location on Anchor Bay. (Courtesy of Bud Goulet.)

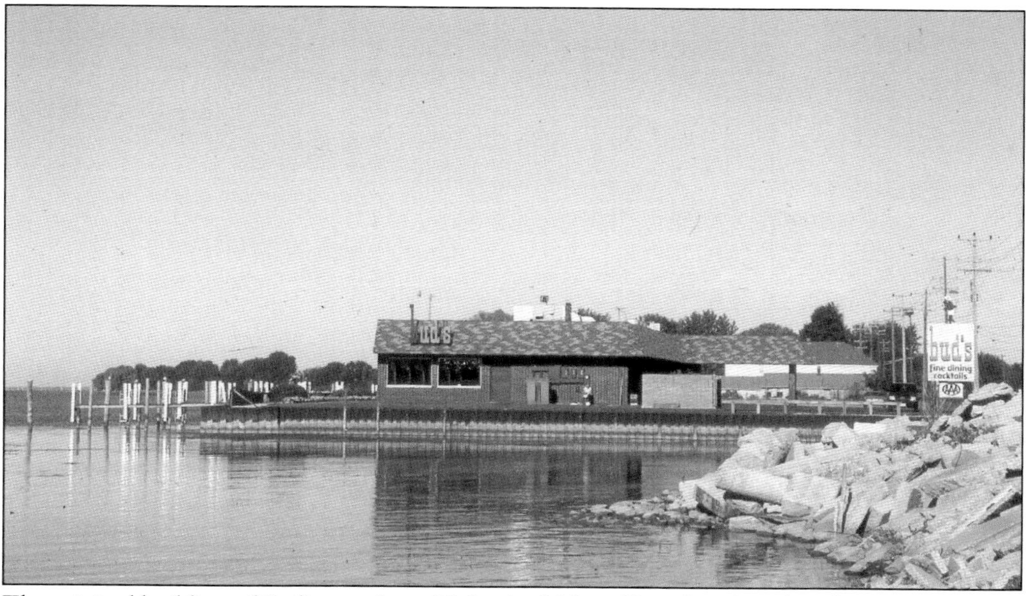

The original building of Bud's was about 20 feet by 20 feet. Here, hot dogs, hamburgers, chili, and soup were served. In 1955, a huge storm caused a flood and washed away a portion of the building and left fish swimming in the dining room. Soon after, it was torn down and replaced with a beautiful new building. A 1972 fire destroyed that structure, and Bud Goulet built the present beautiful, larger building. Today, Bobby Mac's Bayside Tavern and Grill operates there.

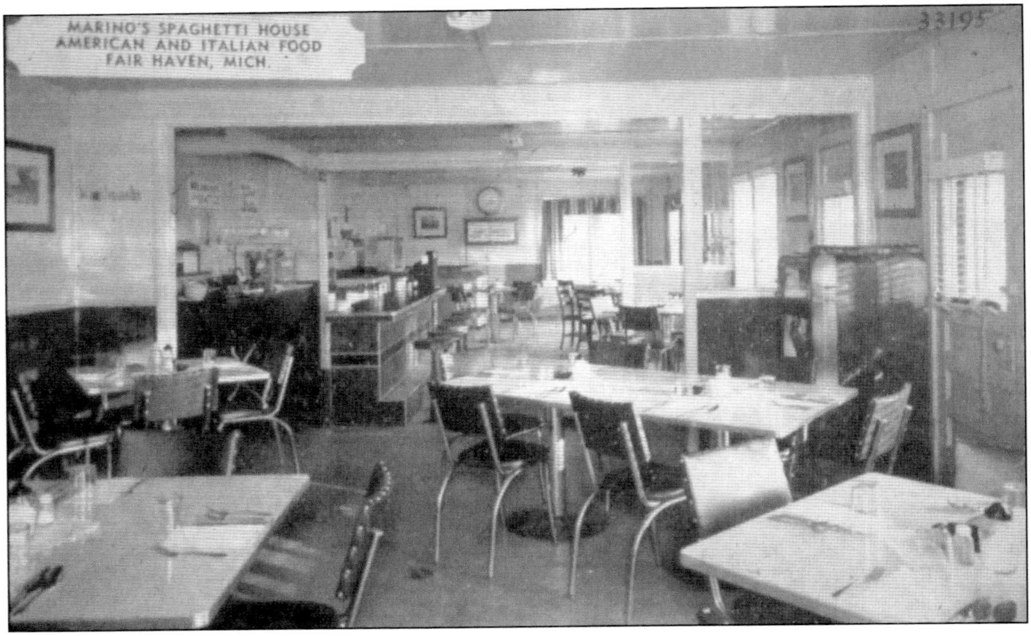

Frank Marino opened Marino's Spaghetti House on Dixie Highway in Fair Haven in February 1946. The house specialty of this popular restaurant was a combination chicken-fish-spaghetti platter. The aroma was always welcoming. Frank Marino was also a well-respected businessman and civic leader and held a position on the Ira Township Water Board and Fire Department. He was instrumental in teaching the local residents and schoolchildren about the importance of fire safety, visiting the schools in Ira Township and giving talks about how to prevent fires, including calling 5-5331 in case of a fire. Ironically, Marino's Spaghetti House was destroyed by fire in 1962 (below). Fifth-Third Bank now occupies the site.

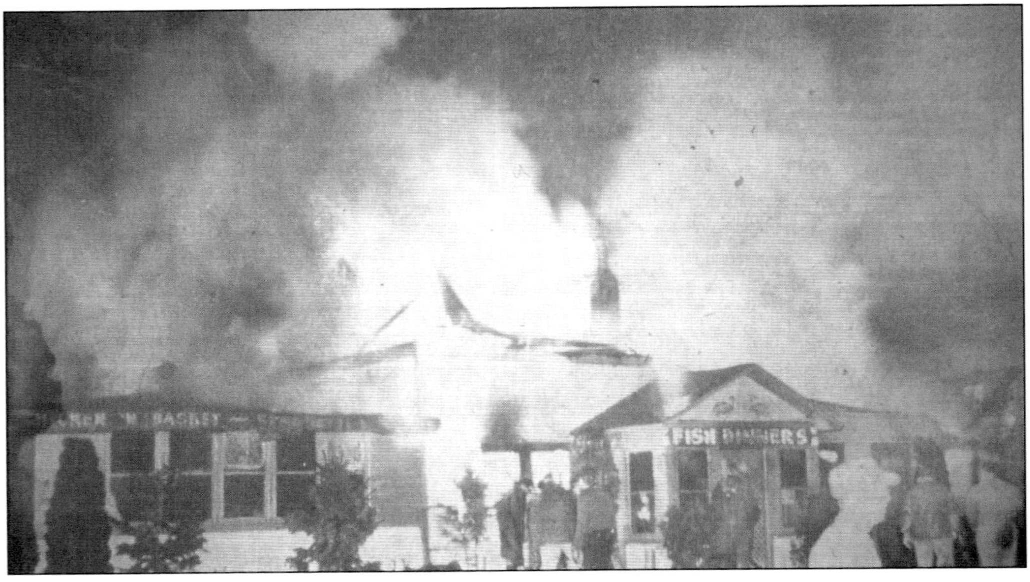

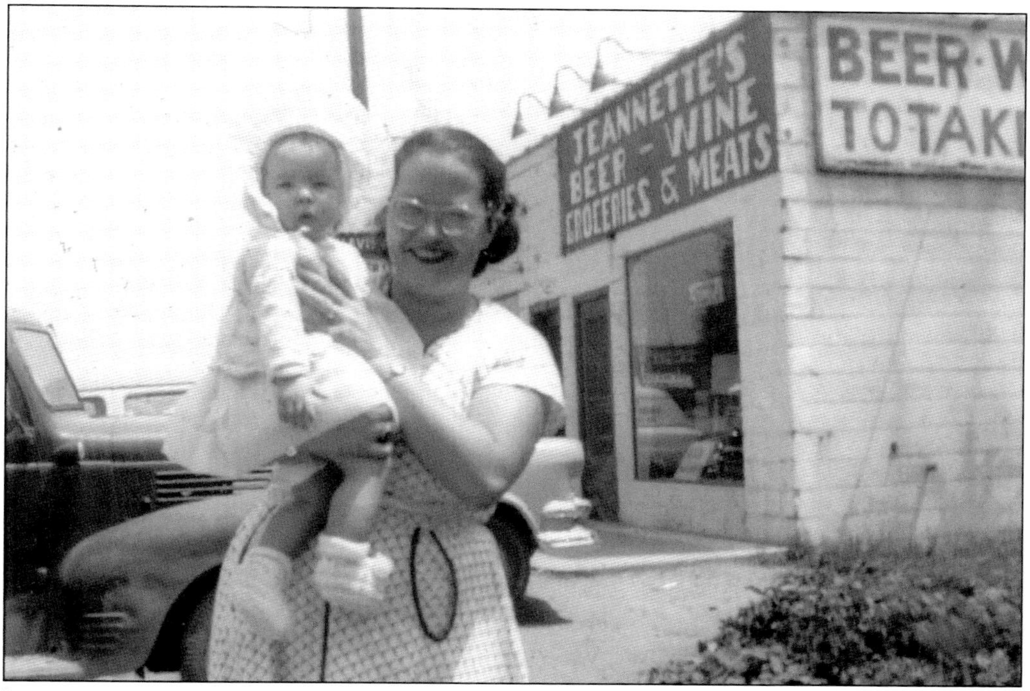

Jeannette's Grocery Store helped establish part of "downtown" Fair Haven when its doors opened at 8861 Dixie Highway in 1942. Vincent and Margaret Jeannette were the owners and proprietors. Providing a little bit of everything, the store sold groceries, meats, household goods, beer and wine, and items for fishermen and tourists. This 1954 photograph shows Fair Haven resident Madeline (DeMars) Zabowski holding her one-year-old daughter, Gail, one of the authors. Jeannette's store closed in 1968.

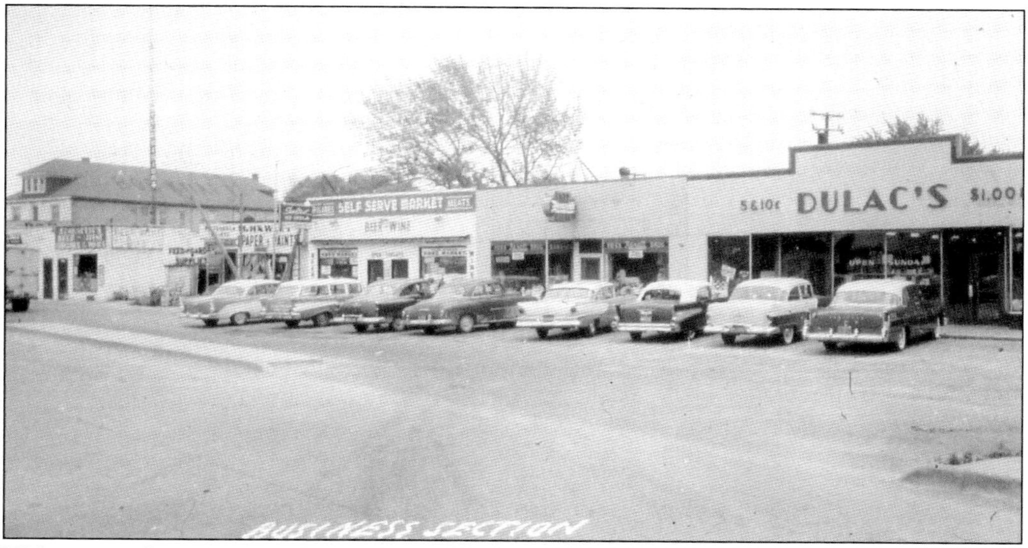

Welcome to downtown Fair Haven! In this 1950s photograph are, from left to right, the Village Tavern, Jeannette's Grocery, a hardware store, Self-Serve Market, Foss' Rexall Drugs, and Dulac's Five & Dime. Locally known as Pijanowski's, the Self-Serve Market was operated for years by Stanley and Florence Pijanowski. It was later called the Fair Haven Food Market and was known for its homemade kielbasa (sausage), which Stanley made religiously every Easter and Christmas.

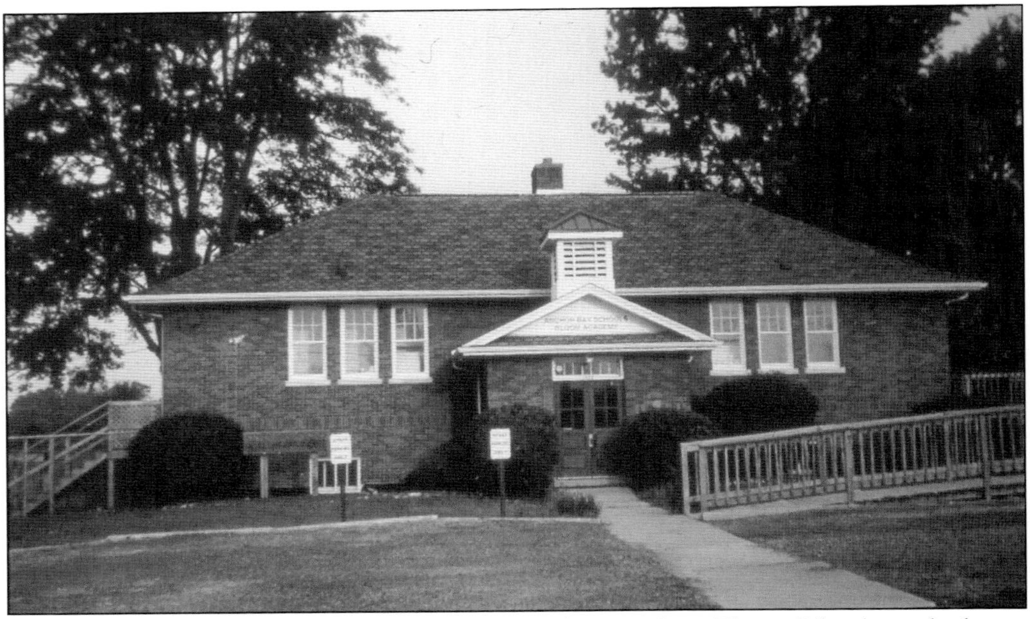

The little red schoolhouse known by many names, but mostly as Bloom School, was built as a school to serve grades one to six. Named for the Bloom family, who originally owned the property, it is located on Church Road just south of Arnold Road in Anchorville. Except for the fact that it had two classrooms, Bloom School was like the traditional one-room schoolhouses that had one teacher instructing all the grades.

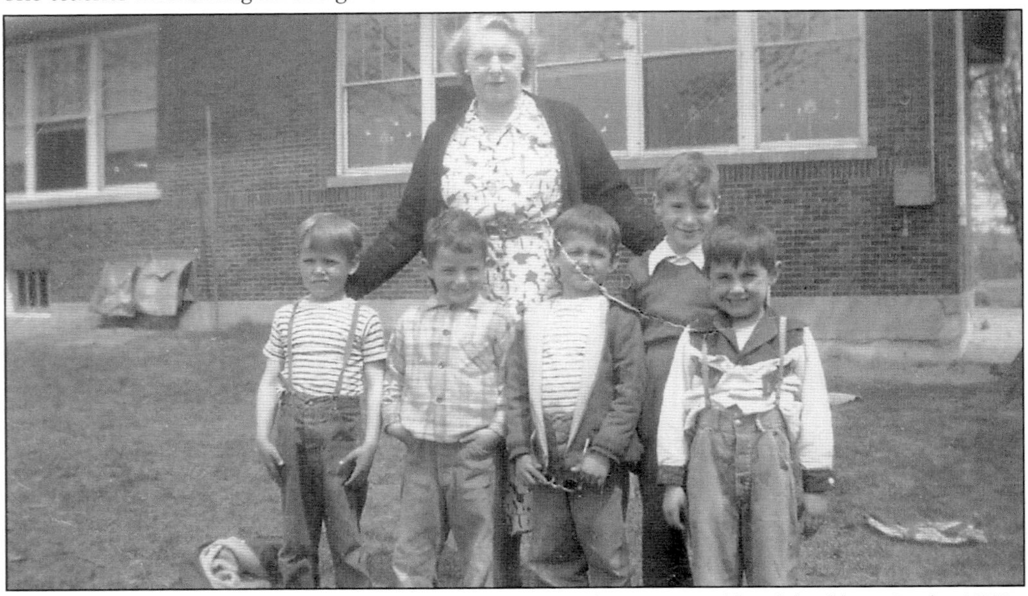

Built around 1912, Bloom School is an exceptionally well-constructed brick building. In the 1950s, the superintendent of Anchor Bay Schools, Dean Naldrett, headed a drive to consolidate Anchor Bay Rural Agricultural Schools. The first to join were Chesterfield Township, New Baltimore, and, finally and reluctantly, Ira Township and its Bloom School. As part of the Anchor Bay School District, Bloom was dubbed "Kindergarten Kollege." Teacher Janet Rae Socia, who taught students for decades at Bloom School, poses here with, from left to right, Fred Furtah, George Torney, David Furtah, John Endres, and Jerry Meldrum. (Courtesy of Stacia Rivard.)

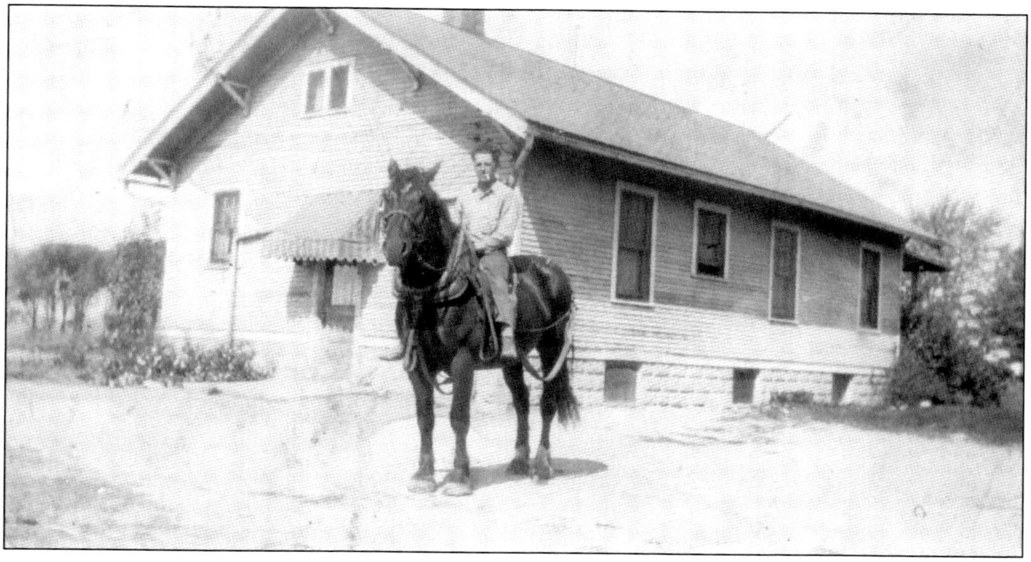

Izzi Farm is located on Marine City Highway, five miles east of I-94 on the northeast edge of Ira Township. It has been in the family since 1971. The corn maze and pumpkin patch offer outdoor fun for all ages, including picking pumpkins, exploring the maze paths, slides, refreshments, picnics, and a farm store offering Michigan products. The Latour family, who started working the land in the 1800s, previously owned the property. Above, Joe Latour and his horse Tops are shown after a day's work on the farm. In 2008, a presidential election year, the subject of the corn maze design was voting. In 2009, the State of Michigan initiated a Travel Michigan advertising campaign, and property owner Carlo Izzi thought it would be a good idea to help celebrate the occasion. He was given exclusive rights to duplicate the Pure Michigan logo (below). Renting a powered parachute from the local Eagle Air Sports Company was another way to view the maze and to take photographs. (Above, courtesy of Joe Latour; below, courtesy of Carlo Izzi.)

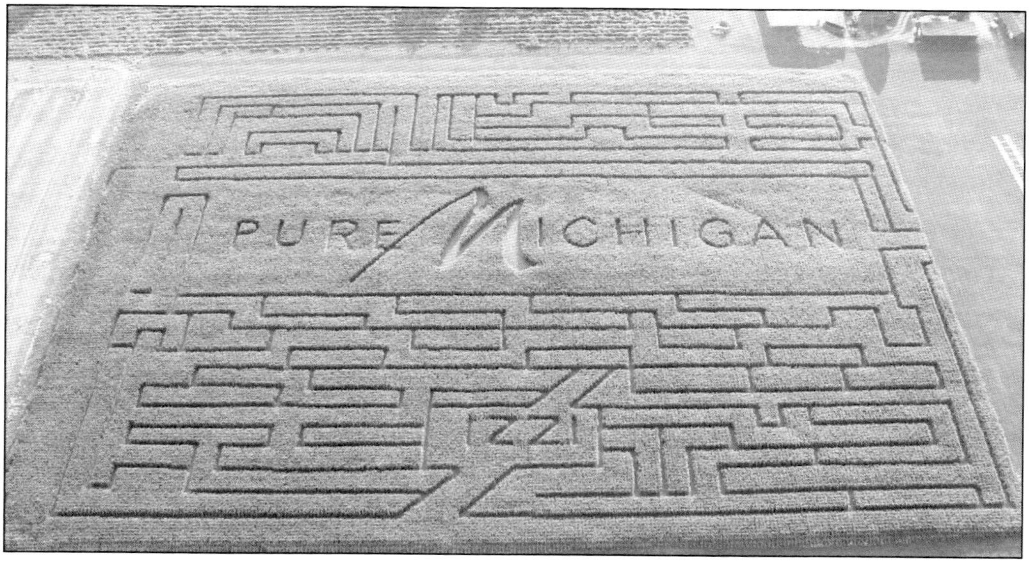

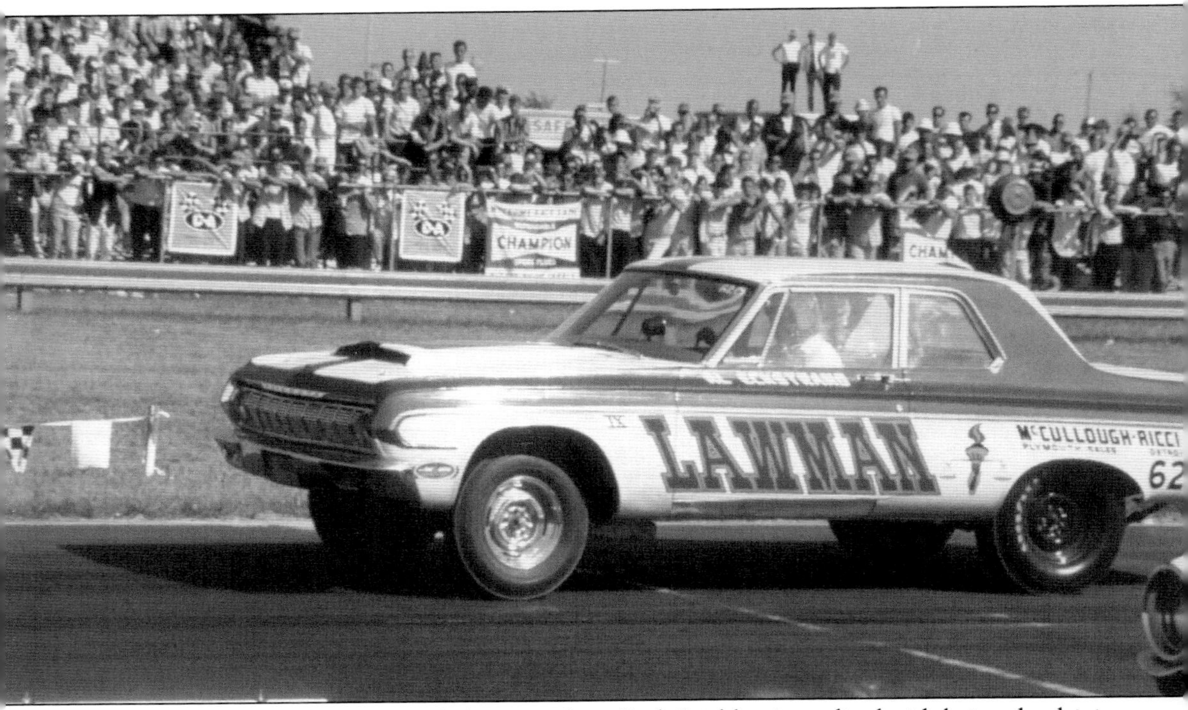

Michigan Hot Rod Association's first president, Dick Stickley, is credited with being the driving force behind the creation of Motor City Dragway. Built in 1956 and officially opened in 1957, it was one of the Detroit area's most popular drag strips in the 1950s, 1960s, and 1970s. It was located on Meldrum Road just south of Marine City Highway in Ira Township. The drag strip was known by different names. In the 1950s, the strip was just "New Baltimore" to those who raced there. It also went by the names Michigan Hot Rod Association Drag Strip and International Raceway Park. Local and big-name drag racers competed there, along with many famous dragsters. Shown here is the Plymouth Fury super-stock "Lawman," driven by Al Eckstrand. The place closed down in the late 1970s due to a decline in drag-racing interest and because of complaints from local residents about the traffic and noise. (Courtesy of Greg Furtah.)

Six

The Interurban Railroad and Short Cut Road

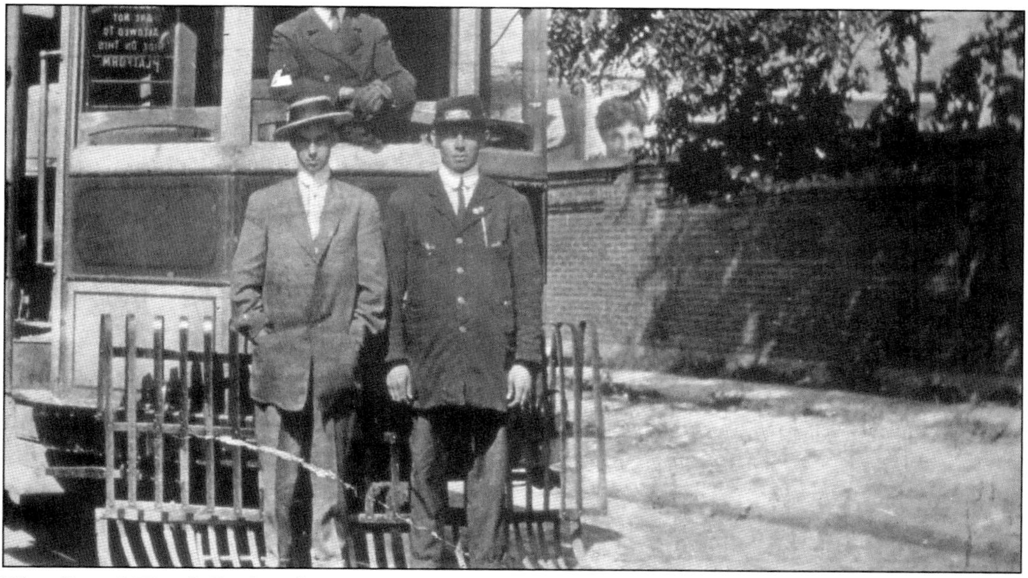

The Grand Trunk Railroad was a great convenience for settlers in the rural areas when this alternative mode of transportation began to proliferate. However, the Grand Trunk did not help the small-time farmer with transportation to markets. A better method soon arose when the interurban railroad companies began laying tracks around the area.

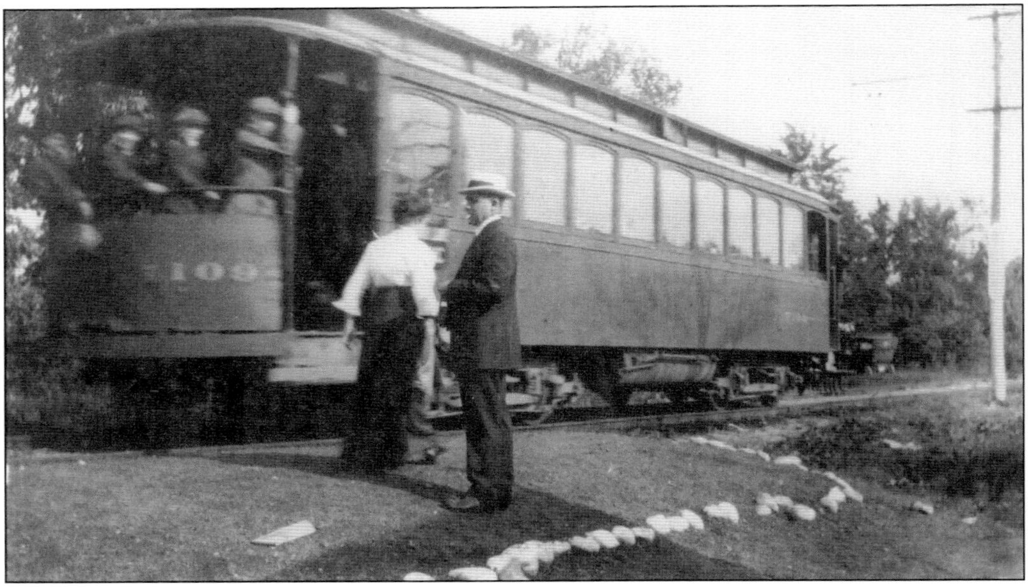

In 1900, the Detroit United Railway began when all the lines within the Detroit area were consolidated into a single corporation. This was a boon not only to commuters who used the interurban railroad to get from Detroit to Port Huron and points between, but to farmers who used the freight cars of the interurban to ship hay, produce, and other crops to markets for a penny per mile. The Grand Trunk was a steam railroad. The interurban railroad used electric current generated in a large powerhouse in nearby New Baltimore. Interurban freight trains would have 40 cars or more. Below, the Beauvais family poses on the tracks in front of their Anchorville home. (Both, courtesy of Carl Beauvais.)

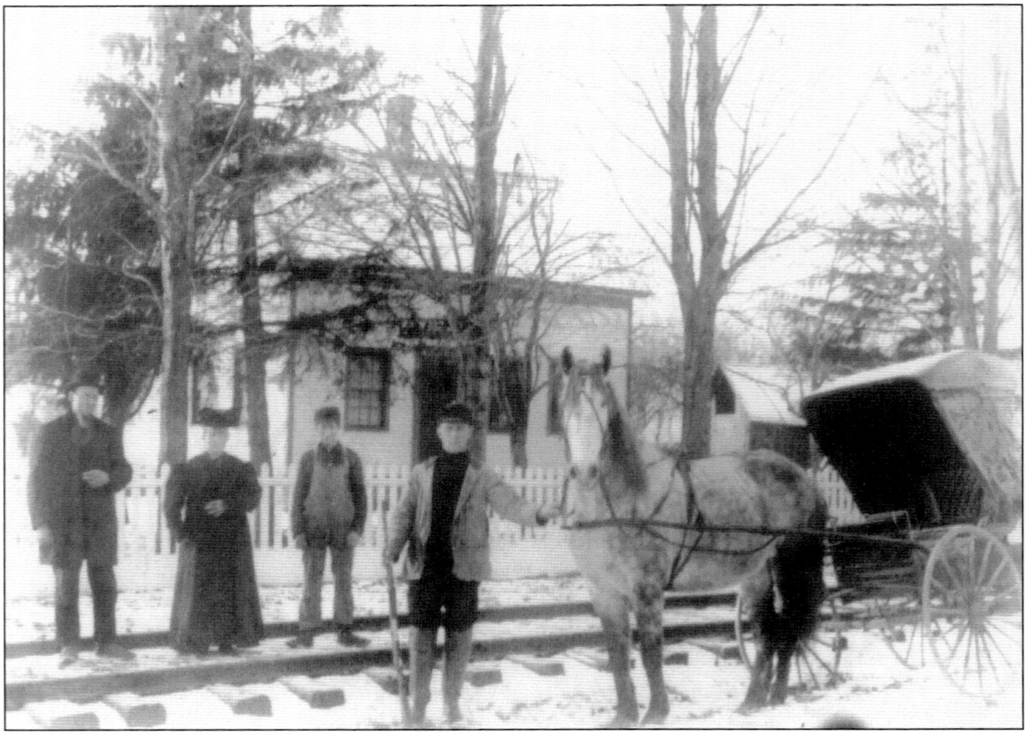

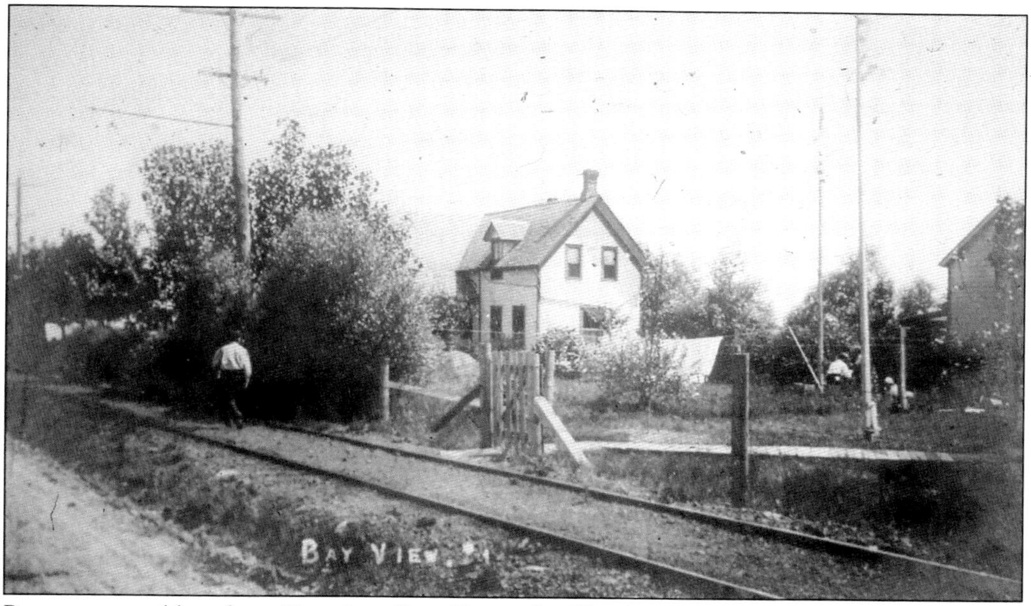

Passengers could go from Detroit to Port Huron for 25¢. A person could take an express route to Marine City, bypassing Algonac, Fair Haven, Pearl Beach, Robert's Landing, and other stops along present-day M-29. It was in Anchorville that the rail line broke off into the longer water route and the quicker inland express route.

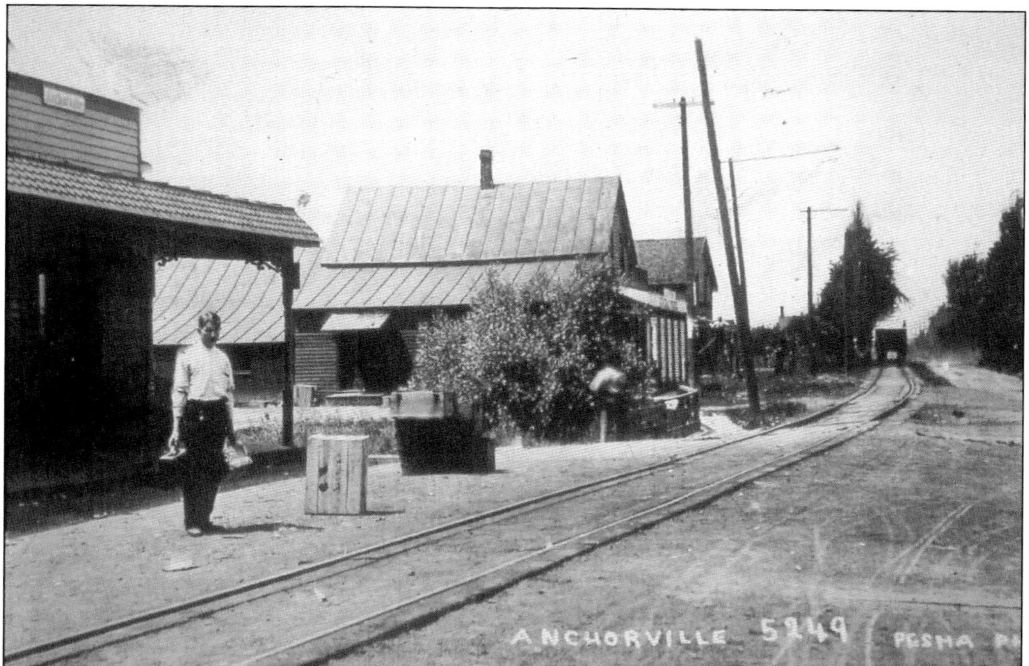

The train turned left onto Church Road, where it would pass Immaculate Conception Church and then turn right onto Meyers Road (Short Cut Road), with tracks running straight toward Marine City. Lifelong resident Carl Beauvais poignantly noted about the interurban, "It killed a lot of our dogs."

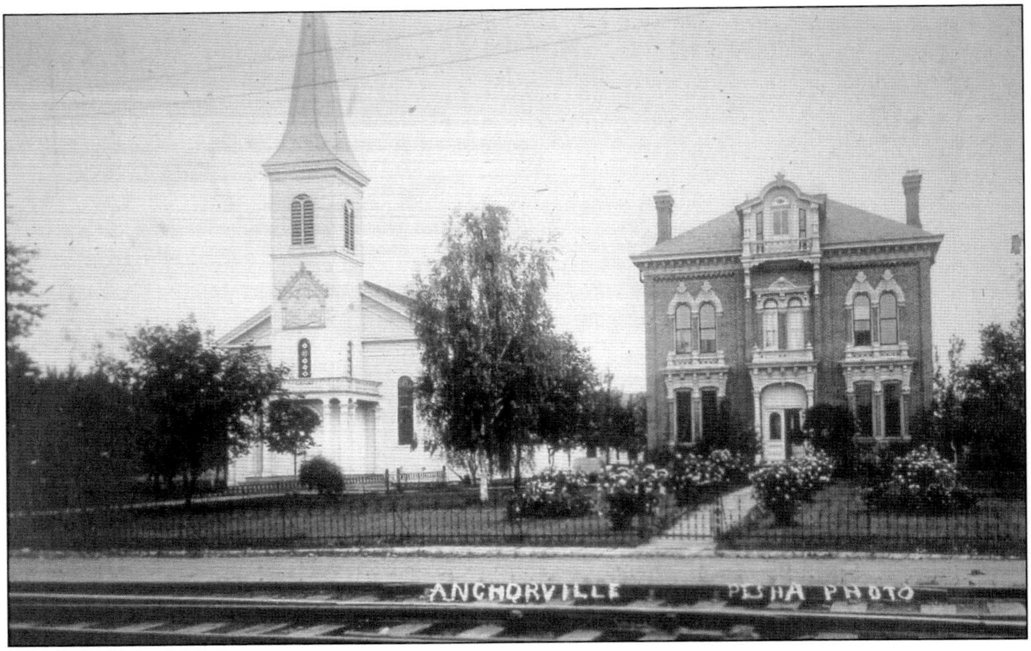

Along the Shortcut route (also known as "Short Cut"), stops in Ira Township and beyond for the interurban included Anchorville, Meyers (which had a large farm), David, Starrville (also known as Starville), Bammel, Smith, and Marine City. Along the scenic Anchor Bay water route, the stops included Anchorville (above), Bay View, Fair Haven, Rose, Mills, Perch Point (below), Crockerville, Dyke, Pearl Beach, Randolph, Nook, Point Duchane, Point Tremble, Algonac, North Algonac, Oak Grove, Harrow, Roberts Landing, Evansmere, Cherry Beach, and Marine City. Not all of these stops were active at the same time.

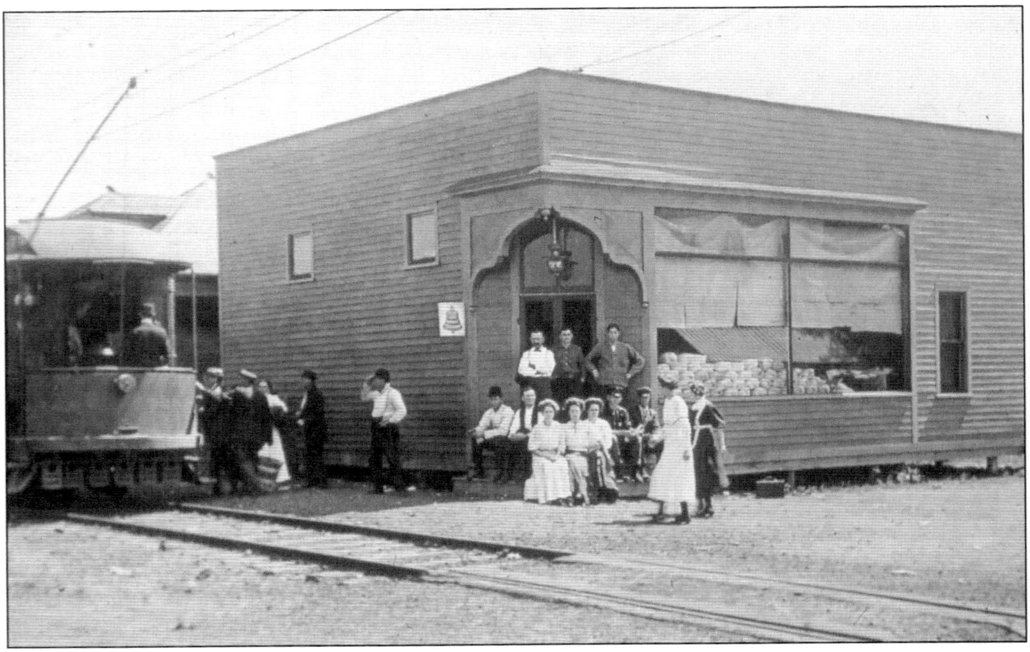

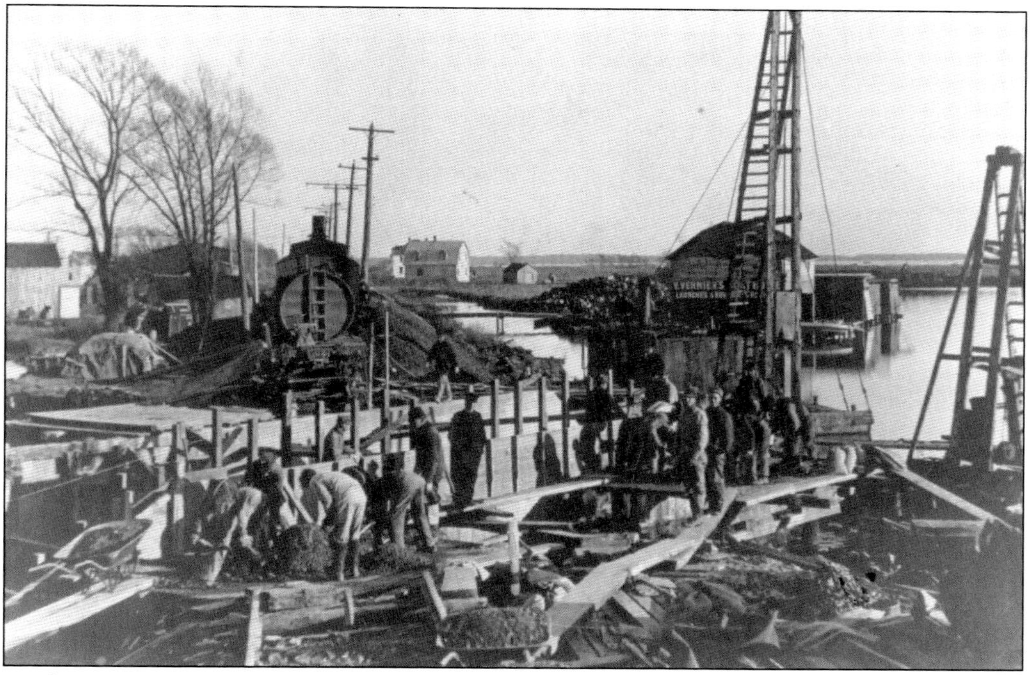

Workers in Fair Haven lay rails for the interurban railroad along M-29. They also built a bridge that spanned the Swan Creek on the Swan Creek Flats. Vic Vernier's boathouse is visible in the upper right. The business rented launches and rowboats for local residents and visitors to gain access to Anchor Bay for fishing and swimming. (Courtesy of Tom Jeannette.)

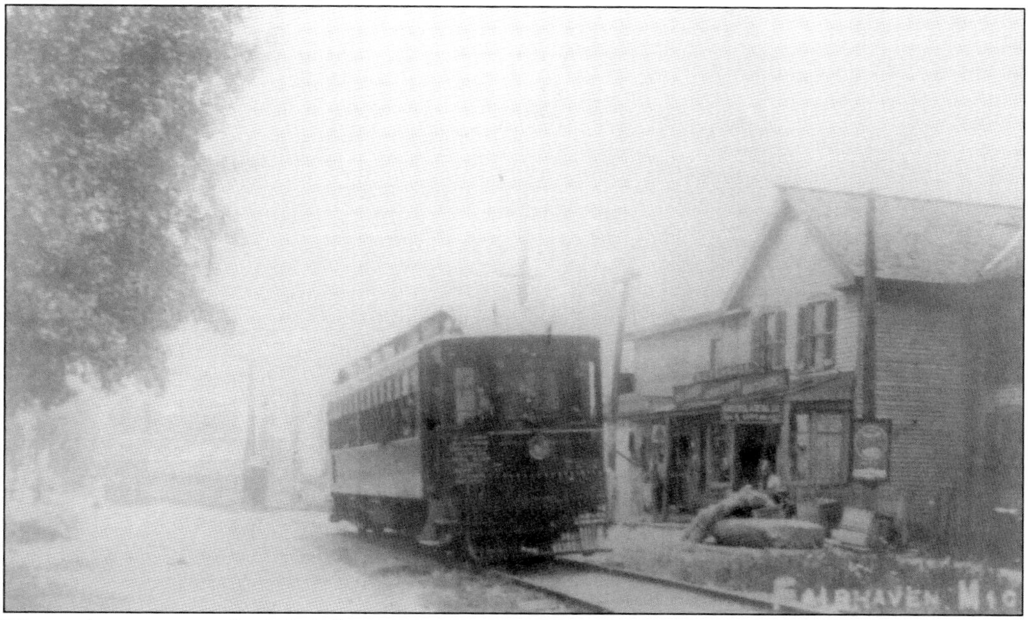

This rail car is stopped at B.J. Schnoor's store around 1900. Next to it is Henry LaBounty's General Store and the post office (LaBounty was postmaster). Henry LaBounty was the postmaster. The photograph illustrates how close the tracks and the general store were to each other. Although probably dangerous, it was convenient for travelers and for store merchandise to be picked up and dropped off. (Courtesy of Bond Schnoor.)

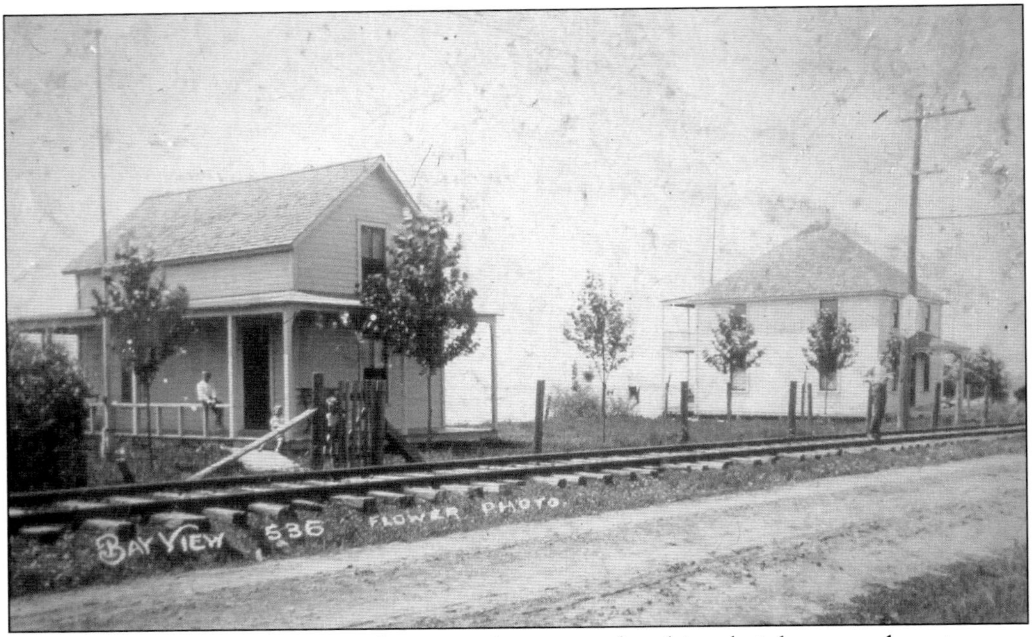

Since the roads were not very good, area residents started to drive their horses and carriages on the tracks. Native Americans were allowed to ride free on the trains. Those cars would be filled with the pleasant smell of sweetgrass, which Native American women used to weave the baskets that they sold on the train and at its stops.

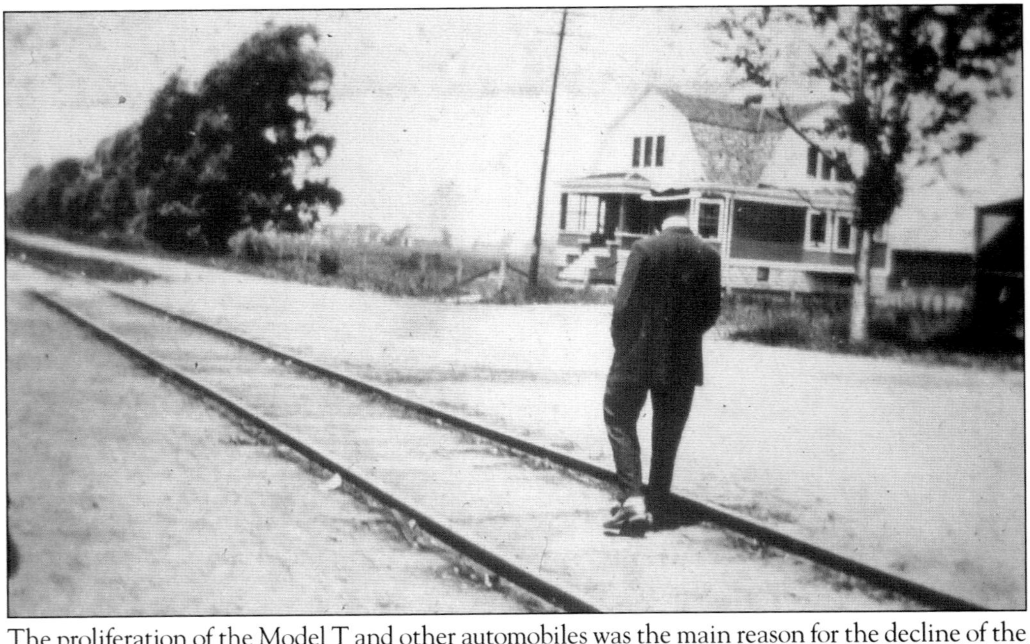

The proliferation of the Model T and other automobiles was the main reason for the decline of the interurban railroads. The Detroit United Railway declared bankruptcy in 1925. Although other companies, such as Rapid Railroad, kept the trains going for a while, the days of the interurban were numbered.

Seven

Shipbuilding and Resorts on the Waterfront

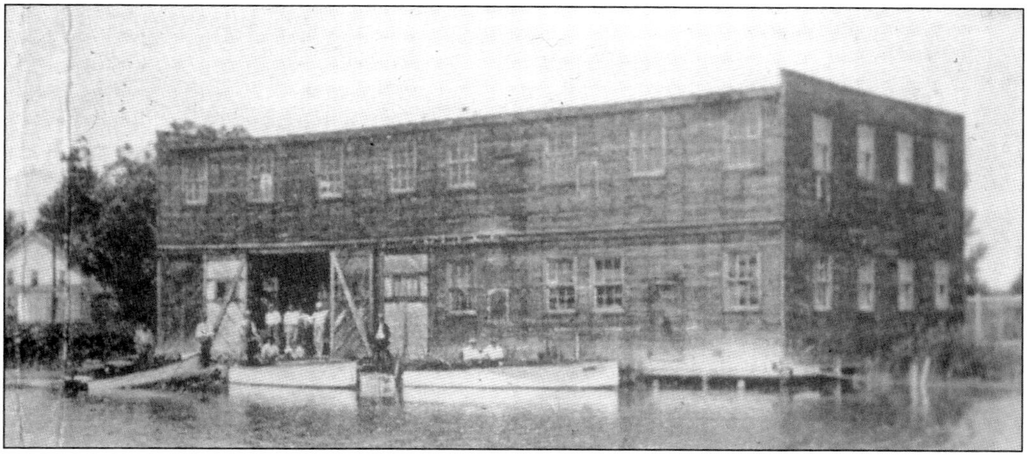

By the late 1800s, Fair Haven shipbuilders produced schooners, scows (a wide-beamed, flat-bottomed boat), and steamships over 200 tons. In 1914, boat maker Louis Mayea moved his company from Detroit to Fair Haven and christened it the Mayea Boat & Aeroplane Works. Still in operation, the Mayeas have assisted in the development of the first hydroplane boat hulls, constructed the first pontoons with the Wright brothers, and built the fastest diesel-powered boats in the world for the US Navy in World War II. They survived the market crash of 1929 and a fire that destroyed their boatyard in the 1960s. During Prohibition, the Mayeas serviced rumrunners' boats, repairing bullet holes and damage from boats run aground.

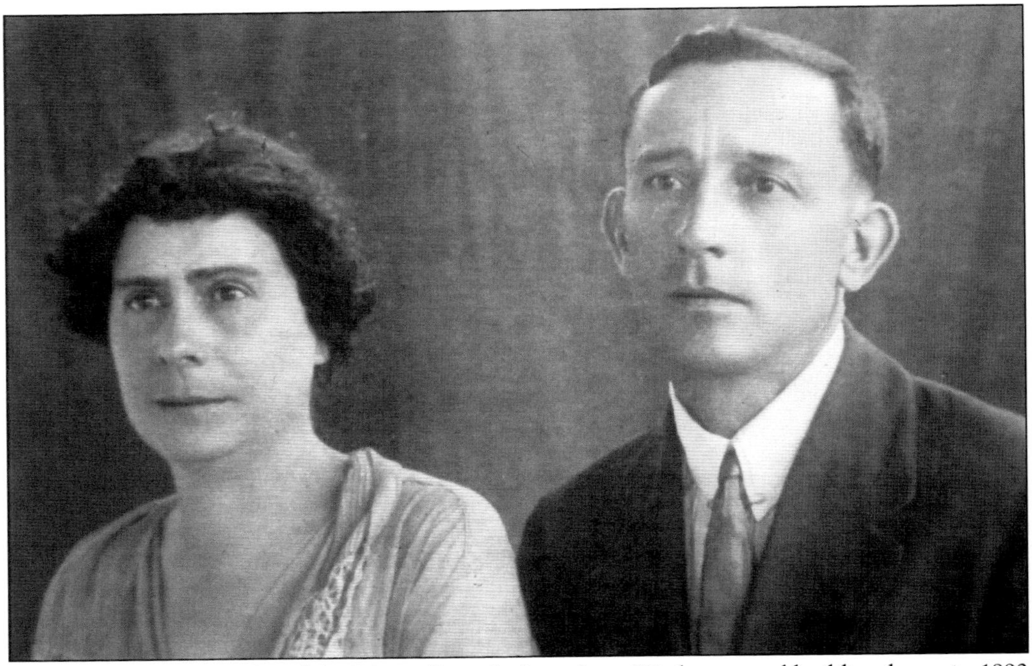

Louis Mayea, the founder of the Mayea Boat & Aeroplane Works, started building boats in 1893 when he was 15 years old. He was recognized as one of the foremost boat-builders of his time. He is shown here with his wife, Mary, in a photograph taken in the 1920s. His company designed and built launches, sailboats, hydroplanes, and cruisers up to 60 feet in length.

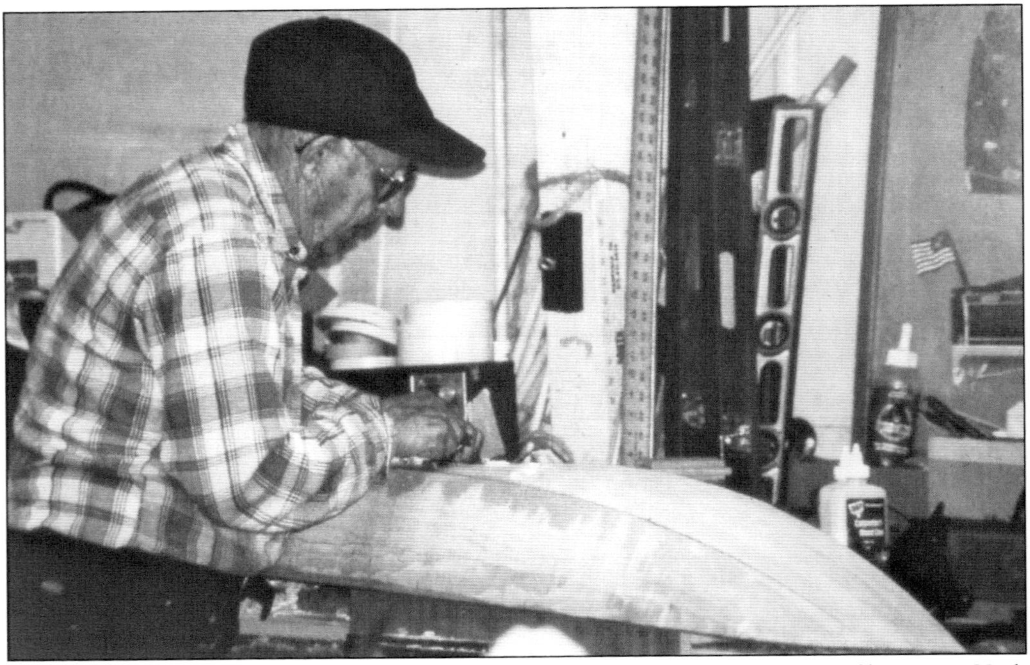

Herb Mayea, son of Louis and Mary, works on a model of a boat. Unlike most of his peers, Herb began his projects using models rather than drawings. The first Mayea boat, called Mays Craft, was designed and built in 1946. The fourth generation of Mayeas continues to create and deliver custom wooden boats for a discerning clientele.

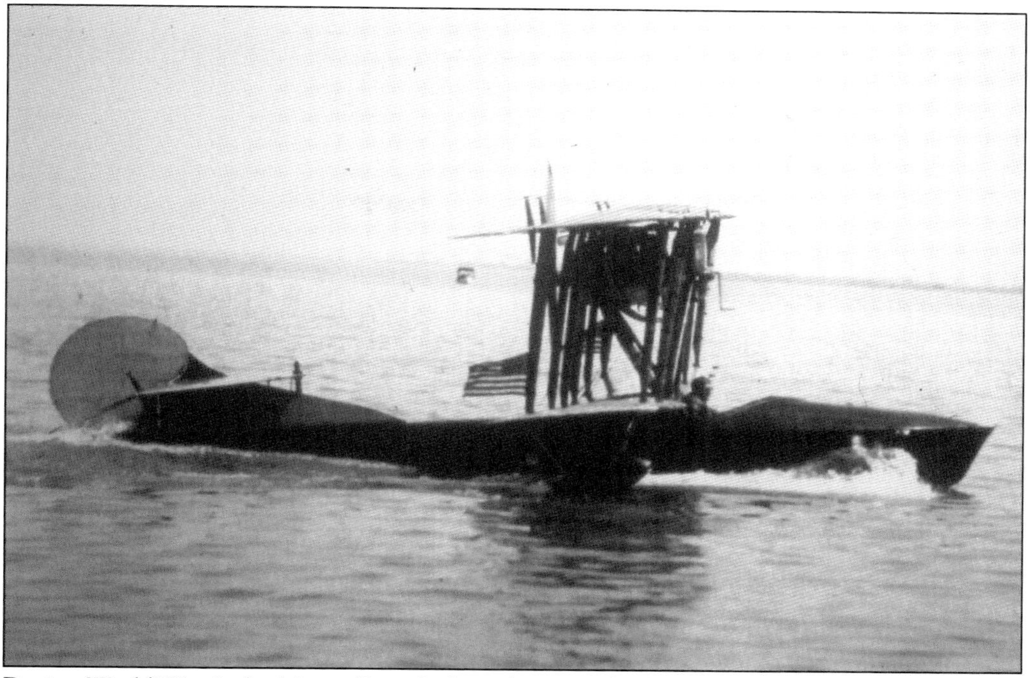

During World War I, the Mayea Boat & Aeroplane Works designed and built seaplanes for the Navy. This photograph, taken in 1916, is an action shot of the Verville Flying Boat, an early seaplane. The flying boat was the first aircraft designed and manufactured in Michigan to be sold to the US armed forces.

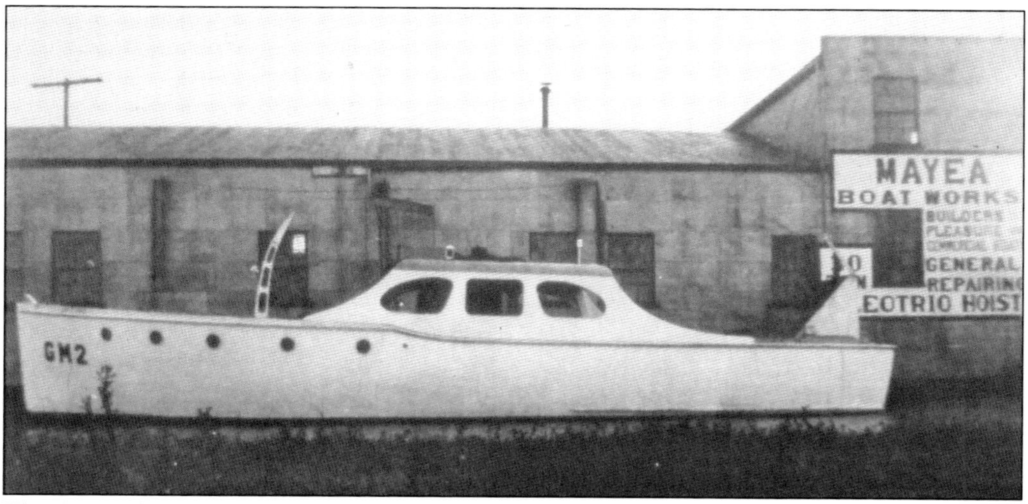

The GM2, shown in this c. 1949 photograph at the Mayea Boat Works in Fair Haven, was a collaboration of the Mayeas and the Gray Motor Company (originally Gray Marine Motor Company), an important marine engine builder. This boat was one of three experimental military craft built in a joint venture of Gray Motor, General Motors, and the Mayeas.

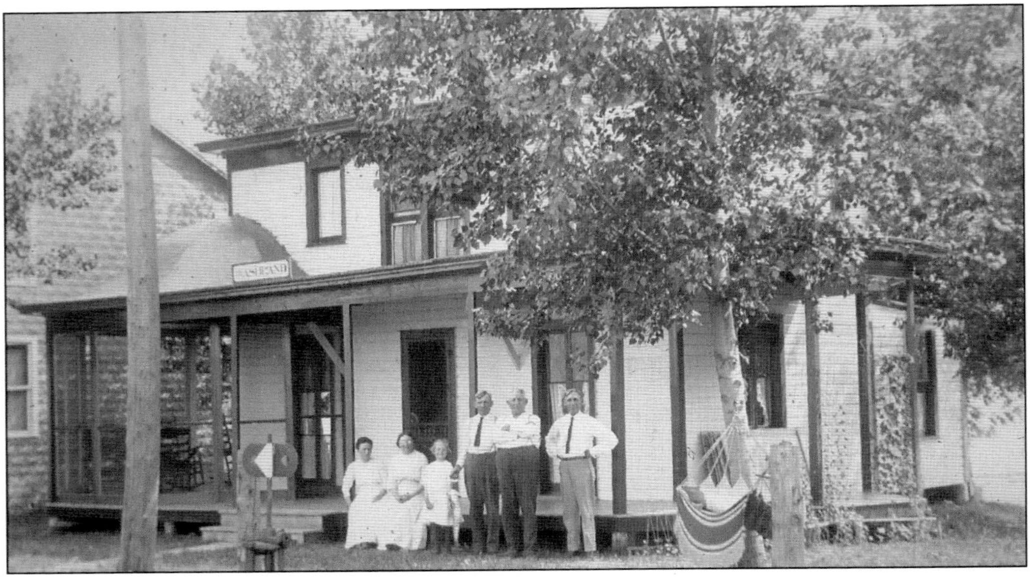

In the 1920s, summer homes and weekend cottages began to spring up along the shores of Anchor Bay, increasing the seasonal population of Ira considerably. Many of these cottages were named in the manner that pleasure boats still are today. Schoolchildren tested their memory skills with each other by calling out the names of the cottages, in advance, on their long walk between Fair Haven and the Catholic school in Anchorville. The name of the cottage was often displayed on a wooden sign that was nailed to the front porch or hung from eaves on hooks (for easy winter storage). One of the last cottages to wear its name was located in Anchorville on Dixie Highway west of Meldrum Road. As pictured above, it was named "The Ashland." Its original owner hailed from Ashland, Kentucky. The cottage of the Meldrum family is shown below.

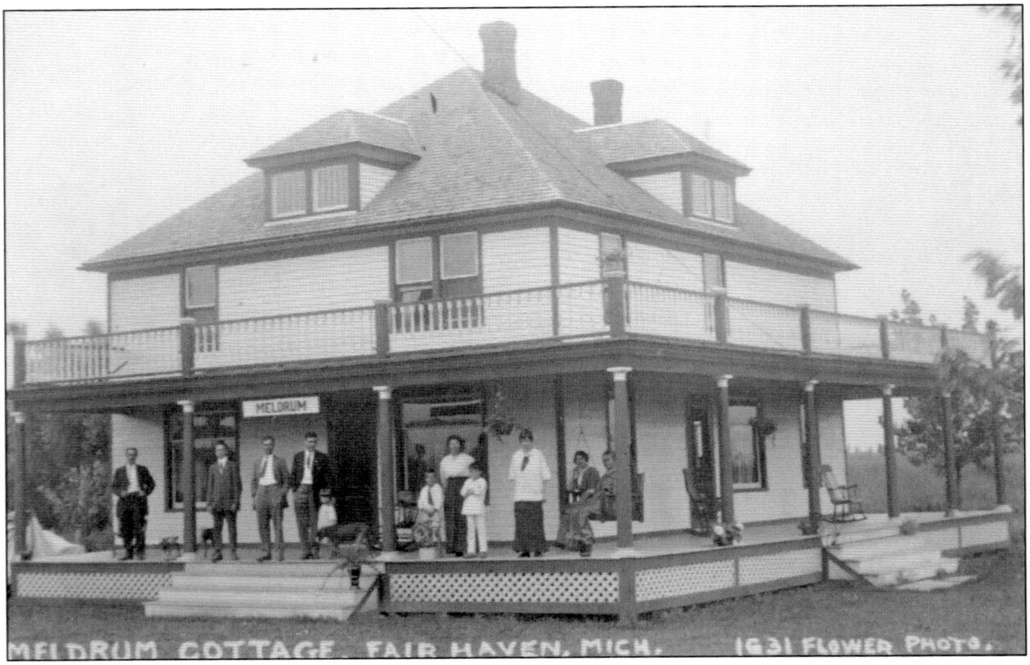

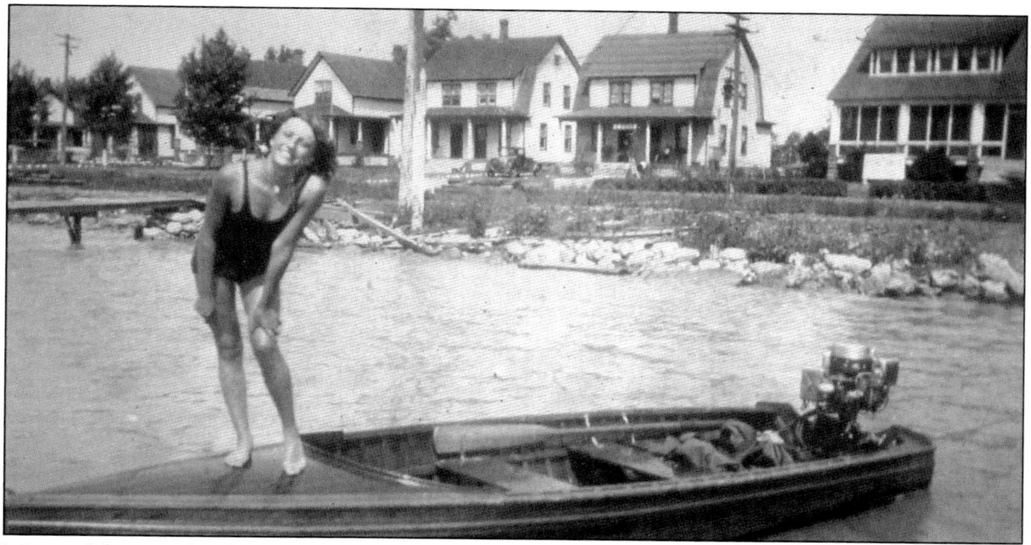

Many of the people who owned summer homes on Anchor Bay were wealthy, as illustrated by this lovely unidentified lady balanced on a speedy outboard boat. These people vacationed above the standard of living of most area residents, and resentments arose because of this. However, after the stock market crash of 1929, some formerly wealthy families who lost their city properties were forced to make their summer houses their permanent residences.

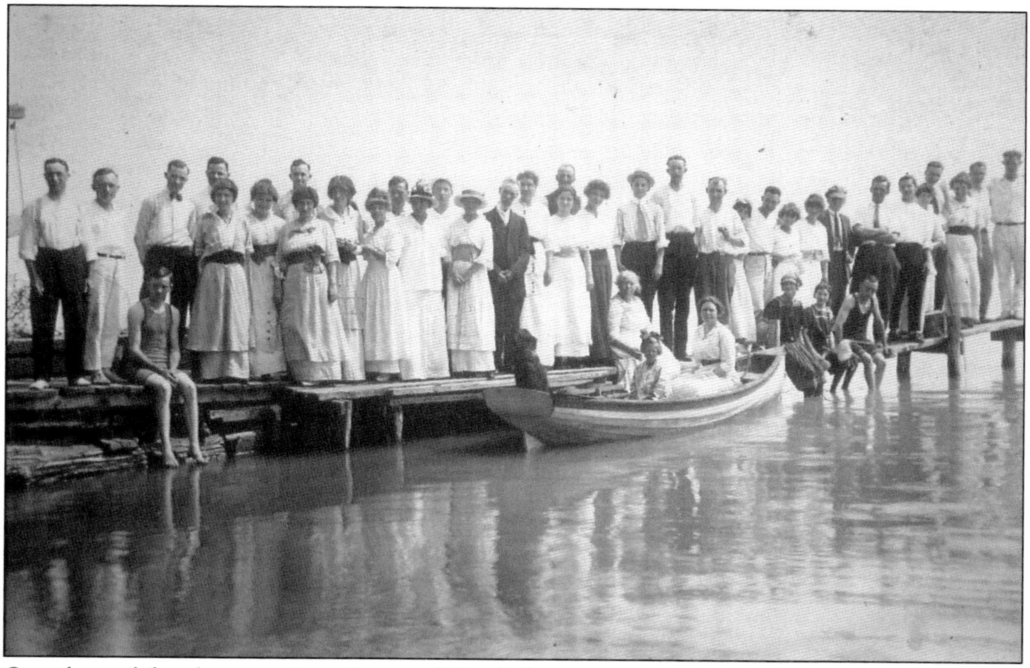

Overdressed for the occasion, these well-heeled vacationers pose for a group portrait before embarking on a day of fun and sun on Anchor Bay and its surrounding area. It can be assumed that no one's attire looked as fresh by day's end. Therefore, visitors often retreated to the bathhouses for bathing and a costume change before nighttime activities.

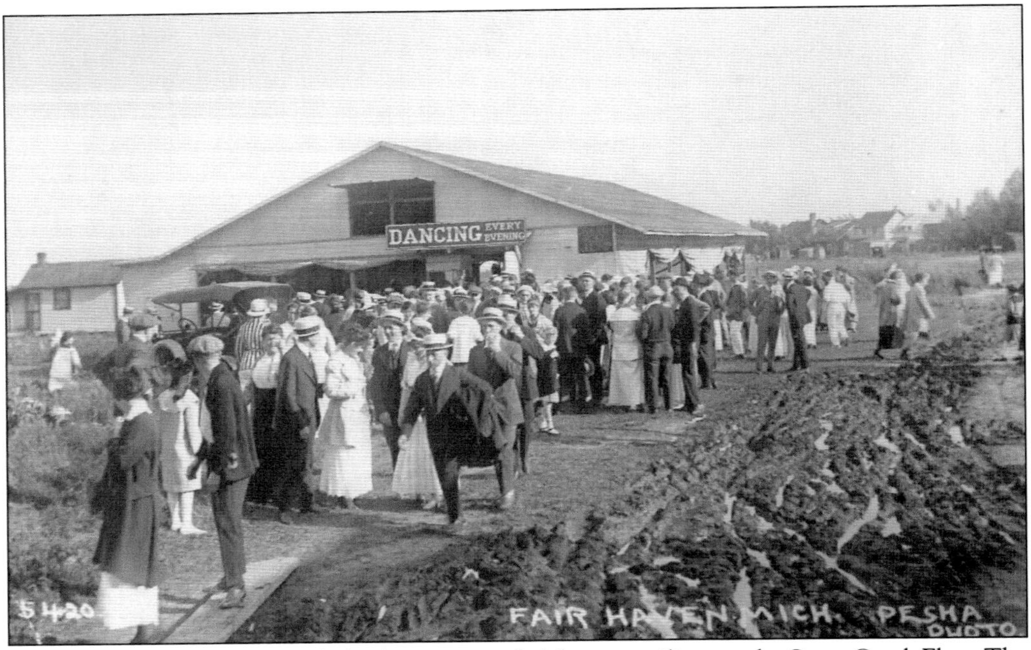

Around 1930, Edward Admaski built an open-sided dance pavilion on the Swan Creek Flats. The very popular dance hall lasted only a few seasons. The owner was forced to close the business because of difficulty with "tough" groups who came to cause trouble rather than to have fun.

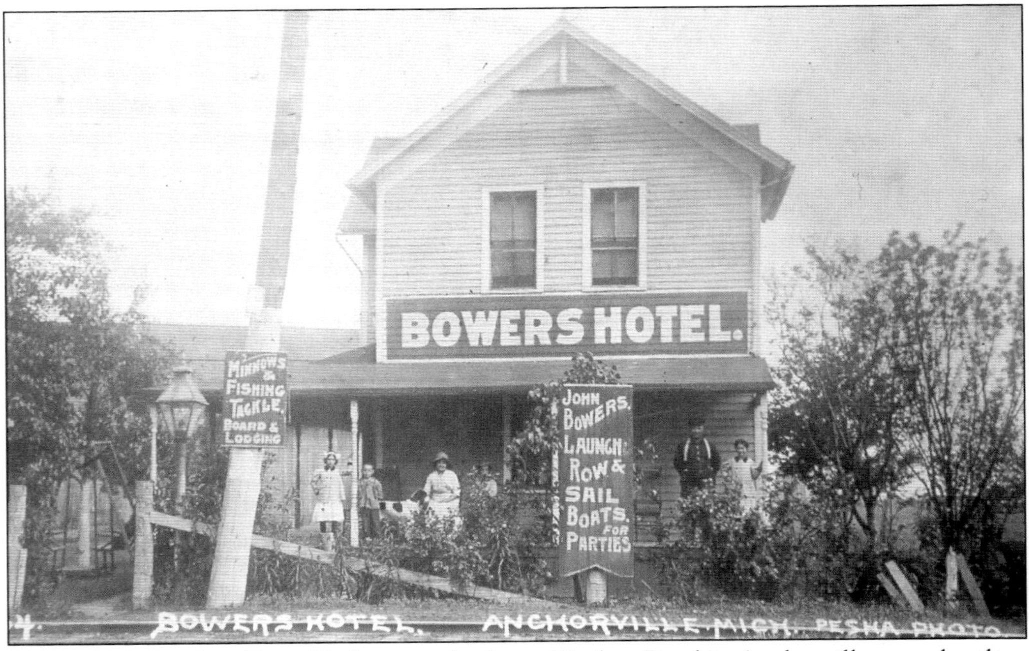

The Bowers Hotel on Dixie Highway at the foot of Bethuy Road in Anchorville was a bustling establishment in the early 1900s. The hotel and boat livery provided room and board to its guests, and meals were served in the dining room. Guests were also provided with boats and, sometimes, a lunch. They then went out to fish, swim, or just enjoy being out on the water.

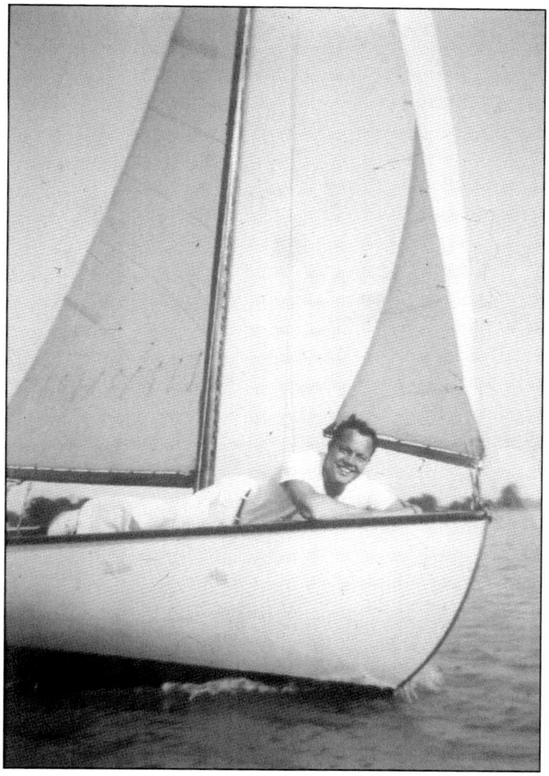

World War II Veteran Joe Stahovec Sr. (right) cruises on a sailboat on Lake St. Clair in 1931. He lived in Detroit and made the two-hour trip to Fair Haven to visit the relatives of his wife, Jermine, at the Schaffer Cottage, located across the street from Bud's Restaurant on M-29. Because of the transportation of the 1930s, it took some planning to make this trip, which was referred to as "going up north to Fair Haven." While at the summer cottage, the couple swam across Anchor Bay accompanied by a boat to provide help if needed. Pictured below in 1955, members of the Fair Haven Ski Club create a pyramid while boating around Anchor Bay. On top is Joyce Eder. The skier on the left is Jack McEwen, and Nick Badonoviac is at right. (Courtesy of Tom Jeannette.)

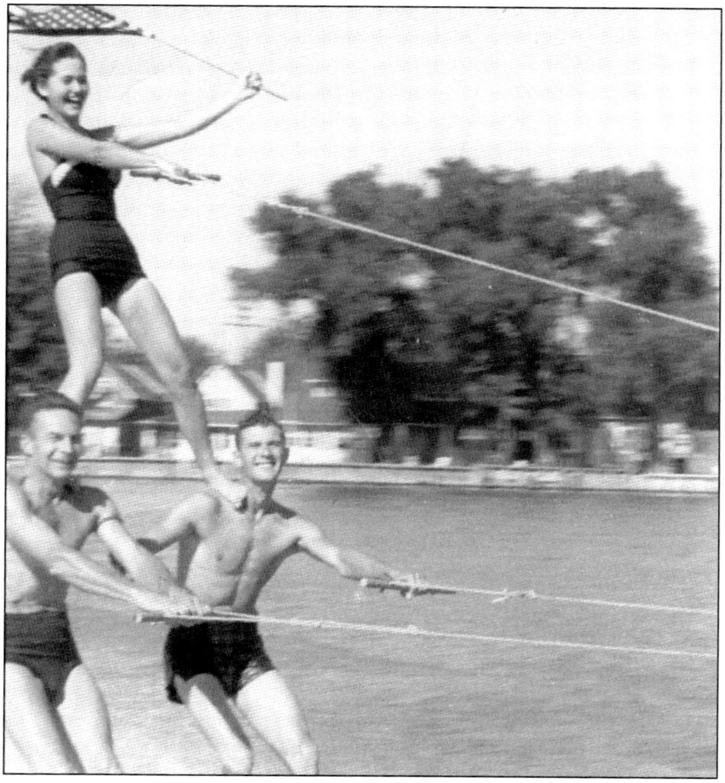

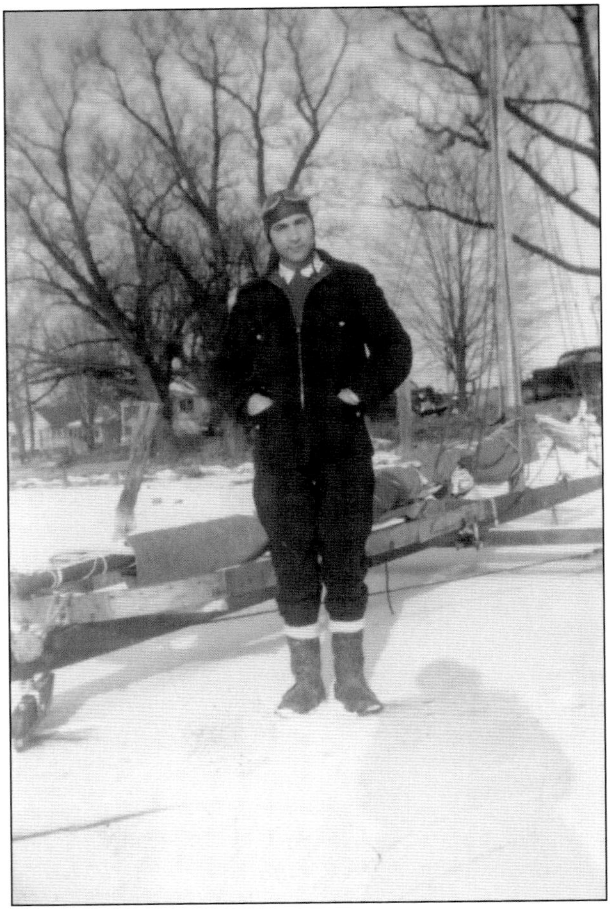

After the summer tourists left the shores of Anchor Bay, local residents made their own kind of fun during the winter when the lake froze. Iceboating was one of the popular pastimes. Pictured at left around 1937 is Anchorville resident Walt Torney, standing in front of a typical iceboat. Racing and joyriding were some of the activities. Depending on the wind velocity, impressive speeds could be achieved. Ice-skaters were known to hitch rides from the ice-boaters. Below, Joe (left) and Jermine Stahovec glide across the ice on Anchor Bay, having fun!

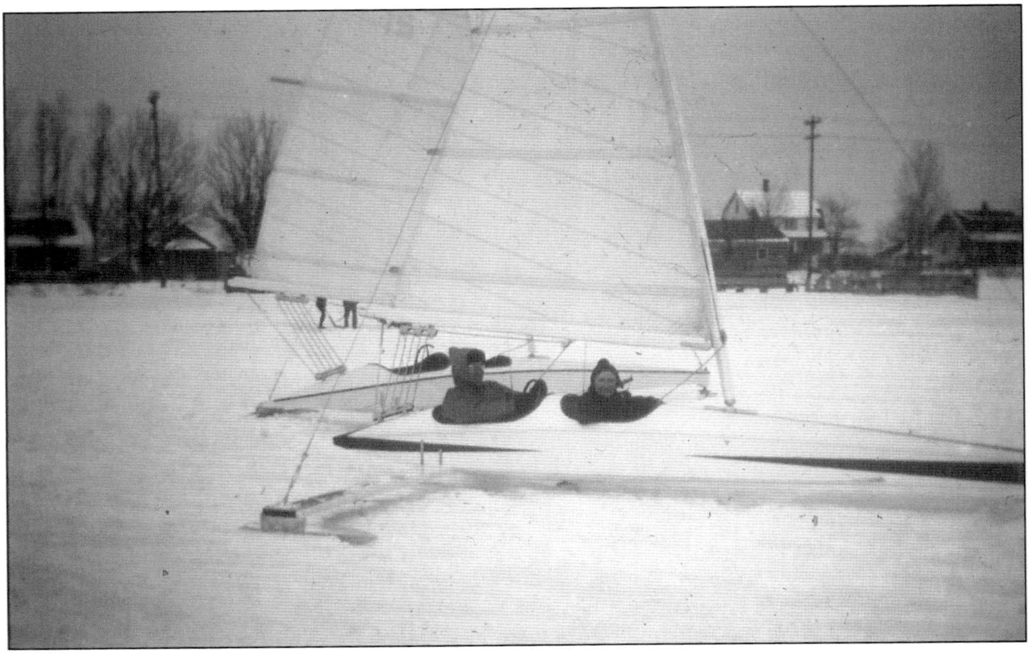

Eight

The Storm of 1955 and Other Great Storms

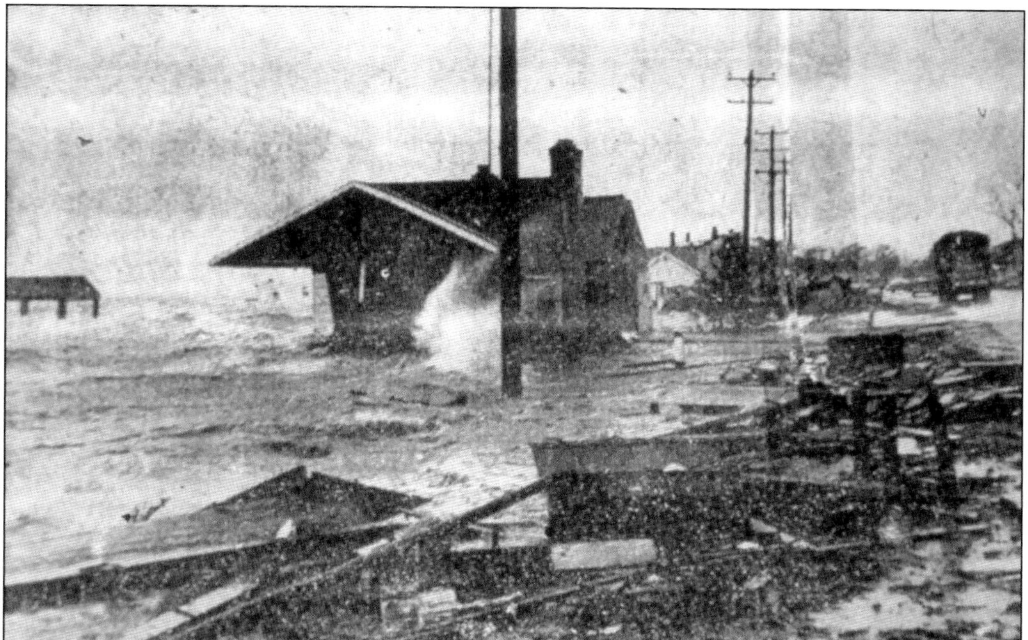

On March 24, 1955, one of the worst storms to ever hit the area occurred. The winds were so strong that the Dew Drop Inn literally dropped into Anchor Bay! The storm's greatest impact was felt along the shoreline, where the 80-mile-per-hour winds caused thousands of dollars of damage to houses, boats, boathouses, and docks. The wreckage littered the shore, and boats were blown miles away from their moorings.

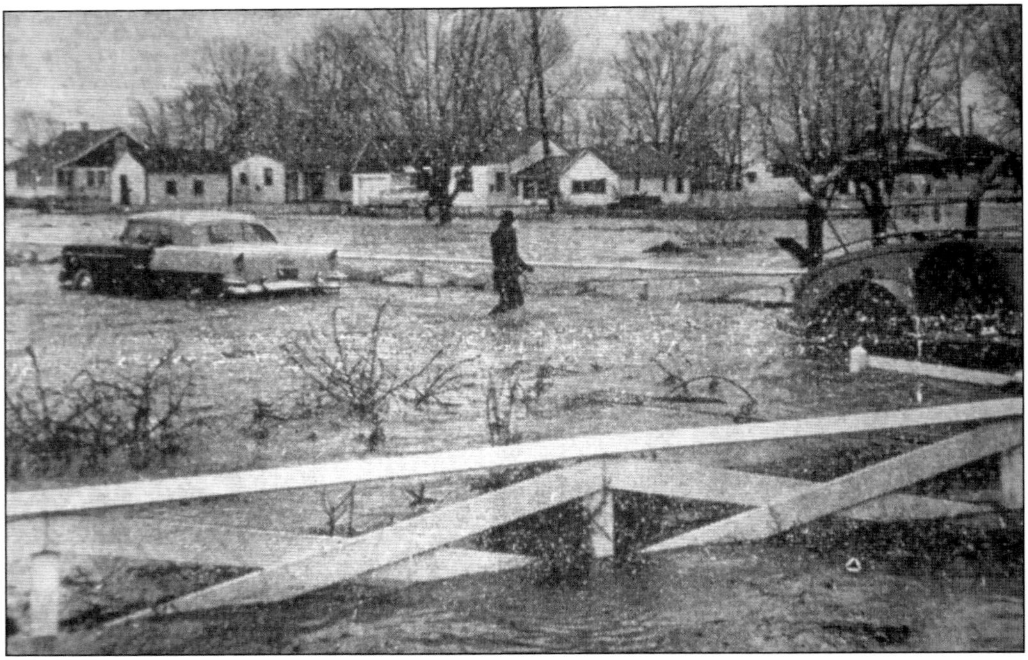

Waves of eight to ten feet pounded anything and everything in their path, destroying houses and sloshing around inside dwellings. Water ruined interiors and caused furniture and other objects to wash out of houses and onto the road and shoreline.

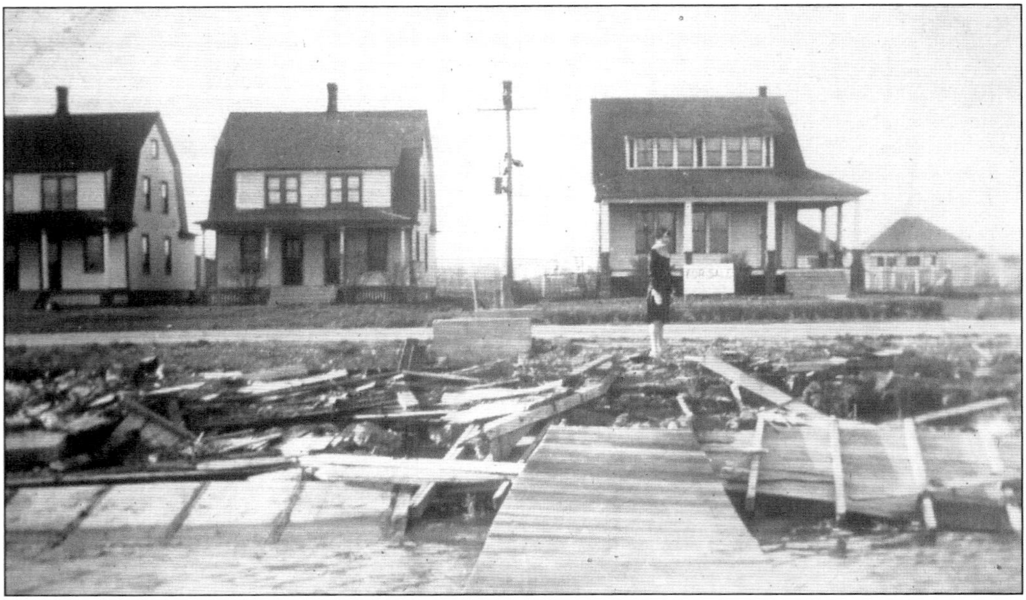

Due to quick and efficient rescue operations, there were no fatalities and few minor injuries. The Red Cross evacuated more than 300 Fair Haven residents, although many refused to leave their homes. Others were cut off from their homes by flooded roads. The Dyke Road was completely submerged for three miles. Evacuated families were housed in the Fair Haven Elementary School (school was called off the day after the storm), the fire hall, and private homes. School was called off the day after the storm. The St. Clair County branch of the American Red Cross set up an emergency canteen in the Fair Haven School.

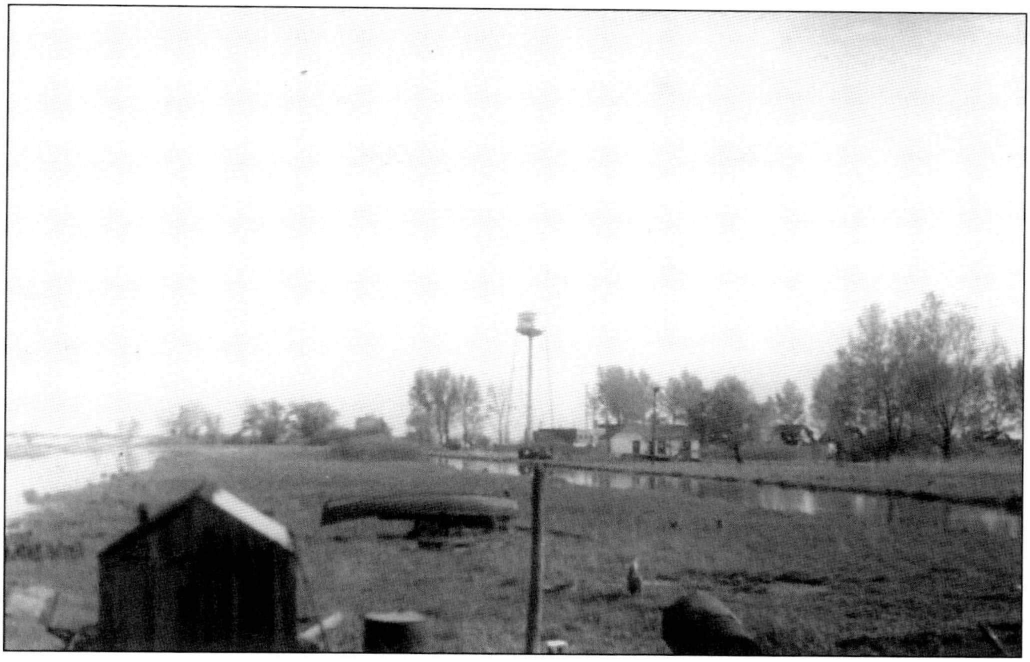

Dozens of repairmen, firemen, and volunteers worked long hours to alleviate the disaster. People came to help from New Baltimore, New Haven, Algonac, and other surrounding communities. A good example of the quickly changing weather in Michigan occurred, as volunteers and rescue workers were hampered by a snowstorm that increased to blizzard proportions as darkness fell. Many evacuees were rowed to safety in a rescue boat recently purchased by the Ira Township Volunteer Fire Department. That was a very timely purchase!

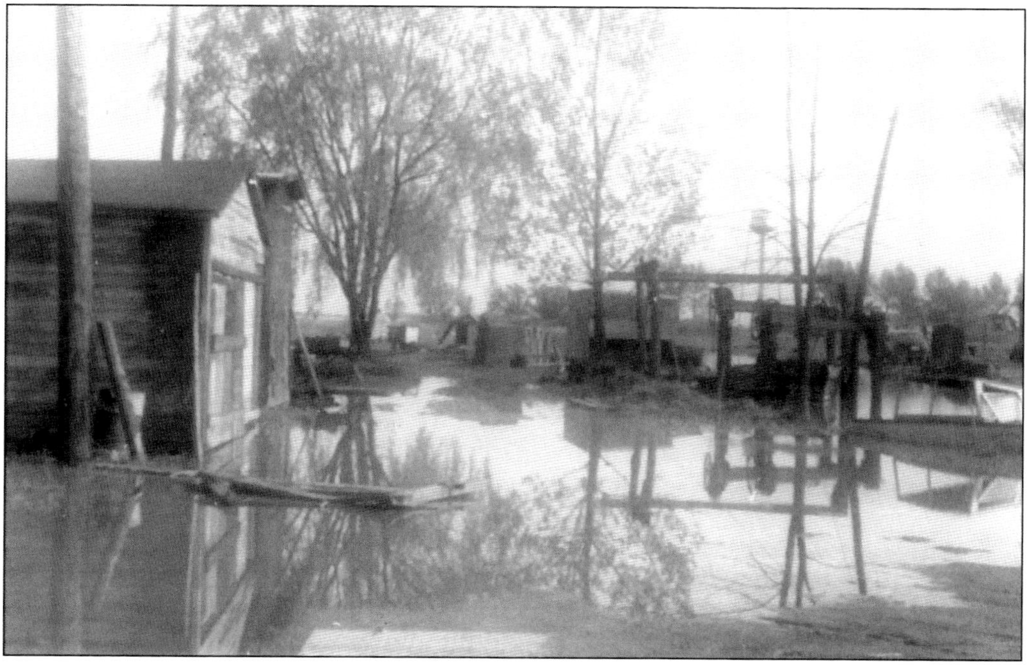

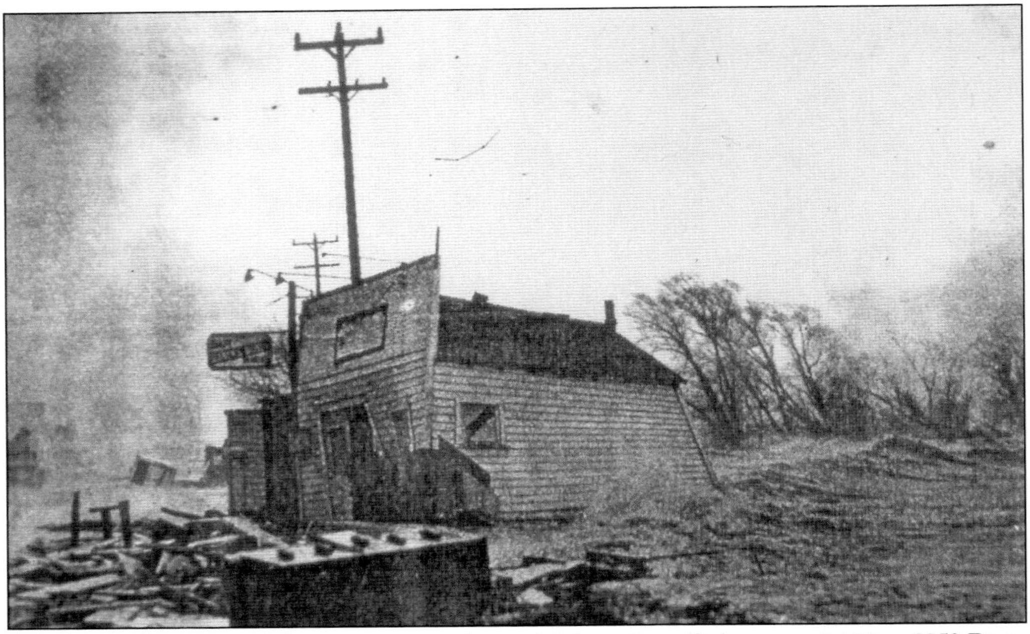

The Dew Drop Inn was a business operated out of Albert Carroll's house on M-29 at 8253 Dixie Highway. The inn was in the southeast corner of Carroll's brick house, and that section was torn off during the storm. Most of the remaining interior of the building was destroyed as well. Next door to the inn was Baker's Boat Livery, which was totally obliterated.

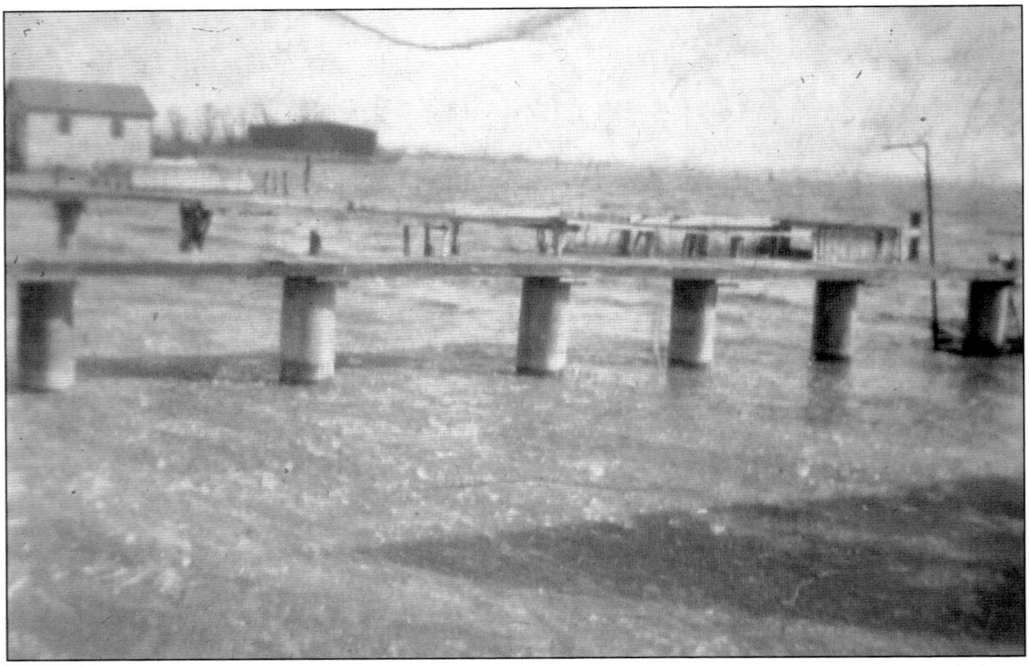

Anchorville had some docks and seawalls destroyed, but the most serious damage occurred along the shoreline from Fair Haven to Perch Point, as Anchorville from Bethuy Road to Meldrum Road is on higher ground than Fair Haven. All along the Ira Township shoreline on M-29, cars were stranded and abandoned, with water up to the fenders. Many cars were stuck in the ditch, as drivers had attempted to escape to higher ground when the flood began.

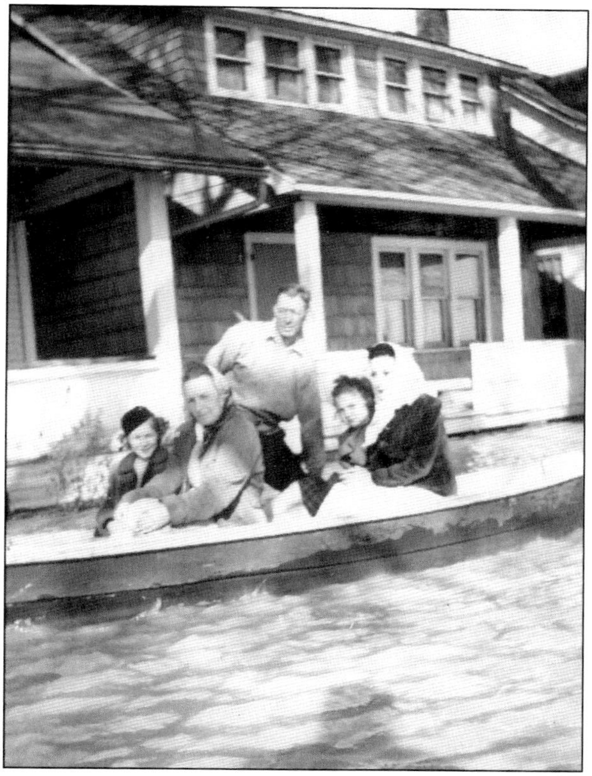

High winds preceded the storm starting at 8:00 a.m. on the fateful day of Tuesday, March 24, 1955. By 10:00 a.m., the rains had begun. At 11:00, a siren was heard as the fire department was called out. At noon, students in all the local schools were sent home. Soon, the flooding caused evacuations to begin and continue throughout the day. The fire department worked without breaks, only to be called at 2:00 a.m. Wednesday morning to Marine City to fight the Colonial Hotel fire. (Both, courtesy of Tom Jeannette.)

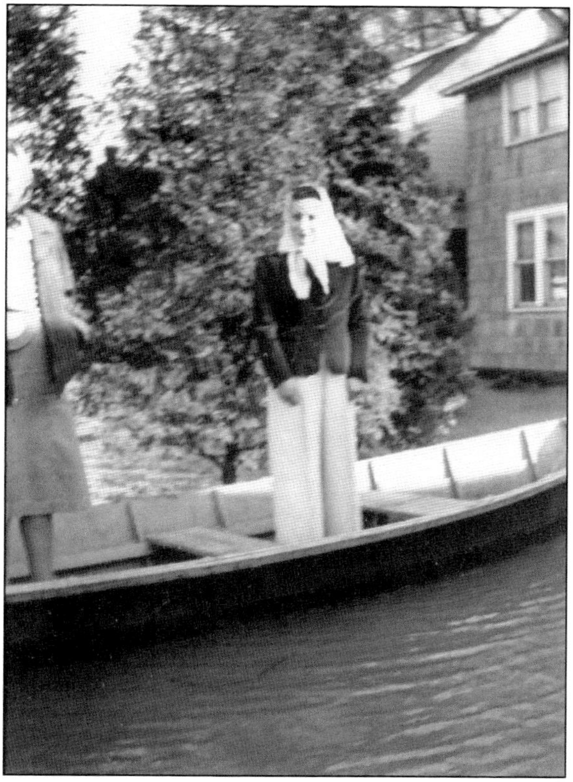

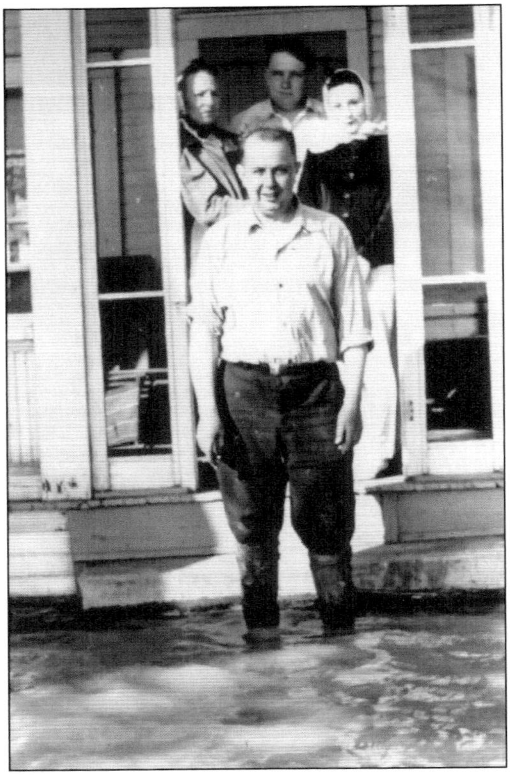

Although the 1955 storm was undoubtedly one of the worst to plague the township, other notable tempests have occurred over the years. A storm in 1913 destroyed 19 ships on the Great Lakes. In 1929, another violent storm destroyed dozens of trees, docks, and businesses from Ira's shoreline to neighboring New Baltimore. These photographs show the aftermath of the 1943 storm, which caused flooding on Long Island Court. Although life on the water is usually great, great storms are one of the pitfalls waterfront communities must endure. (Both, courtesy of Tom Jeannette.)

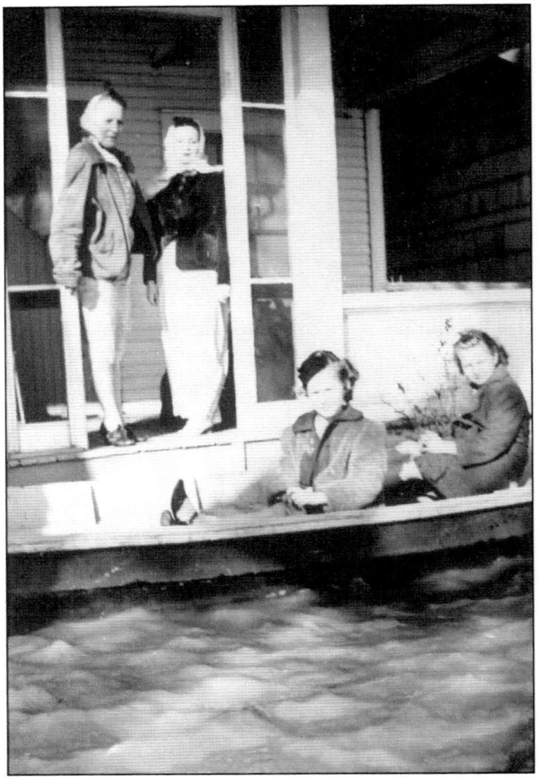

Nine

The Forming of Ira Township Little League

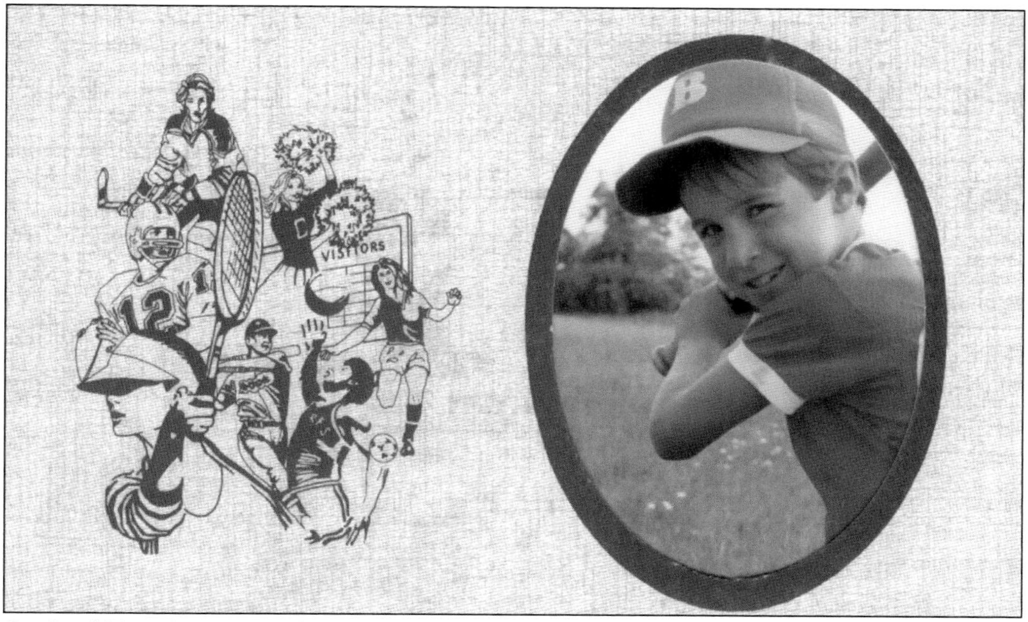

On April 23, 1959, Ira Township residents George Hack and Leo Vernier Jr. applied to Williamsport, Pennsylvania, to establish a Little League program. The boundaries were set, the teams, sponsors, and managers were named, and, for the first time, the youngsters of Ira Township were given the opportunity to play Little League baseball. The first games were played at the athletic field of the Fair Haven Elementary School on Broadbridge Road. Pictured here is Andre "G.J." Furtah. (Courtesy of Greg Furtah.)

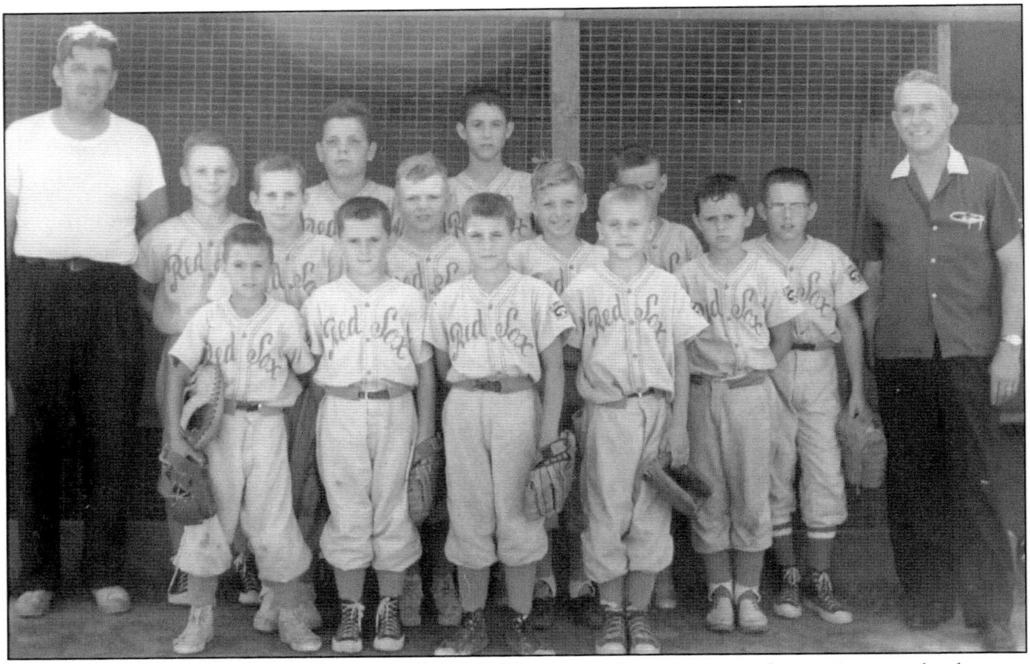

Before the Fair Haven Elementary School field was ready, tryouts and practices took place at Stocker's Field in Anchorville. Some 65 boys from the Fair Haven and Anchorville areas were selected to play on the new teams (Red Sox, Tigers, Braves, and Cubs). The team photograph above shows the 1960 Red Sox. The teams were sponsored by the Ira Township Volunteer Fire Department, Fair Haven–Anchorville Lions Club, the Ira Amvets, and the Fraternal Order of Eagles. The managers were Leonard Bourlier, Mike Green, Nick Bodovinac and George Ignasiak. The coaches were Robert Siefert, Clayton Graebert, Joe Orczykowski, Marv Kettel, Barney Erdman, Joe Elliot, Fred Furtah, and Robert Jarchow. After pregame ceremonies on Sunday, June 14, 1959, Ira Little League launched its summer schedule with a doubleheader. Greg Furtah (below) poses during the ceremonies. That opening day started the long, successful program that continues today. (Both, courtesy of Greg Furtah.)

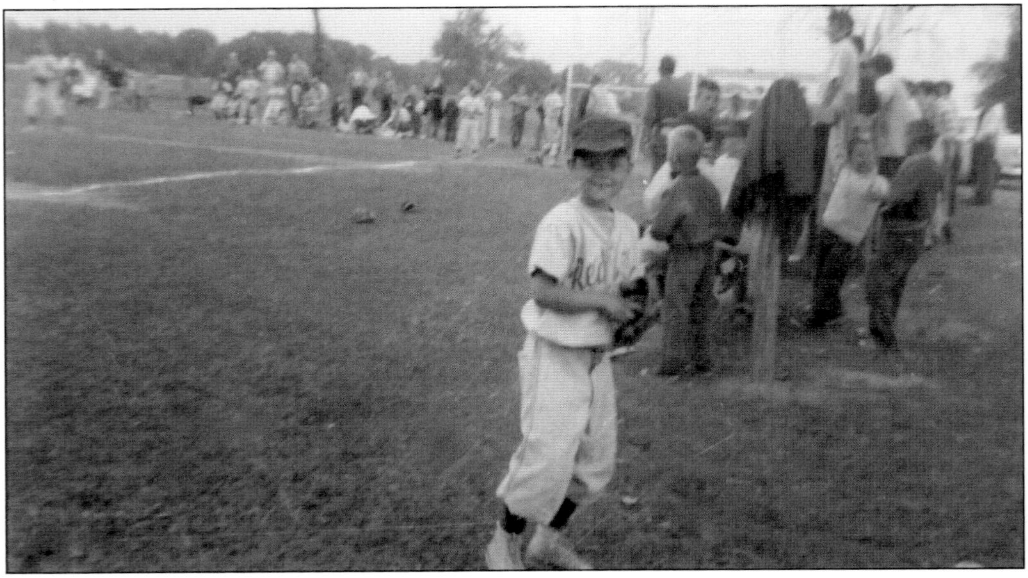

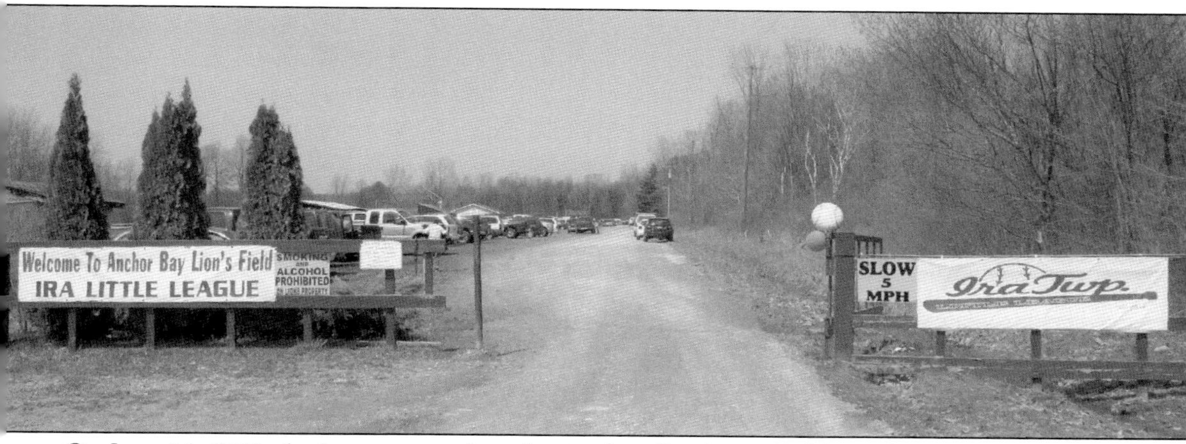

On June 16, 1963, the league moved to the Anchor Bay Lions Field on Short Cut Road in Anchorville. The Lions Club officially dedicated its community recreation center for a Little League baseball diamond. Volunteers donated their time, grooming a new home for the youngsters. George Hack, the league's president, and player agent Leo Vernier Jr. held meetings at the Vernier Hotel in Fair Haven. Parents, umpires, and sponsors held a car wash, with the proceeds going toward new uniforms for the players. The *Anchor Bay Beacon* reported on league events and kept the public aware of registration dates and meeting times. Carol and Nancy Gustin wrote articles for the *Beacon* detailing game results, schedules, and team standings. At the end of each season, the officers organized a banquet and presented trophies to the championship teams.

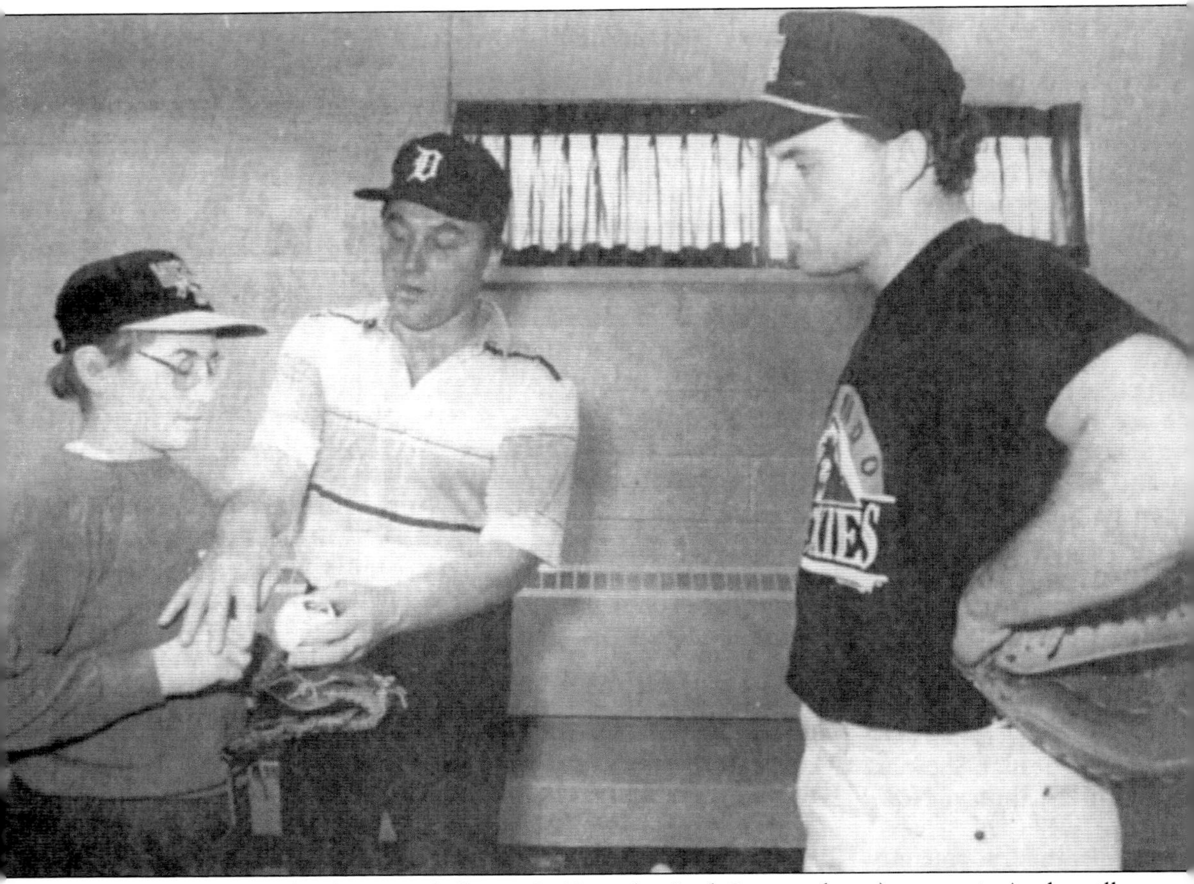

Brothers Gary and Mike Ignasiak (former Ira Township Little League players) grew up in Anchorville and went on to play Major League Baseball. Mike Ignasiak pitched for the Milwaukee Brewers for four seasons, ending his career in 1995. Gary Ignasiak stayed closer to home, pitching part of the 1973 season with the Detroit Tigers. They are believed to be the only former Ira Little League players to make it to the big leagues. In 1940, their father, George Ignasiak, pitched a no-hitter at New Baltimore High School. He also hit a home run in that game. The Ignasiak brothers donated their time to meet with 40 youngsters at the first Ira Township Little League Baseball Clinic held at Fair Haven Elementary School. Their efforts helped raise money to buy a pitching machine. Also, Gary and Mike gave a few pointers about pitching, batting, and fielding. John Gerds of Fair Haven said he "learned to practice a lot and concentrate," and "oh, don't wave to your mother when pitching!"

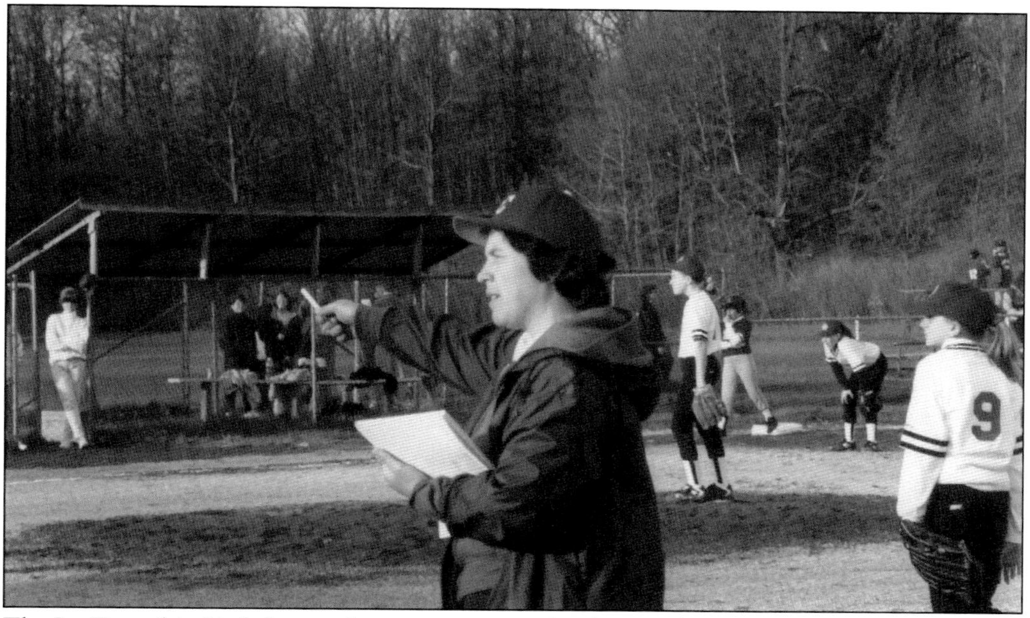

The Ira Township Little League has grown tremendously over the years. Along with expanding its geographic boundaries, it added new leagues, including girls' softball, t-ball, pitching machine, and boys' senior league. The expansions led to an increase in the number of teams, managers, and coaches, warranting a new concession stand, which serves up delicious hot dogs. There are now six baseball diamonds groomed to accommodate some 350 youngsters. A lot of credit goes to the many volunteers and organizations that gave their time and money to support the league.

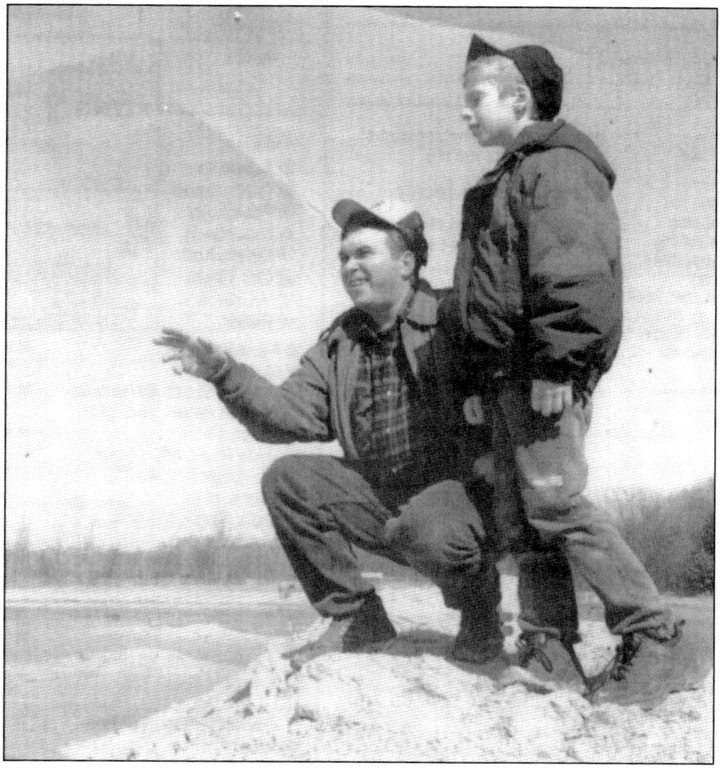

In 1995, local resident Ray Servick spearheaded the development of the Ira Challenged League. This gave mentally challenged children a chance to play baseball at Ira Little League. The Challenged League includes boys and girls ages 5–18 and loosely follows the rules of t-ball. It has been an excellent addition to the program, giving the children the opportunity to enjoy the great game of baseball and create lifelong memories.

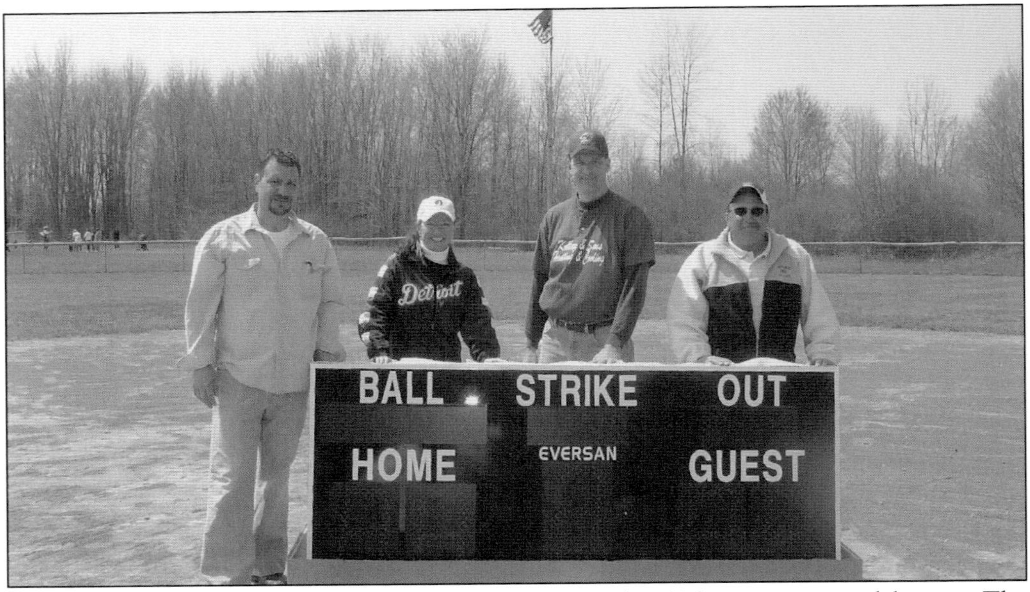

In 2009, Ira Township Little League opened its season with a 50th-anniversary celebration. The festivities started with team photographs, followed by a hit, run, and pitch competition. League president George Sommers invited all former players to come and be recognized, including the Ignasiak brothers, who gave a small speech about hard work and dedication. A new scoreboard donated by the township was also unveiled. Sommers declared all diamonds to be in "tip-top shape." To mark its 50th anniversary, a new logo was designed and placed on each dugout (below) with the words "character, courage and loyalty," setting an excellent example for the players to follow. The Little League Pledge, recited by hundreds of little leaguers eager to play ball, continues to echo throughout Ira Township on opening day: "I trust in God, I love my country and will respect its laws, I will play fair, and strive to win, but win or lose, I will always do my best." The concession stand still serves up hot dogs while the umpires bark out, "Play ball!"

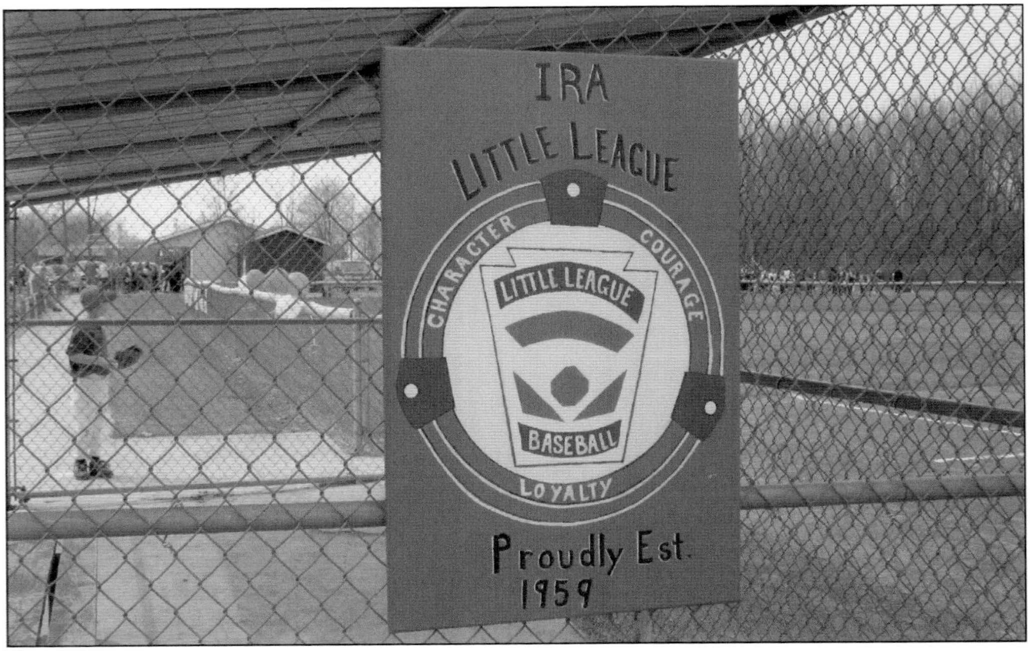

Ten

Township Parades and Celebrations

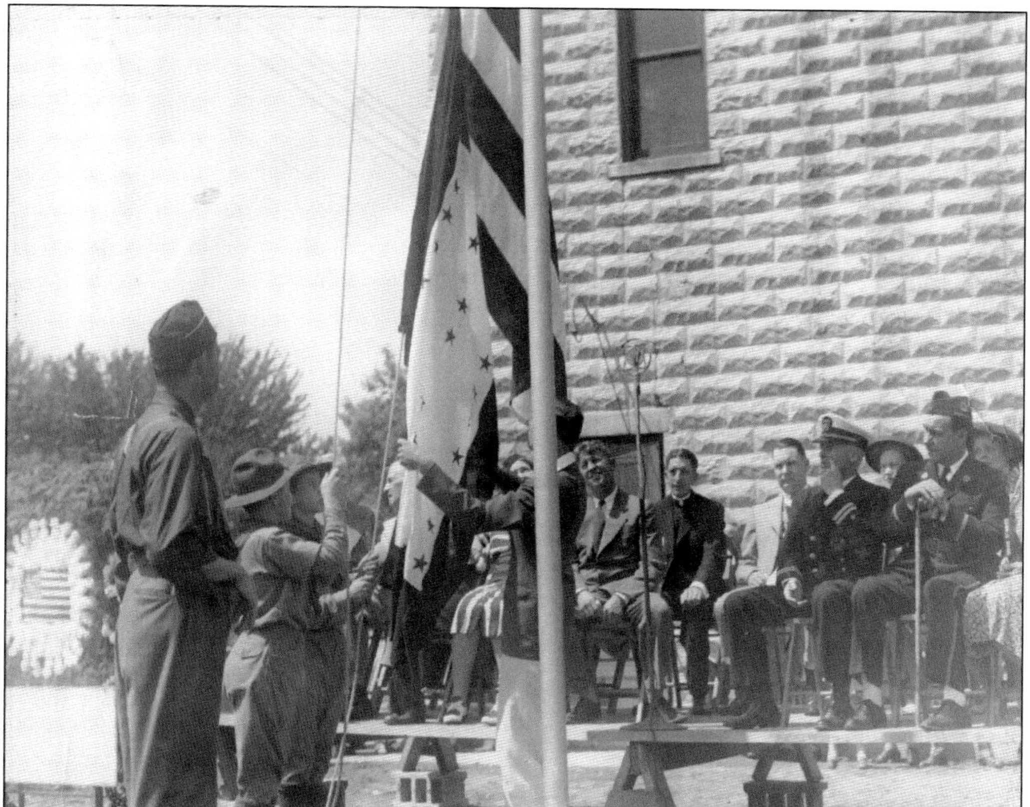

Boy Scouts Robert Comment (left) and Anthony Chryzanowsky raise a 26-star flag to the top of the new 60-foot pole donated by the Ira Township Women's Republican Club in honor of the men from Ira Township who served in the US military. The dedication ceremony was held at the Ira Township Community Hall on May 30, 1946. (Courtesy of Ira Township Library.)

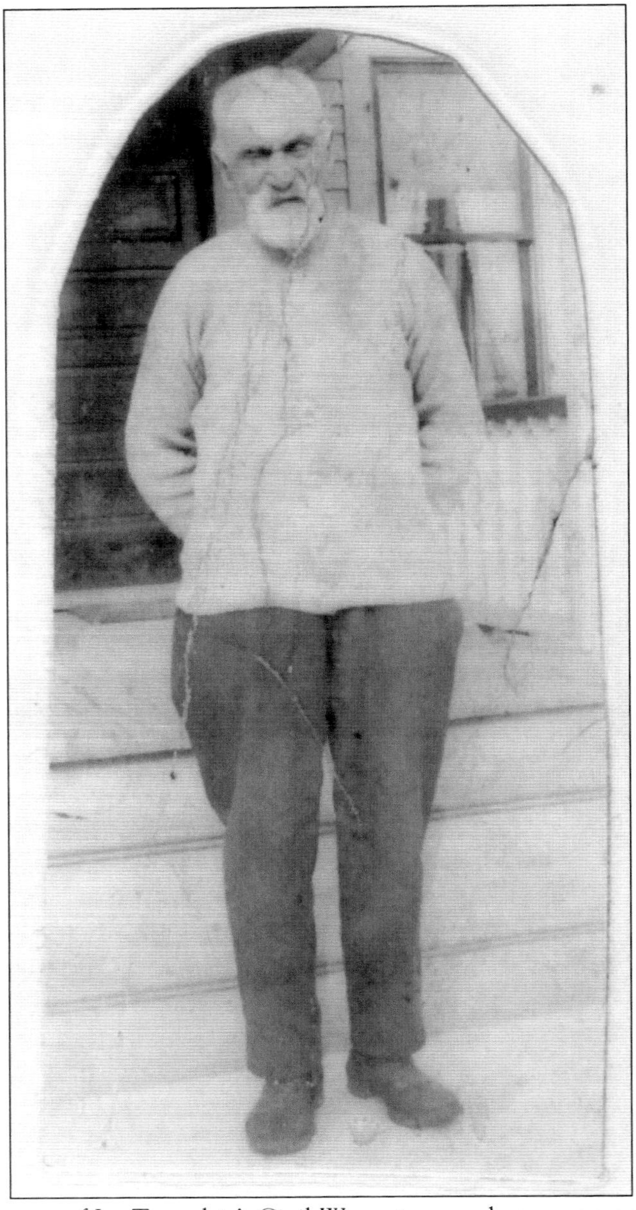

Peter Marcero was one of Ira Township's Civil War veterans whose name appears on the 22nd Michigan Regiment Company G roster, along with six others from Ira Township. Company G totaled 151 men. The 22nd Michigan was one of 10 companies that included soldiers from Ira Township. The whole regiment was made up of 997 soldiers. Company G was formed at Chattanooga, Tennessee, in December 1863, and in the spring of 1864, the regiment was engaged in building railroad bridges, storehouses, magazines, and a sawmill. The 22nd Michigan participated in battles at Kennesaw Mountain, Big Shanty, Golgotha Church, Culp's House, Nickajack Creek, Vining's Station, and Chattahoochee River. It made its way to provide support for the great battle that took place at Atlanta. Peter Marcero served from February 24, 1864, to June 26, 1865, returned home, and in 1867, married Elizabeth Rose. They had 12 children. Besides being a sailor, he farmed his land on Short Cut Road in Anchorville. His wife and four of his children are buried in St. Mary's Cemetery on Church Road in Anchorville.

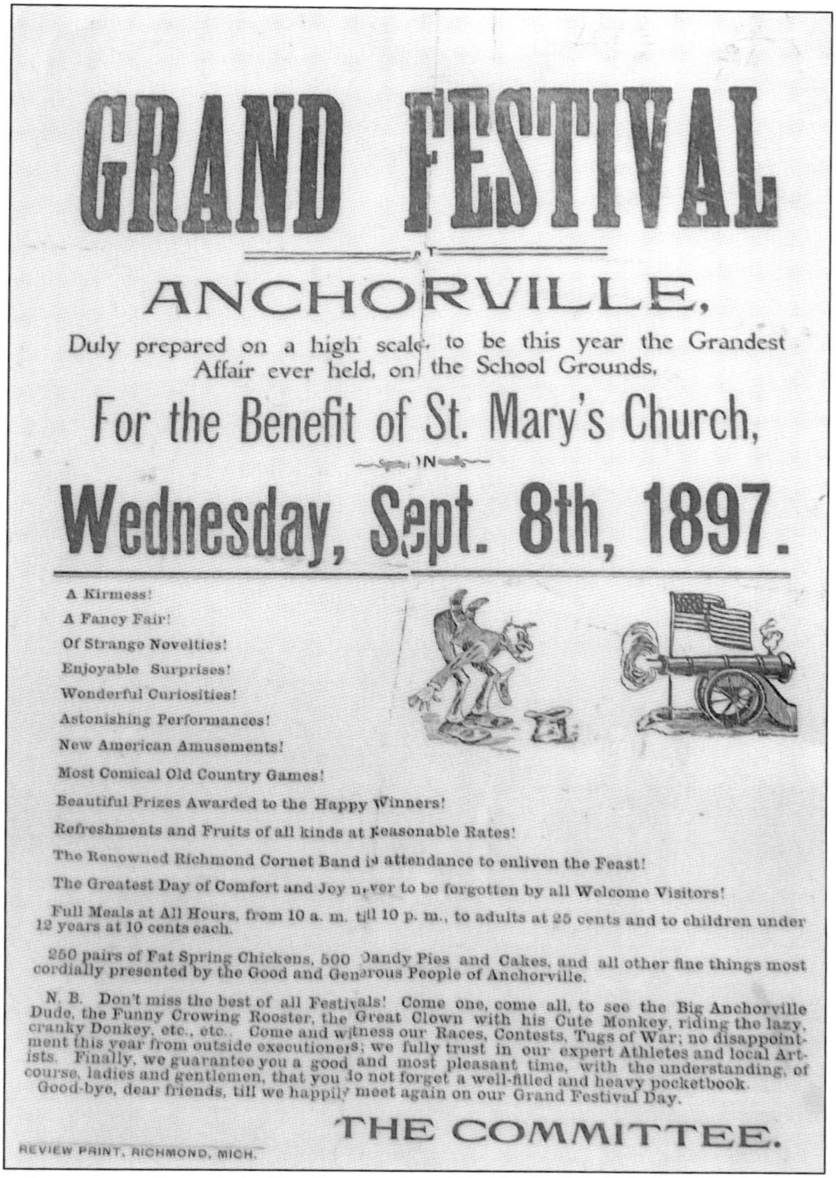

GRAND FESTIVAL

AT

ANCHORVILLE,

Duly prepared on a high scale, to be this year the Grandest Affair ever held, on the School Grounds,

For the Benefit of St. Mary's Church,

IN

Wednesday, Sept. 8th, 1897.

A Kirmess!
A Fancy Fair!
Of Strange Novelties!
Enjoyable Surprises!
Wonderful Curiosities!
Astonishing Performances!
New American Amusements!
Most Comical Old Country Games!
Beautiful Prizes Awarded to the Happy Winners!
Refreshments and Fruits of all kinds at Reasonable Rates!
The Renowned Richmond Cornet Band in attendance to enliven the Feast!
The Greatest Day of Comfort and Joy never to be forgotten by all Welcome Visitors!

Full Meals at All Hours, from 10 a. m. till 10 p. m., to adults at 25 cents and to children under 12 years at 10 cents each.

250 pairs of Fat Spring Chickens, 500 Dandy Pies and Cakes, and all other fine things most cordially presented by the Good and Generous People of Anchorville.

N. B. Don't miss the best of all Festivals! Come one, come all, to see the Big Anchorville Dude, the Funny Crowing Rooster, the Great Clown with his Cute Monkey, riding the lazy, cranky Donkey, etc., etc. Come and witness our Races, Contests, Tugs of War; no disappointment this year from outside executioners; we fully trust in our expert Athletes and local Artists. Finally, we guarantee you a good and most pleasant time, with the understanding, of course, ladies and gentlemen, that you do not forget a well-filled and heavy pocketbook.
Good-bye, dear friends, till we happily meet again on our Grand Festival Day.

THE COMMITTEE.

REVIEW PRINT, RICHMOND, MICH.

There have been many festivals held at Immaculate Conception Parish in Anchorville. This 1897 poster advertises just such an event, the "Grand Festival—Anchorville" to be held at St. Mary's Church (as Immaculate Conception was once called). The festival's poster eloquently states: "Duly prepared on a high scale to be this year the Grandest Affair ever held, on the School Grounds." The church festival brought the community together. There, they were treated to "Wonderful Curiosities! Astonishing Performances! Most Comical Old Country Games! Beautiful Prizes Awarded to the Happy Winners!" The menu alone would have attracted a crowd, with "250 pairs of Fat Spring Chickens, 500 Dandy Pies and Cakes," all to be "presented by the Good and generous People of Anchorville." Stretching beyond its borders, the poster invites the nearby city of New Baltimore. "Don't miss the best of all Festivals! Come one, come all!" Its committee declares, "The Greatest Day of Comfort and Joy never to be forgotten by all. Welcome Visitors!" To the present day, the Church Perch Festival in Anchorville has a long history. (Courtesy of Jerry LeRay.)

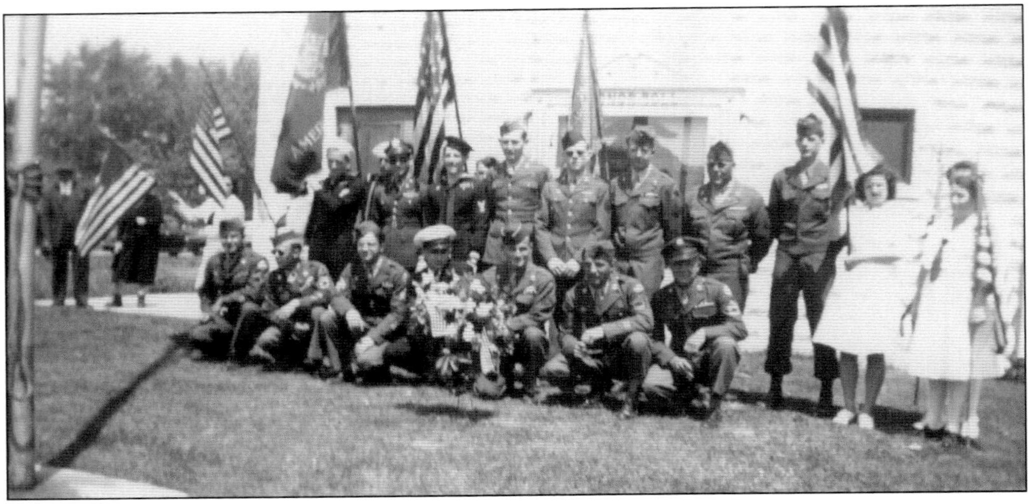

On Memorial Day in 1946, a group of World War II veterans, along with the women's auxiliary unit, gather at the Ira Township Community Hall in Fair Haven (above) to remember the men and women who died while serving in the armed forces. As part of the ceremony, veteran Oscar Stular played "Taps" in memory to the fallen. In 1953, the township converted an old schoolhouse on a 10-acre parcel and chartered an Amvets post to be located on Swan Creek Road in Fair Haven. One of the first commanders, Korean War veteran Bob Meldrum, held meetings at the Ira Community Hall until the building was complete. In the early 1970s, the post was disbanded and the building dismantled.

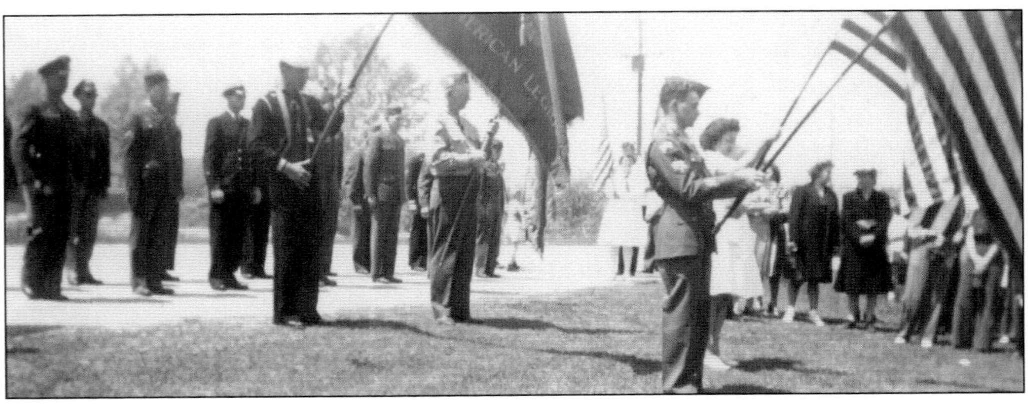

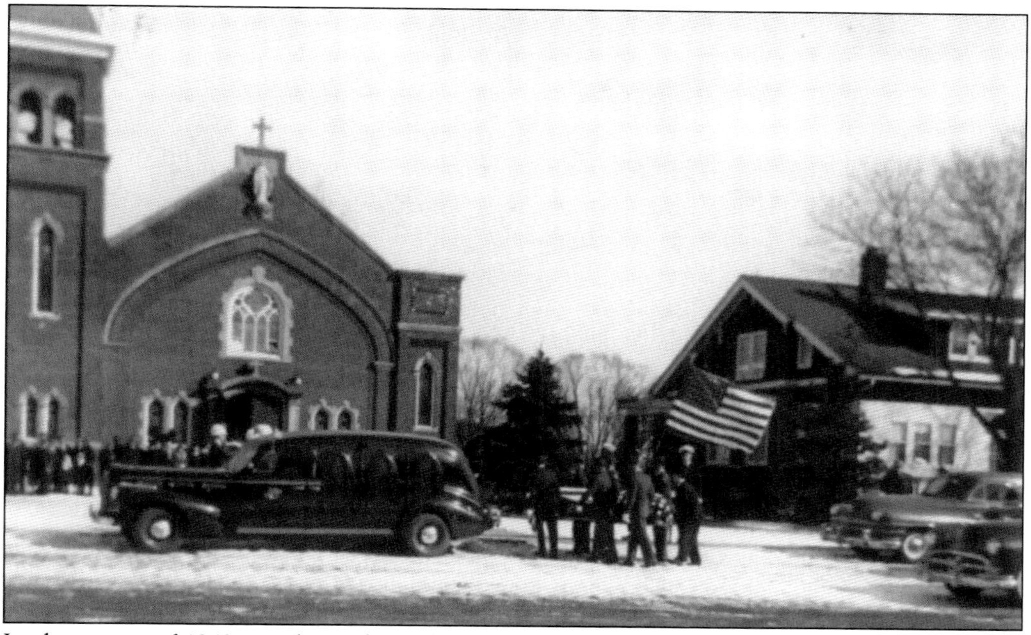

In the winter of 1949, a military funeral was conducted at Immaculate Conception Church in Anchorville. A flag-draped coffin was carried by members of Veterans of Foreign Wars and placed into a black hearse, while family, friends, and neighbors stood by (above). The church service was followed by a procession a quarter mile north on Church Road to Sacred Heart Cemetery. A burial, with full military honors, was given at the cemetery, including the playing of "Taps" and an 18-gun salute. Among the veterans pictured are Harry David and Oscar Stular.

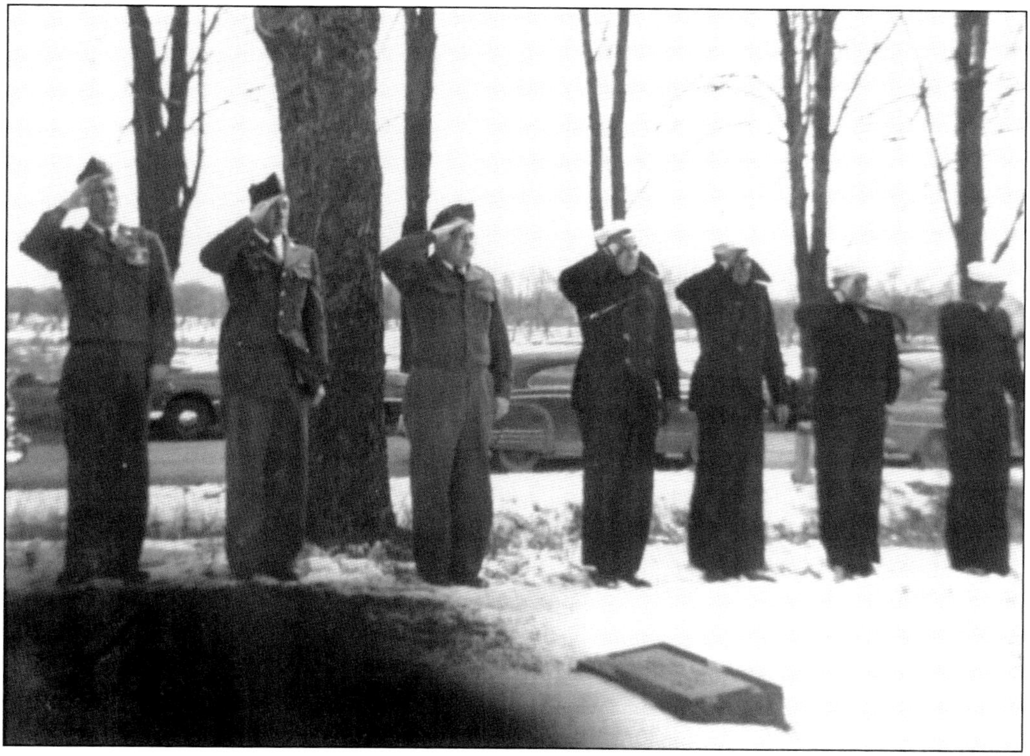

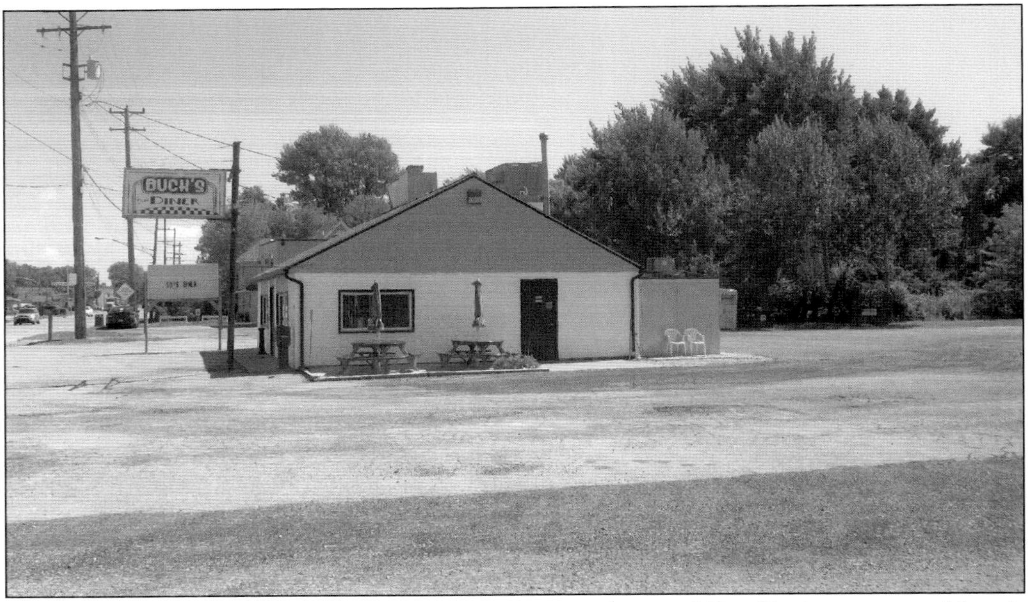

The Memorial Day parades of the 1960s were organized around Dee Dee's restaurant (above), now known as Buck's Diner, in Fair Haven. The Algonac Marching Band performed the music; other participants in the parade were Boy Scouts, Girl Scouts, and members of the Ira Township Veterans Club. The parade route started at Dee Dee's and went east down M-29 a short distance to the Ira Township Community Hall. There, the parade's organizers gave speeches commemorating the veterans who were killed in foreign wars. The community came together to acknowledge the sacrifice of our veterans and to share the solemn moment with fellow citizens. (Both, courtesy of Chuck Gregory.)

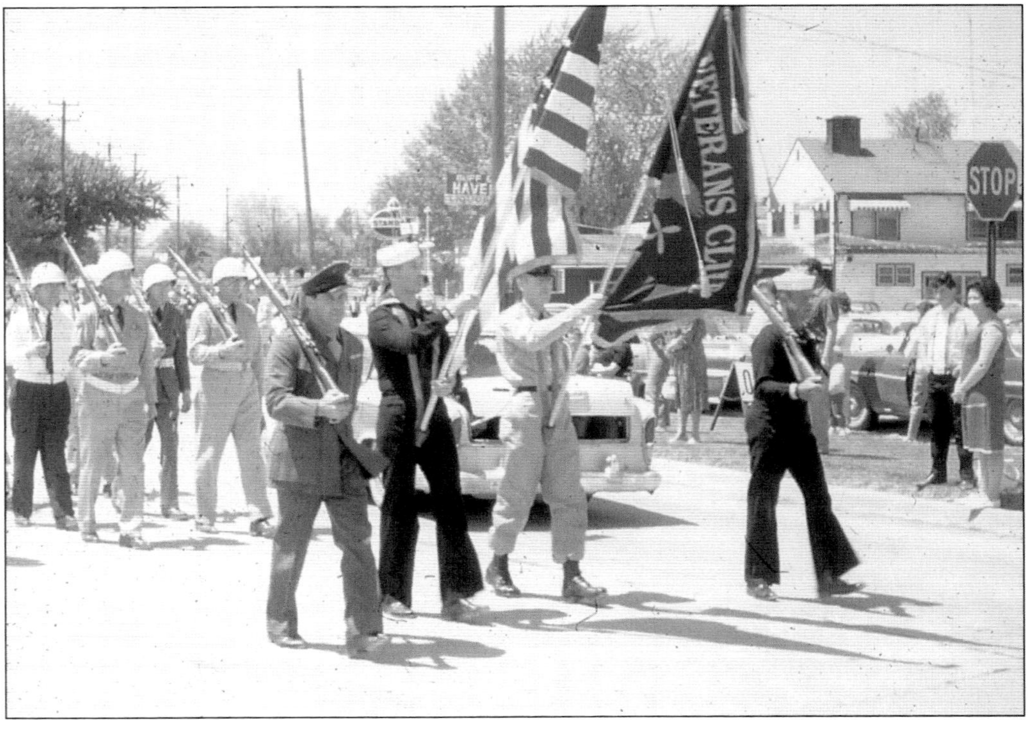

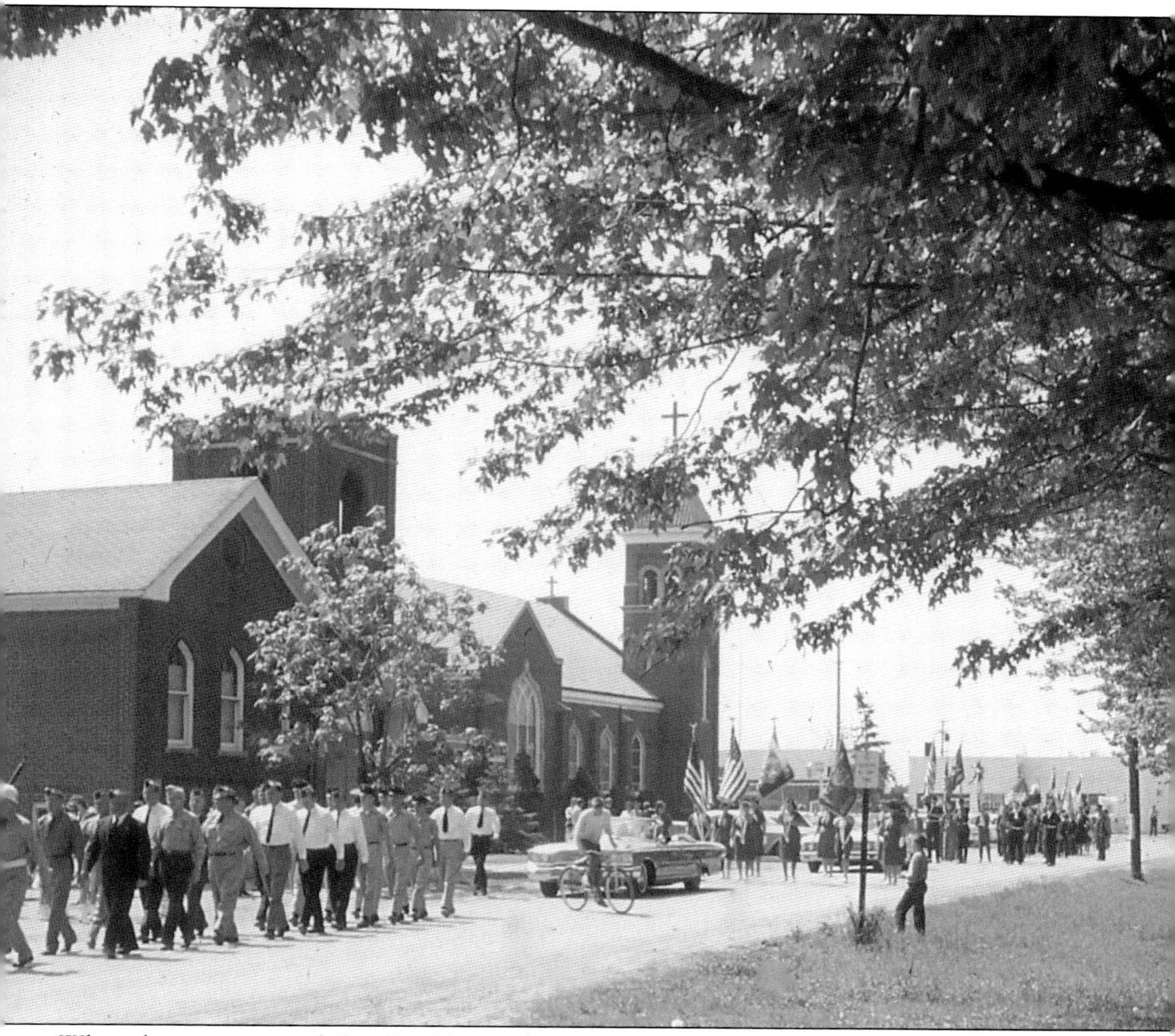

When the ceremony ended in Fair Haven, the parade packed up and drove two miles west and regrouped at Immaculate Conception Church in Anchorville. The parade then continued up Church Road to Sacred Heart Cemetery, about a quarter mile north of M-29. The procession gathered around the small hill where former pastor of Immaculate Conception, Father James Downey, is buried. Flags representing the Boy Scouts, Brownie troops, Veterans Club, and the United States are on display. Father Harry Paul said a prayer in honor of the fallen, and an 18-gun salute was delivered. Veteran Oscar Stular played "Taps." It was common for local children attending the ceremony to block their ears at the sound of the rifles and then run and pick up the fired cartridges. (Courtesy of Chuck Gregory.)

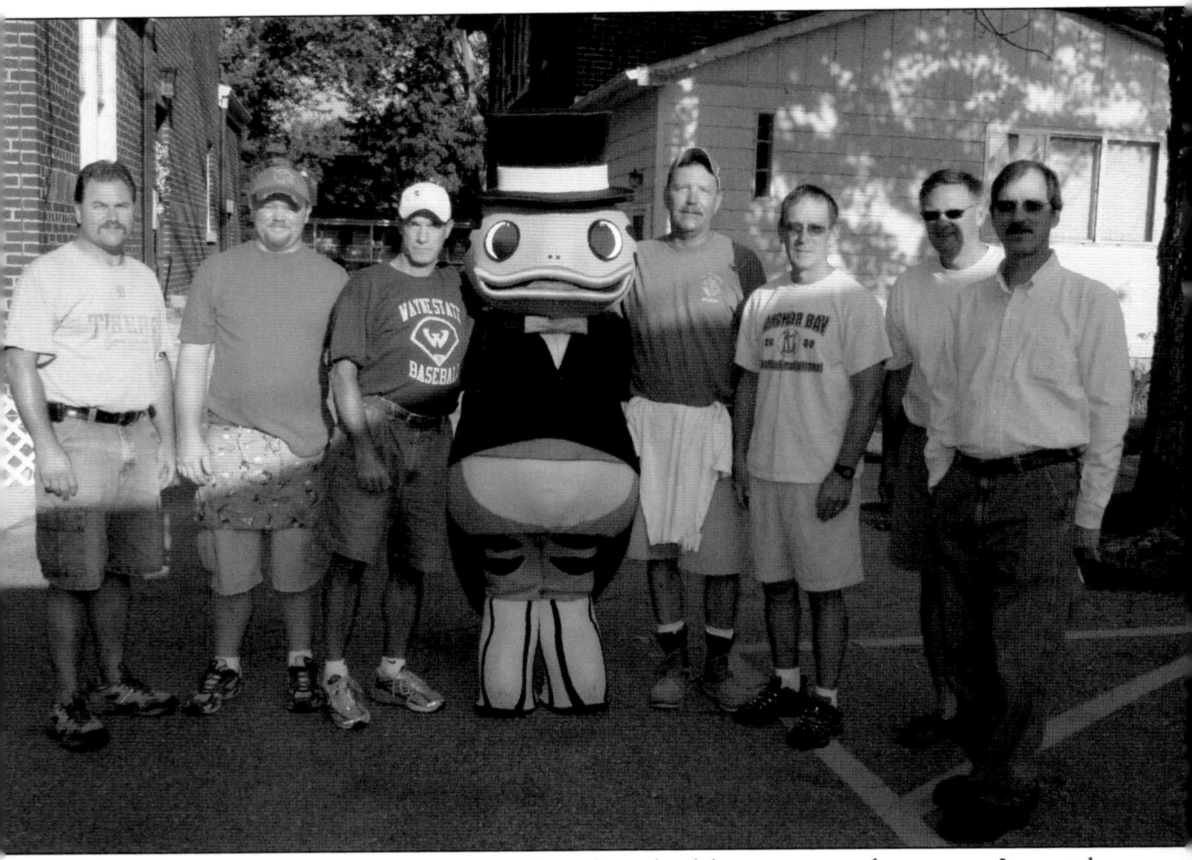

There have been many carnival-type festivals and celebrations over the years at Immaculate Conception Parish, but in 1972, when Father Harry Paul was pastor, a committee was established and a small group of volunteers put together the church festival that eventually became known as the Family Fun and Perch Festival. The organizers held a fishing contest for the applicants to see who could catch the biggest perch in Lake St. Clair. The winner received a prize and a year's bragging rights. In 2014, the parish celebrated its 42nd festival year. It has grown into a popular event in the Anchor Bay community that all anticipate. Here, the festival mascot, Mr. Fins, poses with members of the Knights of Columbus Au Lac Council.

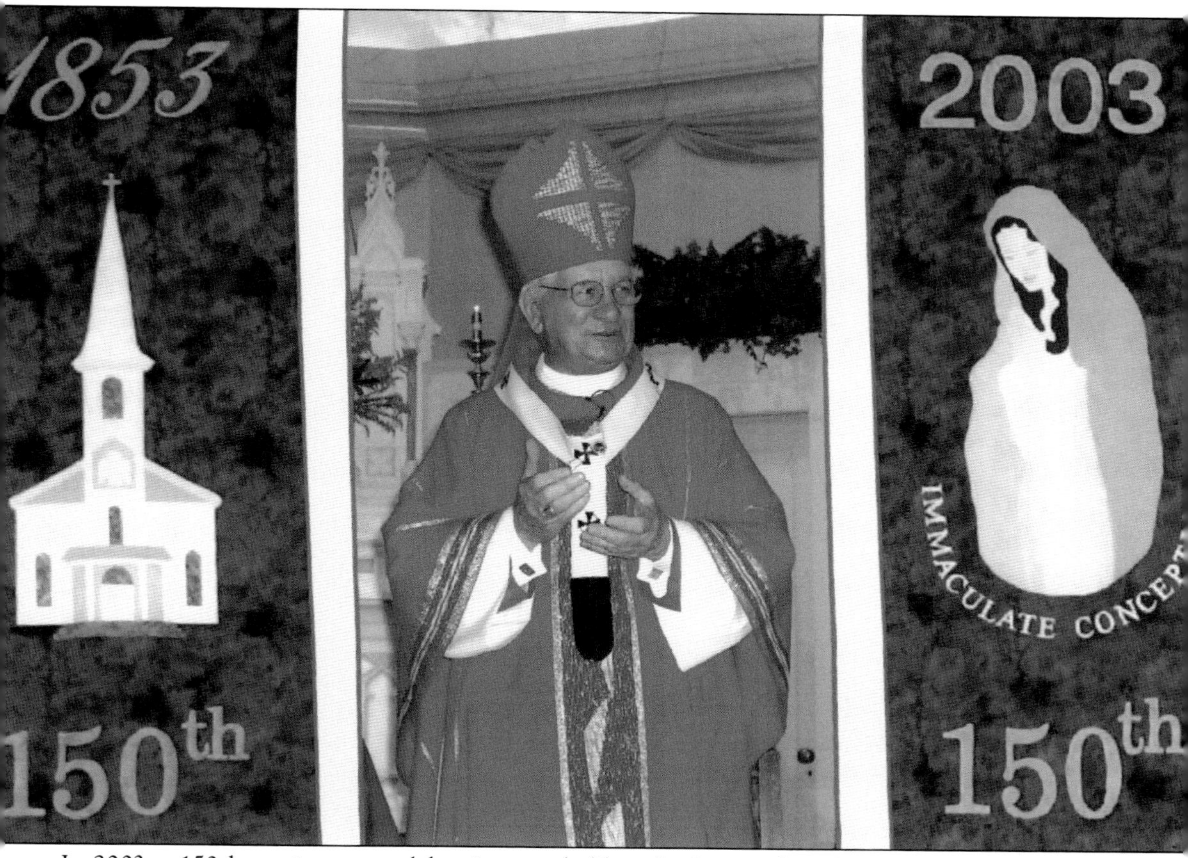

In 2003, a 150th-anniversary celebration was held at the Immaculate Conception Church in Anchorville. The church renewed its mission and celebrated with planned special events that included a complete and comprehensive history book containing photographs of all its former pastors. The book is still available at the parish office. A play was written that highlighted some of the church's history, and was performed in the sanctuary. In September, former cardinal Adam Maida, archbishop of Detroit, came to say mass to recognize the long history of the church. In his sermon, he acknowledged the strong roots of the parish, from the early pioneers to today's faithful. A new logo was created in celebration of the occasion witht these words: "150 years Grounded in Hope—Nurtured in Faith, the Journey Continues . . . 1853–2003."

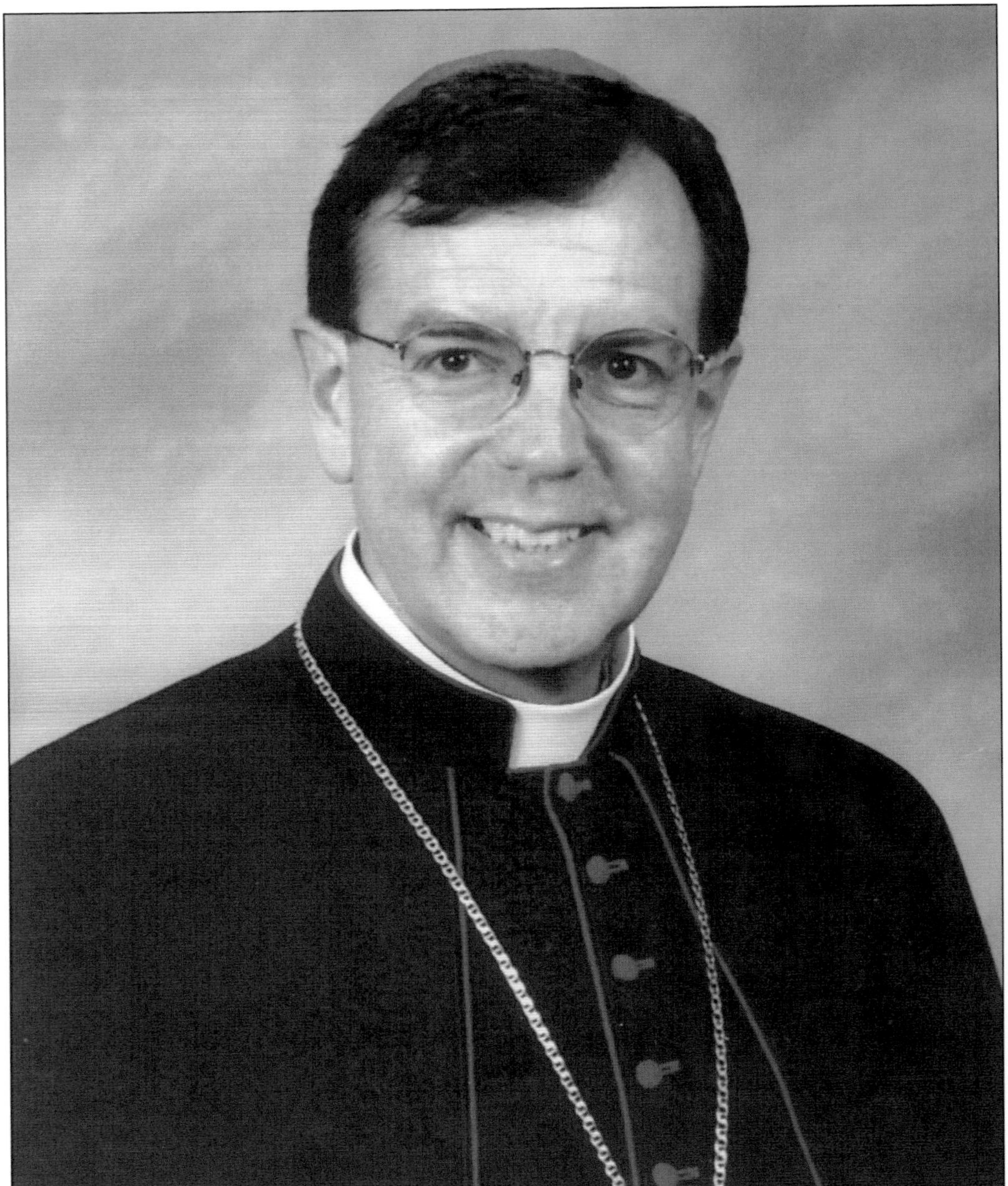

On January 5, 2009, the Most Reverend Allen Henry Vigneron, native son of Ira Township, was named by Pope Benedict XVI to succeed Cardinal Adam Joseph Maida as the next chief shepherd of Detroit. On January 28, 2009, he was installed as the fifth archbishop to serve the Detroit Archdiocese. The installation mass took place at the Cathedral of the Most Blessed Sacrament in Detroit. On June 29, 2009, in a ceremony at Saint Peter's Basillica in Rome, the archbishop received the pallium from Pope Benedict XVI, a vestment worn by metropolitan bishops. In 2010, the archbishop returned home to Immaculate Conception Parish, where the parishioners welcomed him with open arms and the new archbishop celebrated a mass of Thanksgiving. As metropolitan archbishop for the Province of Detroit and chairman of the Michigan Catholic Conference, he will also serve as chairman of the board of Sacred Heart Major Seminary and SS. Cyril and Methodius Seminary in Orchard Lake, Michigan. (Courtesy of Immaculate Conception Church.)

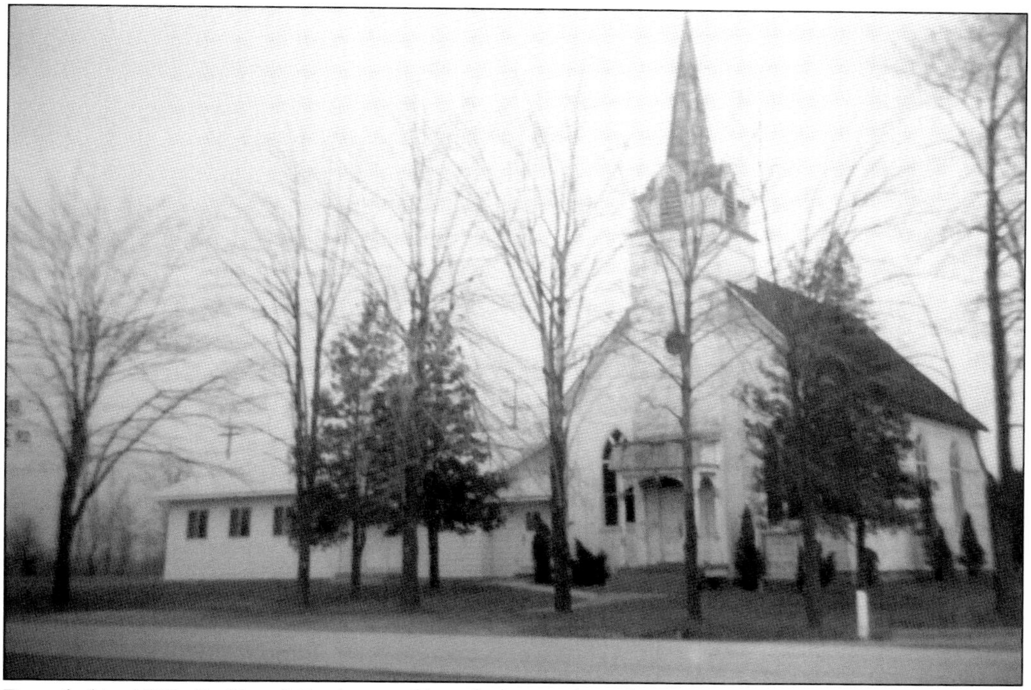

Founded in 1880, St. Peter's Lutheran Church, located on the corner of Palms and Markel Roads in Fair Haven, has served the communities of Fair Haven, Algonac, Marine City, Casco, and Ira Township for over 130 years. The church had two schools: the Jacob School, which closed in 1912, and the Poplar Grove School, which closed in 1960. After the latter closed, the student body was moved to Palms Elementary School on Palms Road. St. Peter's Lutheran Cemetery is located in Section 12 of Ira Township, behind the church, at the northeast corner of Palms and Markel Roads. In 2005, the church celebrated its 125th anniversary. Below, Rev. Robert Wagner stands in the historic sanctuary of St. Peter's Lutheran Church of Ira Township.

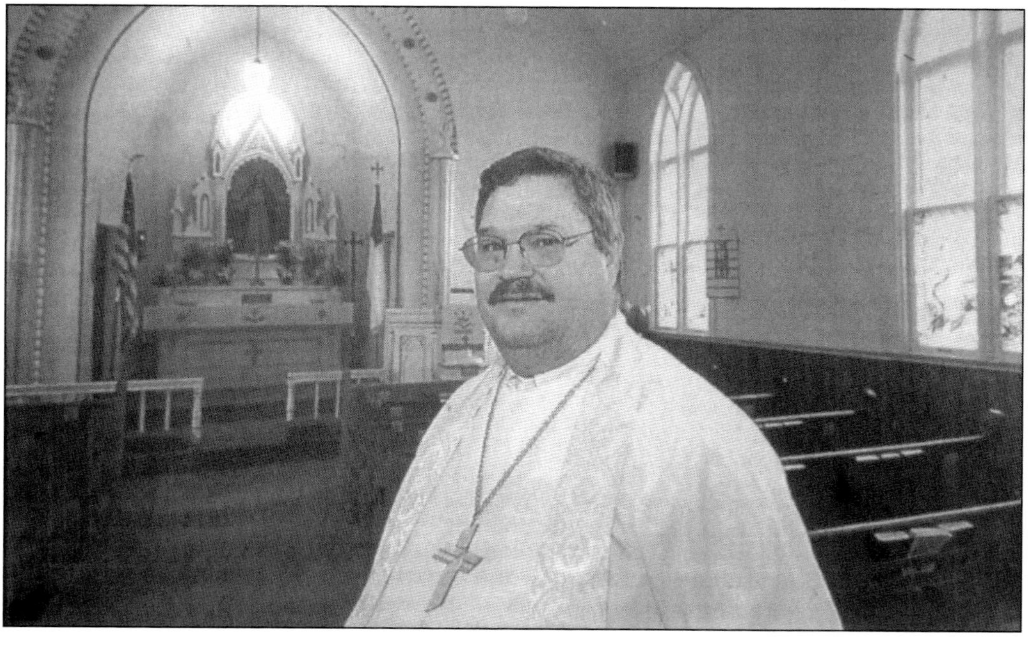

THE HERITAGE OF IRA

A Sesquicentennial History

Ira Township Sesquicentennial Committee

1990

In 1982, Marjorie Thomas, Frances Fritz, Mildred Schmidt, and volunteers from Ira Township, Algonac, and nearby New Baltimore formed A Sesquicentennial History Book Committee. Its purpose was to write and celebrate the 150-year history of Ira Township, from 1837 to 1987. The Ira Township Board of Trustees appointed the committee in 1986. After four years of research and dedicated work, a comprehensive book, *The Heritage of Ira: A Sesquicentennial History*, was published in 1990. The book contains 16 chapters covering the first settlers, churches and cemeteries, schools, transportation, business and industry, maps, and family histories. The book is highly recommended to those who have ties, past or present, to Ira Township and to all who have an interest in its history. To celebrate the book's arrival, the committee, the Ira Board of Trustees, and fellow citizens of Ira attended a dinner party sponsored by the Fraternal Order of Eagles, which is located on Palms Road in Fair Haven.

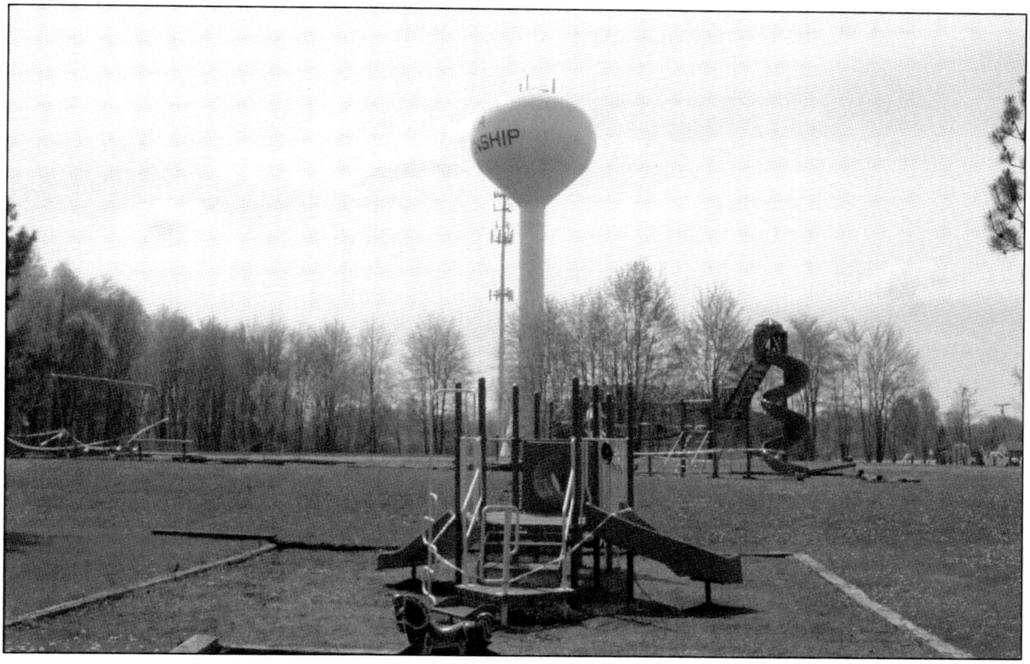

Ira Township Municipal Park was built on a 25-acre parcel adjacent to the municipal offices on Meldrum Road in Fair Haven. The site includes a pavilion, toddler and child playscapes, a sandbox, picnic tables, grills, and cleared picnic areas. A nature trail follows the path of Swan Creek through the woods. The path is available year-round. There are several benches and two foot bridges for residents to enjoy. To honor the veterans of Ira, the township has installed a monument. The names of veterans who lost their lives are engraved on the stone.

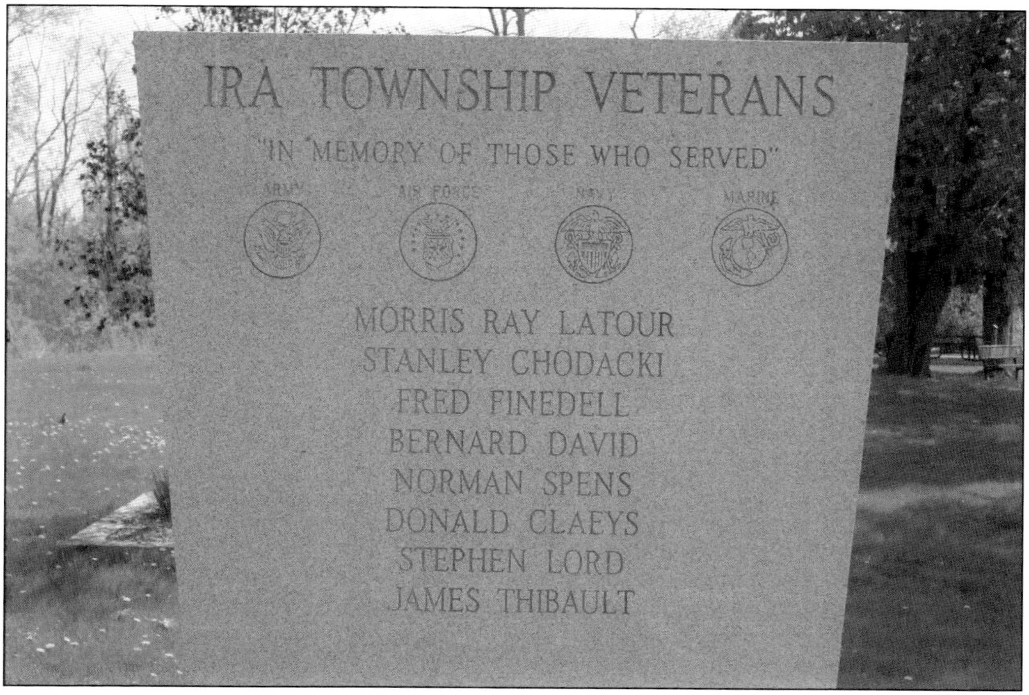

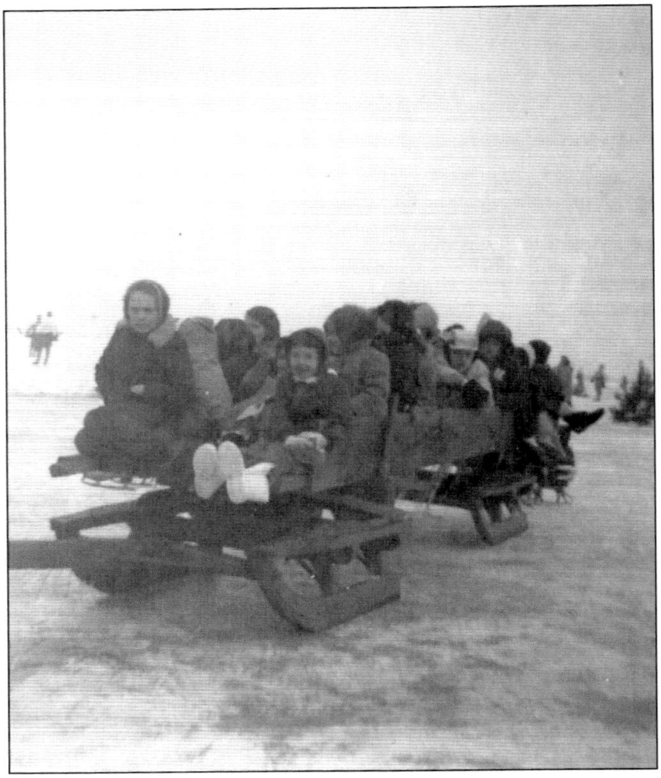

The Fair Haven Fishing Site was for many years the access point of the annual midwinter Shantytown Carnival. Thick ice and good fishing brought hundreds of wooden shanties out on Bouvier Bay. Competition for landing the largest muskellunge was the main event; all entries were displayed on ice for the crowd's perusal. A local radio station would broadcast from Walt's Fish House. The big tent was crowded and hot from the kerosene heaters, while one step outside made attendees feel the deep freeze. There were ice-wagon rides and skating on the bay, food and music in the tent, and cold beer. It is a warm memory now. Below, Anchorville businessman and civic leader George Hart has a lively conversation with Madeline Zabowski.

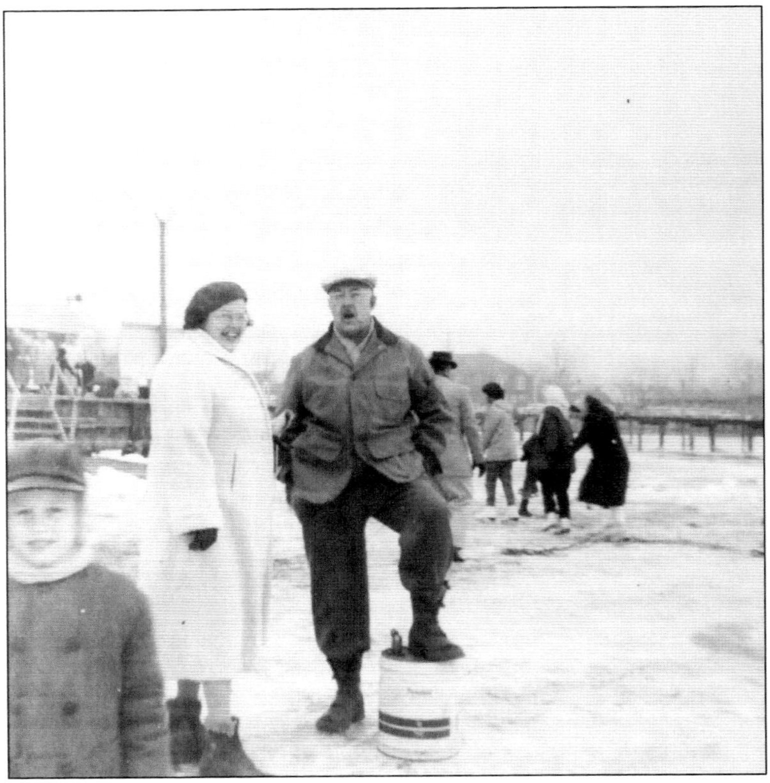

The St. Clair County Library Board established a branch library for Ira Township in February 1965. The original library building was formerly Hamlin's store and, later, John Kandler's meat market in Fair Haven. In 1981, Ira Township built a new township hall. With the old hall now vacant, it was decided to move the library there. It was remodeled to include bookshelves, new carpeting, and a restroom. In 1989, the library became even more patron-friendly, as the community united to build an addition. The added space allowed for a community room, children's library room, additional computer space, new restrooms, and a utility room. In 2015, an additional room was added to this century-old building.

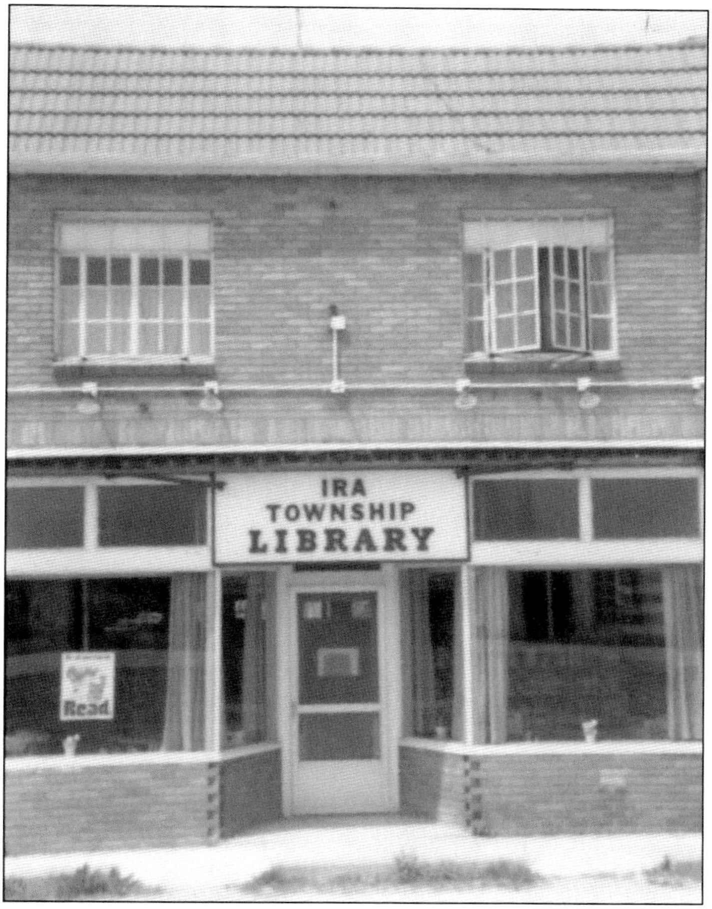

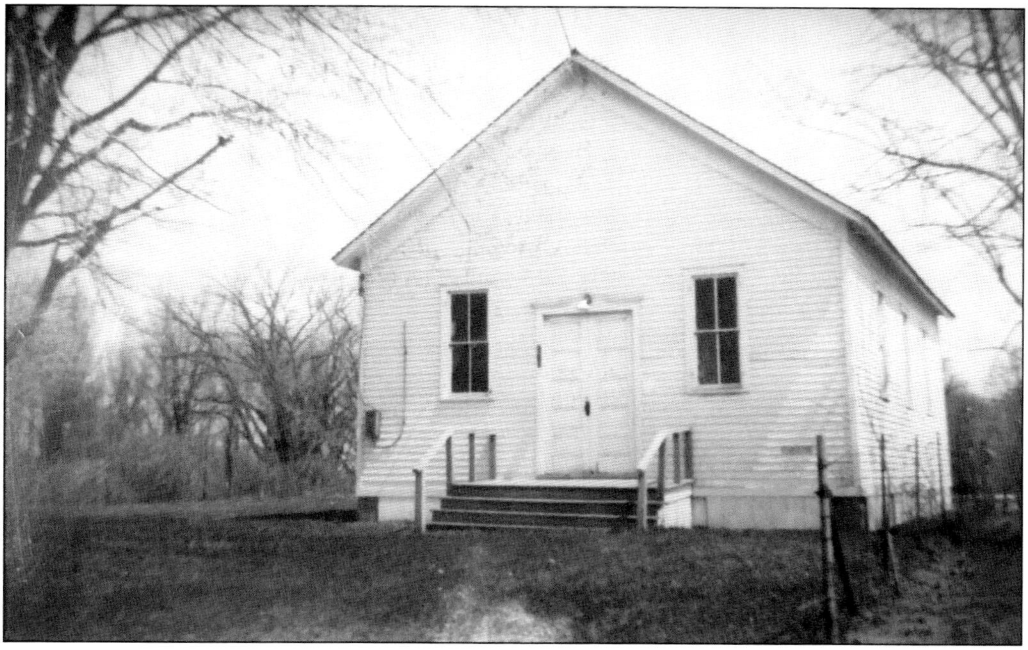

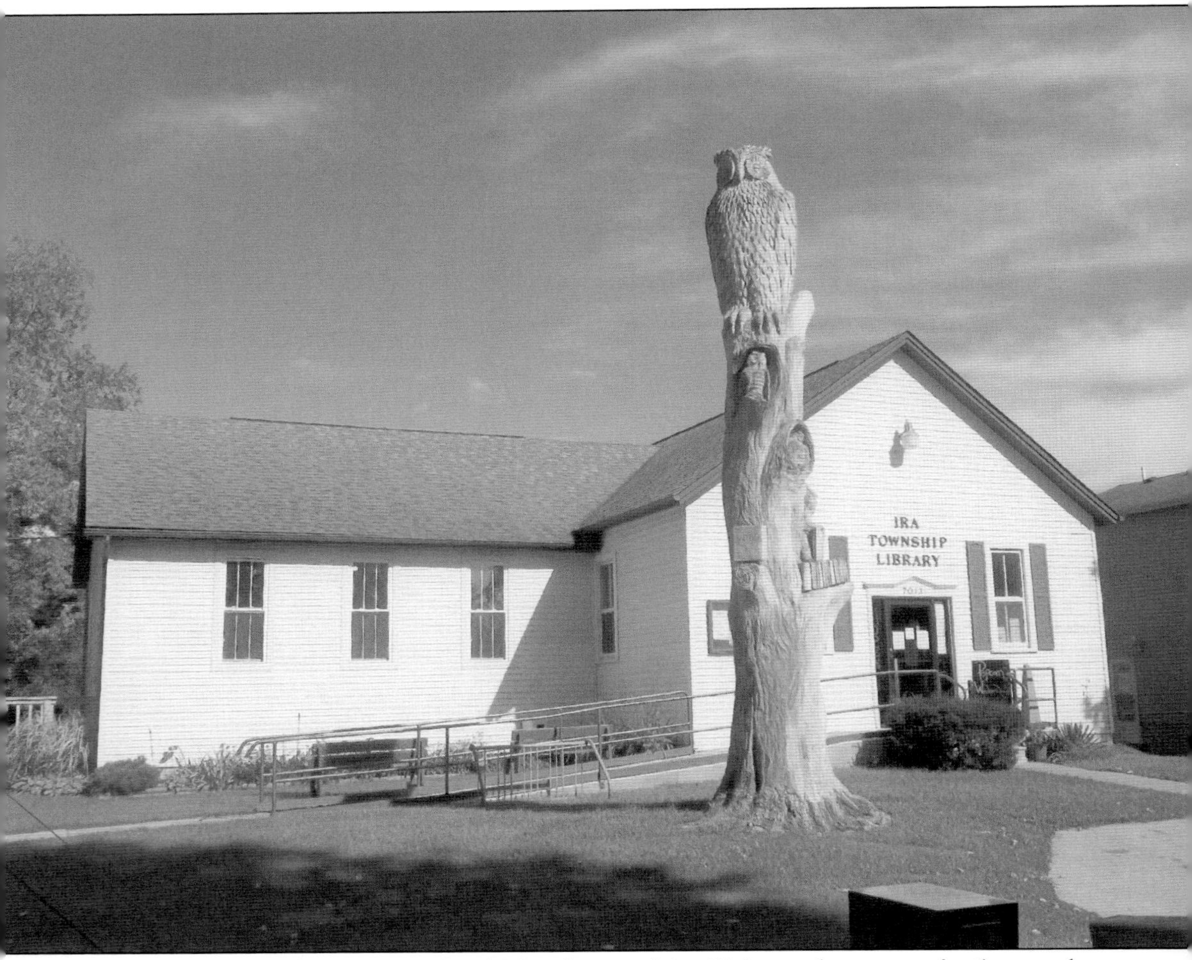

In January 2012, chainsaw artist Emil Szkipala carved this 22-foot sculpture out of a silver maple tree that had stood on the corner of Short Cut and Meldrum Roads for over 150 years. Commissioned and paid for by two private Anchorville citizens, this may be Ira Township's first piece of public art. Topped by a great horned owl (named "Guardian" in a library-sponsored contest), it also holds two smaller owls, two raccoons, and stacks of books. There are two observations often made by Ira Township residents: "Be careful who you talk with, they may be your cousins;" and, "So the journey continues."

Bibliography

Dixon, Michael E. *Life on the Flats*. Fair Haven, MI: Mervue Publications, 1987.

Greenman, Emerson F. *The Indians of Michigan*. A John M. Munson Michigan History Fund Publication.

Immaculate Conception Parish 150-Year Anniversary and History Book (1853–2003). Roseville, MI: Skip Printing Co., 2003.

Ira Township Sesquicentennial Committee. *The Heritage of Ira: A Sesquicentennial History*. Algonac, MI: Reference Publications Inc., 1990.

Mayea, Chad E. *Since the Beginning: Mayea Boats*. (Second edition.) 2005.

Romig, Walter. *Michigan Place Names*. Detroit, MI: Wayne State University Press, 1986.

Rynearson, Dr. Elton James Jr. *The History of the Anchor Bay School System*. Unpublished, 1973.

Skinner, Grace C., and Elmer L. Skinner. *History Stories of New Baltimore, 1845–1951*. Port Huron, MI: Kerr-Albert Office Supply, 1961.

Trinity, Bernard. *Many Yesterdays*. Dublin, OH: Trinity Enterprises, 1986.

Western Historical Co. *History of St. Clair County*. Chicago, IL: A.T. Andreas and Co., 1883.